Celtx: Open Source Screenwriting
Beginner's Guide

Write and market Hollywood-perfect movie scripts the free way!

Ralph Roberts

BIRMINGHAM - MUMBAI

Celtx: Open Source Screenwriting
Beginner's guide

First published: March 2011

Production Reference: 1040311

Published by Packt Publishing Ltd.
32 Lincoln Road
Olton
Birmingham, B27 6PA, UK.

ISBN 978-1-849513-82-1

www.packtpub.com

Cover Image by Asher Wishkerman (a.wishkerman@mpic.de)

Credits

Author

Ralph Roberts

Reviewers

Sabine Asanger

Dave Burgess

Deondre Ng

Nicholas Zorro Iway

Acquisition Editor

Dilip Venkatesh

Development Editor

Meeta Rajani

Technical Editor

Azharuddin Sheikh

Copy Editor

Neha Shetty

Indexers

Tejal Daruwale

Rekha Nair

Editorial Team Leader

Akshara Aware

Project Team Leader

Priya Mukherji

Project Coordinator

Srimoyee Ghoshal

Proofreader

Aaron Nash

Graphics

Nilesh Mohite

Production Coordinator

Kruthika Bangera

Cover Work

Kruthika Bangera

About the Author

Ralph Roberts is a decorated Vietnam veteran and worked with NASA during the Apollo moon program. He built his first personal computer in 1976 and has been writing about them and on them since his first published article "Down with Typewriters" in 1978. He has written over 100 books along with thousands of articles and short stories. His best sellers include the first U.S. book on computer viruses (which resulted in several appearances on national TV) and Classic Cooking with Coca-Cola®, a cookbook that has been in continuous print for the past 16 years and sold half a million copies. He is also a video producer with over 100 DVD titles now for sale nationally on places such as Amazon.com, and has also produced hundreds of hours of video for local TV in the Western North Carolina area, and has sold scripts to Hollywood producers.

About the Reviewers

Sabine Asanger, born and raised in Germany, was interested in film at an early age, making short videos with the family camera. She received an award for her short film Canberra, A Guided Tour, at the age of 16, winning a trip to Australia. Then she moved to San Diego, California where she attended San Diego State University Film School graduating with a Masters in Film, TV, and New Media. She has successfully completed several film projects with four of them currently being shown world wide at film festivals. Her most noted film to date "The Cave" has won several awards, including 1st place Short Films (Experimental) 2009 Indie Gathering, Cleveland, OH Aug 2009; The Indie Merit Award, La Jolla, CA Sep 2009; 3rd Place Student in SkyFest II, Asheville, NC Sep 2009; Silver Sierra Award 2009 Yosemite Film Festival, CA Oct 2009; Special Mention, Festival de Cine de Granada, Spain, Apr 2010; Silver Palm Award, Mexico IFF, May 2010; Golden Ace Award, Las Vegas IFF, NV, June 2010.

Dave Burgess is a professional writer and systems engineer living in Omaha, Nebraska. He retired from the Air Force in 1999, where he was a computer programmer for his entire career. He works for his wife's consulting company, Cynjut Consulting Services, as a principal telephony engineer producing custom library systems. Dave has written several books, mostly in the fiction genre. His most successful book is based on the life of Barack Obama's childhood friend, Keith Kakugawa, who Barack called "Ray". In addition, he is an aspiring screenwriter and playwright. His screenplay "Dreams for the Sandman" was a finalist in the both the Omaha Film Festival and at the SkyFest Film and Script Festival last year. His play "Bad for Business" was performed in Ontario, Canada to sold out audiences.

Deondre Ng is a student and a blogger who enjoys living with technology. He enjoys blogging about reviews on software, as well as tutorials of some things he learned from fiddling around with things like WordPress. He is currently teaching himself programming.

Deondre is also fond of writing fiction. Deondre enjoys theater, and so he sometimes writes just for fun, in Celtx, scripts. He has been using Celtx to write scripts for quite some time now.

Beside these, Deondre also occasionally enjoys photography and videography.

www.PacktPub.com

Support files, eBooks, discount offers and more

You might want to visit www.PacktPub.com for support files and downloads related to your book.

Did you know that Packt offers eBook versions of every book published, with PDF and ePub files available? You can upgrade to the eBook version at www.PacktPub.com and as a print book customer, you are entitled to a discount on the eBook copy. Get in touch with us at service@packtpub.com for more details.

At www.PacktPub.com, you can also read a collection of free technical articles, sign up for a range of free newsletters and receive exclusive discounts and offers on Packt books and eBooks.

 PACKTLiB®

http://PacktLib.PacktPub.com

Do you need instant solutions to your IT questions? PacktLib is Packt's online digital book library. Here, you can access, read and search across Packt's entire library of books.

Why Subscribe?

- ◆ Fully searchable across every book published by Packt
- ◆ Copy & paste, print and bookmark content
- ◆ On demand and accessible via web browser

Free Access for Packt account holders

If you have an account with Packt at www.PacktPub.com, you can use this to access PacktLib today and view nine entirely free books. Simply use your login credentials for immediate access.

Table of Contents

Preface

This book is about dreams: yours, mine, all sorts of creative people's dreams. Today's inexpensive yet powerful software, computers, cameras, and so forth create visual productions—whether they are movies, audio-visual, audio plays, stage presentations, and more—and now bring them within the reach of most of us.

Here's the secret for turning an amateurish mish mash into a sharp professional piece people will pay you money for—write it down. Script it. In that aspect, Celtx makes dreams come true.

Writing screenplays—especially the free part—is what first attracted me to Celtx a few years ago. However, Celtx is much more than just script writing software! Here are just a few of the many things you can create with Celtx automatically formatted to industry standards:

- Feature movie screenplays
- Television shows
- Stage plays
- Audio-visual productions
- Podcasts
- Comic books
- Documentaries
- Commercials

Some of these things will make you money, and some you will just do for fun. These and more we'll look at in the course of this book—how to do them, what to do with them (marketing tips), and all sorts of other good stuff. We'll have fun, all while becoming downright proficient with Celtx.

While this book emphasizes Celtx as script formatting software, the entire package adds production scheduling, story visualization tools, and more—all of which we'll see in action and use.

In the **Overview** section of the official Celtx website (`http://celtx.com/overview.html`), the Celtx developers describe this software package as "the world's first all-in-one media pre-production system." We are told that Celtx:

◆ Can be used for the complete production process

◆ Lets you write scripts, storyboard scenes, and sketch setups

◆ Develop characters, breakdown and tag elements

◆ Schedule productions plus generate useful reports

Celtx is powerful software yet simple to use. It can be used in writing the various types of scripts already mentioned, including everything independent film makers and media creators of all types need. This includes writing, planning, scheduling, and generating reports during the various stages of all sorts of productions. The following screenshot is an example of a Celtx report screen:

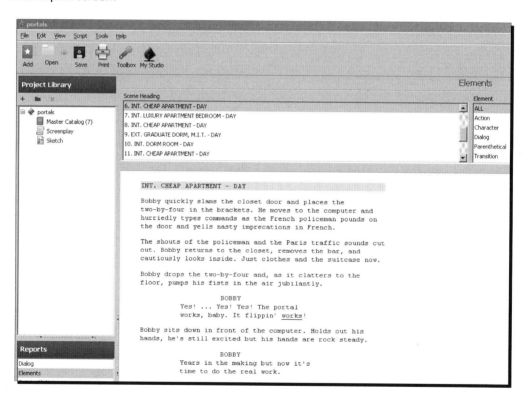

An important concept of Celtx's power is that it's a client-server application. This means only part of Celtx is in that download installed on your computer. The rest is out there in the cloud (the latest buzz term for servers on the Internet). Cloud computing (using remote servers to do part of the work) allows Celtx to have much more sophisticated features, in formatting and collaboration especially, than is normally found in a relatively small free piece of software. It's rather awesome actually and we'll see how it works throughout this book.

A major reason Celtx can be an open source program is that it is built on non-proprietary standards, such as HTML and XML (basic web mark-up languages) and uses other open source programs (specifically Mozilla's engine, the same used in the Firefox browser) for basic operations.

Celtx is really a web application. We have the advantage of big computers on the web doing stuff for us instead of having to depend on the much more limited resources of our local machine. This also means that improvements in script formats (as final formatting is done out on the web somewhere for you) are yours even if you haven't updated your local software. Yes, we'll discuss this more to better get our heads around it, but it's very much to your advantage.

In writing scripts, getting it in the industry standard format is critically important, especially if you're trying to sell scripts to producers or getting an agent interested in representing your work.

Celtx generates your finished scripts as a PDF file (automatically sending your script out on the web, converting it to PDF in the proper format for whichever type of project you are writing, and back to your computer very quickly indeed). We then have a nice finished product like the one shown in the following screenshot, which is a snippet from one of my own scripts:

```
INT. DORM ROOM - DAY

Max looks around at the messy dorm room as Bobby and Fred
beam proudly.

                    MAX
          Does this new trade involve
          cleaning?

                    FRED
          No, no. It's-

                    BOBBY
          He's kidding again. He's fast on
          the uptake.
```

Scene heading, action, character names, dialog—Celtx puts it all in exactly the right format for you!

The name Celtx, by the way is an acronym for Crew, Equipment, Location, Talent, and XML.

Celtx is supported by the Celtx community of volunteer developers and a Canadian company, Greyfirst Corp. in St. John's, Newfoundland.

The Celtx website says that more than 500,000 media creators in 160 countries use Celtx in 33 different languages. Independent filmmakers and studio professionals, and students in over 1,800 universities and film schools have adopted Celtx for teaching and class work submission.

What this book covers

Chapter 1, Obtaining and Installing Celtx. By the end of this chapter, we will have a fully running version of Celtx, ready for action and know which of the six major project types to use depending on what we want to accomplish! Celtx, by the way, has you covered for PC, Mac, all kinds of Linux, and even eeePC Netbooks, as shown in the following screenshot:

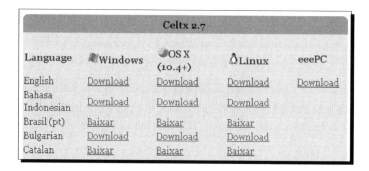

Chapter 2, All Those Wonderful Writing Features. We learn all the features that aid in writing, such as the various editing formats, using the electronic index cards, templates, the typeset feature, and more ways Celtx helps free you up to create, by taking a lot of the drudgery out. The index cards, for example (see the following screenshot), are great for plot notes, keeping track of characters, and so on:

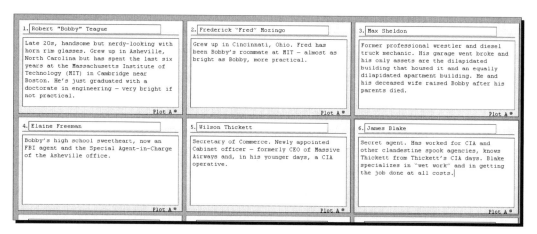

Chapter 3, Visualizing Productions Ahead of Time. Using the built-in storyboarding techniques, attaching media files (pictures to describe costumes for example, or an audio file showing how a bit of dialog should really sound), and all the other pre-production visualization techniques in Celtx. Storyboarding lets us actually draw a representation of what the setup for a scene looks like (like the following scene setup)—a great aid in planning production:

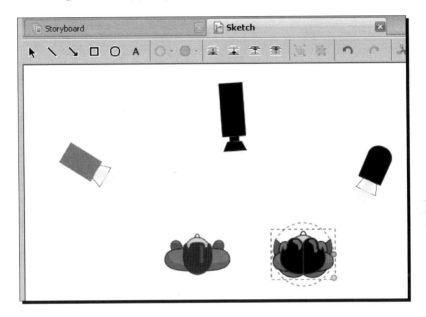

Chapter 4, Tools for Getting Organized. By the end of this chapter, we will be able to schedule production activities and generate reports based on your scripts using the scheduling features in Celtx. We'll also have the ability to move documents between projects, and understand how to create or add custom tools.

Chapter 5, Tooling Up for Scriptwriting. We explore and learn about the basic menus, as shown in the following screenshot, and tools provided by Celtx to make our writing experience much easier:

Chapter 6, Advanced Celtx. We will look at adding and working with multiple projects in a single container, importing scripts in detail, and taking a comprehensive look at exporting scripts.

Chapter 7, Writing Movies with Celtx. This chapter shows us how to use the features of Celtx for outlining and writing an entertainment industry standard feature movie script, short film, or animation—all properly formatted and ready to market. We will actually start a script and learn practical, real-world examples.

To emphasize, this chapter shows not just how to format a script but how to write a screenplay (for feature or short). The very best way of all to learn about both Celtx and writing scripts is by following real world examples. I've got several scripts in progress and completed, which we'll share as examples, as shown in the following illustration:

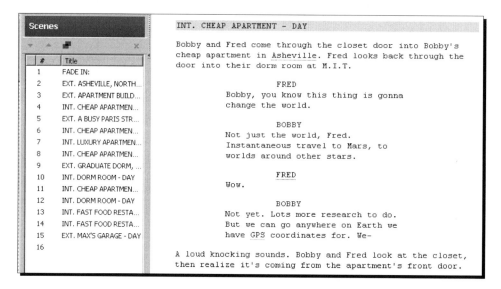

Chapter 8, Documentaries and Other Audio Visual Projects. Writing documentaries and other nonfiction scripts is a bit different than movies. Celtx's integral Audio-Visual editor is perfect for docs, commercials, public service spots, video tutorials, slide shows, light shows, or just about any other combination of visual and other content (not just sound).

Chapter 9, Raising the Curtain on Plays. Plays are pretty much like movies except for the car chase scenes (just kiddin'). There are differences but Celtx assists us in mastering and writing for the stage.

Chapter 10, Audio Plays, Podcasts, and Other Great Sounds. Celtx's Audio Play editor makes writing radio or other audio plays a breeze. It's perfect also for radio commercials or spots, and absolutely more than perfect for podcasts. Podcasts are easy to write, require minimal knowledge to produce, and are a snap to put on the Internet. Learn all that and more in this chapter.

Chapter 11, WAP! POW! BANG! Writing Comic Books with a Punch. How to use Celtx in writing comic books, graphic novels, comic strips, or any other mode of this widely popular method of storytelling. We comic fans know that writing for comic books is very close to writing for the movies. In fact, for a writer, marketing scripts for the comics is at least somewhat easier and has less competition than trying to sell a script.

Chapter 12, Marketing Your Scripts. Okay, your script is finished and polished, looks and reads great. So? How do you sell your baby? This chapter gives you some of my hard-won secrets in marketing—how to inexpensively get the attention of agents, managers, producers, and others who will not only read your script but actually pay you money if they like it.

Appendix A, List of Recommended Books on Screenwriting and Productions and Online Resources. This appendix provides a comprehensive list of some recommended books and also useful online resources on screenwriting, which will help you to learn and grow as a screenwriter and/or movie professional.

Appendix B, Celtx's New Web Look and Smartphone Apps. Celtx offers a new add-on. It's an **app (application)** that allows you to write scripts on your Smartphone and synchronize it with Celtx on your desktop or laptop computer. This appendix also shows you the new look of Celtx's official website.

Appendix C, Future Development of Celtx. This appendix will give you information about the future developments in Celtx.

Appendix D, Pop Quiz Answers. The answers to the pop quiz are given in this appendix.

What you need for this book

The only software required is Celtx, which can be downloaded from `http://celtx.com`. Installation of the software is covered in *Chapter 1, Obtaining and Installing Celtx* with download links for the language of your choice.

Who this book is for

This book will help anyone interested in writing, planning, making, and producing just about any type of movie, audio-visual production, play, podcast, radio play, comic book, and almost any other type of visual, sound, or print media. Celtx is the Swiss Army Knife of pre-production software, and it's free.

As this book goes to press

This book is based on Celtx Version 2.7. On February 8, 2011-as this book was receiving its final edits-Celtx 2.9 was released.

The only major difference between 2.7 and 2.9 is the renaming of Text to Novel. There were also 22 Bug Fixes and improvements (see `http://www.celtx.com/#/desktop/nav-releasenotes` for the complete list).

None of these changes make this book any less timely or useful. All of the suggested uses for Text, such as in outlining screenplays in Chapter 7 and marketing uses in Chapter 12, still work exactly the same in Novel.

Novel is essentially Text with Index Cards and Title Page included, both of which are covered in this book. Thus we can proudly state: Celtx: Open Source Screenwriting explains and enhances Celtx 2.7, 2.9, and future releases with valuable screenplay and other marketing tips found in no other book.

Conventions

In this book, you will find several headings appearing frequently.

To give clear instructions of how to complete a procedure or task, we use:

Time for action – heading

1. Action 1
2. Action 2
3. Action 3

Instructions often need some extra explanation so that they make sense, so they are followed with:

What just happened?

This heading explains the working of tasks or instructions that you have just completed.

You will also find some other learning aids in the book, including:

Pop quiz – heading

These are short multiple choice questions intended to help you test your own understanding.

Have a go hero – heading

These set practical challenges and give you ideas for experimenting with what you have learned.

You will also find a number of styles of text that distinguish between different kinds of information. Here are some examples of these styles, and an explanation of their meaning.

Code words in text are shown as follows: " For Windows, the downloaded file (currently) is named `CeltxSetup-2.9.exe`."

Any command-line input or output is written as follows:

```
sudo apt-get remove xandros-scrim
```

New terms and **important words** are shown in bold. Words that you see on the screen, in menus or dialog boxes for example, appear in the text like this: " For example, in Ubuntu, left click on the desktop, click on **Create Launcher**, and follow the directions".

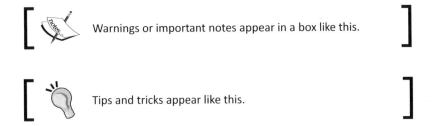

Warnings or important notes appear in a box like this.

Tips and tricks appear like this.

Reader feedback

Feedback from our readers is always welcome. Let us know what you think about this book—what you liked or may have disliked. Reader feedback is important for us to develop titles that you really get the most out of.

To send us general feedback, simply send an e-mail to feedback@packtpub.com, and mention the book title via the subject of your message.

If there is a book that you need and would like to see us publish, please send us a note in the **SUGGEST A TITLE** form on www.packtpub.com or e-mail suggest@packtpub.com.

If there is a topic that you have expertise in and you are interested in either writing or contributing to a book, see our author guide on www.packtpub.com/authors.

Customer support

Now that you are the proud owner of a Packt book, we have a number of things to help you to get the most from your purchase.

Errata

Although we have taken every care to ensure the accuracy of our content, mistakes do happen. If you find a mistake in one of our books—maybe a mistake in the text or the code—we would be grateful if you would report this to us. By doing so, you can save other readers from frustration and help us improve subsequent versions of this book. If you find any errata, please report them by visiting http://www.packtpub.com/support, selecting your book, clicking on the **errata submission form** link, and entering the details of your errata. Once your errata are verified, your submission will be accepted and the errata will be uploaded on our website, or added to any list of existing errata, under the Errata section of that title. Any existing errata can be viewed by selecting your title from http://www.packtpub.com/support.

Piracy

Piracy of copyright material on the Internet is an ongoing problem across all media. At Packt, we take the protection of our copyright and licenses very seriously. If you come across any illegal copies of our works, in any form, on the Internet, please provide us with the location address or website name immediately so that we can pursue a remedy.

Please contact us at copyright@packtpub.com with a link to the suspected pirated material.

We appreciate your help in protecting our authors, and our ability to bring you valuable content.

Questions

You can contact us at questions@packtpub.com if you are having a problem with any aspect of the book, and we will do our best to address it.

1
Obtaining and Installing Celtx

We've all watched a disappointing movie and said, "I could write it better than that." Perhaps you can! The trick is, getting your great idea into a professional format acceptable to producers, agents, managers—those gatekeepers of Hollywood, Bollywood, Euro studio, indie, and elsewhere. It doesn't matter how good your script might be if it doesn't look right. Yes, they are that particular. They won't read it.

The answer (and it's an easy one) to writing screenplays in the rigid format required is software. The two big name "professional" scriptwriting programs—Final Draft and Movie Magic—each retail for over $200. What if you could get software that not only lets you turn out scripts just as professional as the big money programs but does a lot more? What if you get it for free? Well, Celtx (pronounced kel-tiks) costs nothing but a few seconds of downloading time.

Is that worth a shot or what?

Of course, you like that whole concept of a no-cost solution or we wouldn't be here this book. Sell one screenplay and the cost of this book will be a pretty good investment. The purpose of these pages is to gift you with the knowledge and skills to use Celtx to its full advantage.

In this chapter, we shall:

- ◆ Discuss system requirements needed to run Celtx
- ◆ Find Celtx's home on the web
- ◆ Check out the languages available
- ◆ Decide on and download our new software for our specific operating system

- ◆ Install Celtx on our computer(s)
- ◆ Test our installation to make sure that it works and check out some of the neat and useful features
- ◆ Summarize what we've learned and find out some other sources for additional information

By the end of this chapter, we will have a fully running version of Celtx, ready for action, and we'll know which option to use depending on what we want to accomplish. This is all easy and fun. So hold on to your keyboard, because here we go!

System requirements

First, we need a computer.

Okay, yeah, but Celtx fits a much wider range of computers than most software; certainly more than the big commercial packages that only work on PC or Mac. Unless you're still running an Apple II from 1980, chances are Celtx has you covered.

The very best thing about Celtx is that it's free! There are two definitions of free that people throw around—free beer and free speech. Celtx is free in both ways. There's no cost for Celtx, like free beer, and you can do whatever you want with it, within certain limits, like free speech. Later, we'll talk about other additional services and products that are almost free, but for now, Celtx is free.

 Unlike commercial scriptwriting software, which limits you to only one or two active installations on one type of operating system, you can install Celtx on as many computers as you have with no limits whatsoever on how many run at a time.

By the way, Celtx requires 75 MB of free hard disk space for installation. In these days of multi-hundred-gigabyte disks, this is a very light footprint indeed.

PC

Any relatively recent PC from the last ten years or so handles Celtx with no problem. Celtx runs on XP, NT, 2000, Vista, and the latest, Windows 7.

Mac

Just about any Apple Mac OS X (also know as **Tiger**) machine since 2002, runs Celtx. Celtx is a *universal binary*, meaning it works equally well on X86 (Intel based) or Power PC Macs.

Linux

Hundreds of Linux **distributions** or **distros** (versions of Linux from different groups or companies) exist. Celtx works fine on pretty much all of them (at least all the X6 or Intel processor machines) so long as certain supporting **library** packages (collections of common routines programs needed to operate) are installed. Don't worry, this takes about ten seconds, and we'll check and do this, if needed, in this chapter concerning installation of Celtx on Linux.

eeePC

Since 2008, **Netbooks** (subcompact notebook computers) have been available. Many of the earlier ones run Windows XP, although more recent offerings provide Vista or even Windows 7. Netbooks also might have various "lite" versions of Linux. Celtx loves them all, and we'll sort this out in the eeePC installation section forthcoming in this very chapter.

So, let's download Celtx and install it.

Choosing and downloading the right version of Celtx

The current version (at the time of writing) of Celtx is 2.7, which was released in early 2010. You'll want to check occasionally to make sure the Celtx on your computer is up to date.

Let's go get Celtx!

Time for action – finding the download choices

Here's what we will be doing. After connecting to the Internet, we perform the following steps:

1. Open our browser and go to `http://celtx.com`. (The webmasters at Celtx have set it up, so that you can use "www" if you want, but it's not needed.) The following screenshot shows the Celtx home page at the time of this writing:

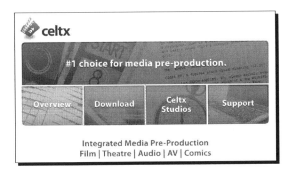

2. Below the big green banner (refer to the preceding screenshot) reading **#1 choice for media pre-production**, there is a row of four smaller banners. Click on the second from the left, the orange one marked **Download**. We now have the download matrix similar to the one shown in the following screenshot:

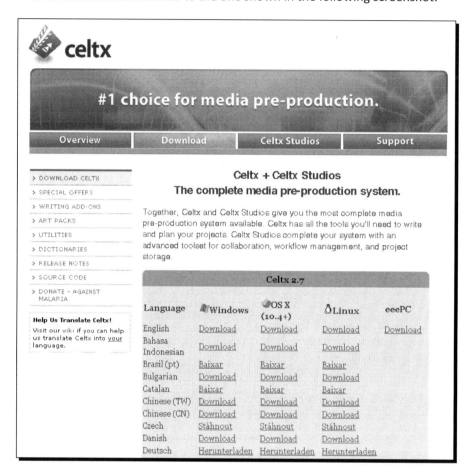

3. Now we have a couple of choices to make with reference to language and computer version and for our machine. By the way, in the preceding screenshot, please note that both **Celtx** and **Celtx Studios** are shown. Celtx, the program, is the free part. Celtx Studios is the commercial collaboration system that Celtx can use to store files on a safe server on the Internet. It is entirely optional, as are some of the "for pay" add-ons, which we'll discuss later.

Celtx speaks your language

Using software is much more pleasant if the instructions on the screen and the menu choices make sense. Celtx currently offers 33 choices of language (see the first column on the Download page) in every operating system version except for eeePC (which is only available in English).

These language selections, of course, only affect the on-screen instructions and menu selections, not whatever language you write. For example, let's say you are Dutch (I am always awed by how well so many Dutch folk speak English) and you write scripts for Hollywood in English but prefer to have Celtx's choices in your native language just to speed things up. No problem; choose **Nederlands** off the download matrix and **Downloaden** in the right operating system column for your computer.

Write in Hindi for Bollywood? Well, you still can, but there is no Hindi version yet, so, for now, the instructions will be in English or whatever other available language you might be more comfortable in. One caveat to this—the software may have been translated into these languages, but not all of them are supported by Celtx's online PDF generation. (Typeset does not support non-Latin characters at the moment. So, although the program may be in Hindi, it isn't possible to use the Typeset feature as of yet. Cyrillic and Phonym languages such as Russian, Chinese, and Japanese are also affected.)

 Want a version of Celtx in Hindi or some other language not yet available? Well, the Celtx people seek volunteers to help out with translations. Hindi is a work in progress as are a number of other languages. Visit the following URL for more information:

```
http://wiki.celtx.com/index.
php?title=Category:Translating_Celtxhttp://wiki.celtx.
com/index.php?title=Category:Translating_Celtx.
```

The right operating system

In the first column of the **Download** page, again, is our choice of language. The remaining four columns—Windows, OS X (for Mac), Linux (see the little Linux mascot penguin?), and eeePC—are where you choose the right version for your computer.

Time for action – downloading Celtx

Now, since our choices are made with regards to language and operating system, it's time to download Celtx.

1. Go down column one to the language you want.

2. Move over to the column under the name of your operating system.

3. Left click your mouse on **Download** or the equivalent word in your language (**Baixar, Downloaden, Lataa**, and so on).

A new page comes up and the download should have started automatically. If not, see the line **If your download doesn't start automatically, please click here**.

There are several commercial offers on this page for the Writers Pack, Art Pack, and Celtx Studios. Celtx itself is free but the company that develops Celtx, Greyfirst Corp. in St. John's, Newfoundland, Canada, uses the revenue stream of selling add-ons and providing the Celtx Studio service to support their work. That's fine but it's your choice as to whether or not you buy anything; Celtx itself is free. Once you become proficient in using Celtx, the various add-ons will become more useful and you can consider a purchase at that time.

Installing Celtx

With the download now on the computer we want Celtx to reside on, we're ready to install. You can skip ahead to your operating system.

 It's always good to know where files download onto your computer, as you need to access your download in order to install Celtx. Using Firefox as your browser, for example, is as easy as typing *Ctrl-J*, which shows a list of downloaded files. Just double-click on the top one (if it's Celtx) to begin the installation.

Time for action – installing Celtx on a PC

For Windows, the downloaded file (currently) is named `CeltxSetup-2.7.exe` (and is an executable file; that is, it will perform the action of installation when you open it by double-clicking on it). A later version might be named `CeltxSetup-2.8.exe` or `CeltxSetup-3.0.exe` or whatever the latest version is.

If you have a virus scanner that can scan self-installing executables, you should scan the file before you run it. This is true for any executable, and you never know when someone might be doing something sneaky. While we trust the people that produce Celtx, you can't trust everyone on the Internet, so always be careful.

So, we double-click and a security warning most likely pops up reading **The publisher could not be verified**... This is a Microsoft thingy—Celtx is not one of the big, commonly installed programs, so Windows does not recognize it. As we downloaded it directly from the Celtx site ourselves, we know it to be safe. Just click on the **Run** button in that dialog box, which looks like the following screenshot:

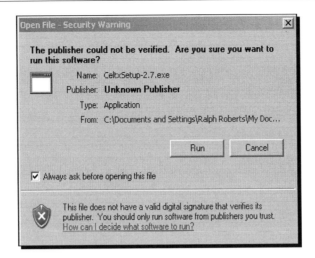

A small window comes up briefly and shows the program extracting, then another window welcomes us to the Celtx Setup Wizard. Hit the **Next** button (preferably just with the mouse cursor).

The License Agreement pops up. Check (by clicking in it) the License Agreement accept box, and click on the **Next** button. Choose **Standard** on the Setup Type dialog, hit **Next** again. In the Summary dialog box, click on **Install**. It takes a short amount of time, then click on **Finish** on the Completion dialog box, and yes, that's it.

Easy!

Nothing can go wrong, right?

Well, there is one thing you should know about, if you get an error message reading as follows:

```
The application has failed to start because MSVCR71.dll was not found.
Restarting the application may fix this problem.
```

No, restarting won't fix it. You'll need to get the library files `msvcr71.dll` and `msvcp71.dll`. These files can be found at the following URLs:

```
http://www.driverskit.com/dll/msvcr71.dll/2373.html and http://www.
driverskit.com/dll/msvcp71.dll/2371.html
```

The DLLs go in your `C:\Windows\system32` directory.

One more thing, if you have an earlier version of Celtx, uninstall it before installing the new version. This will not affect any of your scripts, storyboards, or any other files you might have created (although regularly backing them up is always a good idea).

What just happened?

We are now ready to use Celtx on our Windows computer.

Time for action – installing Celtx on Mac OS X

The Mac file is named `Celtx-2.7.dmg`. This could be 2.8 or 3.0, by the time you read this book and get the file.

To install is a snap. Just double click on the `.dmg` file to mount the drive to your system. Then drag the Celtx icon to your `Applications` folder. Eject the mounted drive and you can delete the `.dmg` file. That's it!

What just happened?

We are now ready to use Celtx on our Mac computer.

Time for action – Linux installation

How you install on a Linux system, any Linux system, depends on your access and permissions.

If you are just a regular user on the system, download to your home folder (usually `/home/yourusername/`). The file is `Celtx-2.7.tar.bz2`.

First, however, download Celtx. The following screenshot shows downloading in progress:

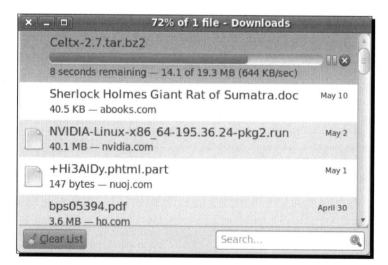

What just happened?

That completes the installation of Celtx on Linux for a single user.

Time for action – installing on a Netbook

Celtx for eeePC Netbooks, again, is only available in English, so far. For a Netbook, we'll be downloading `Celtx-2.7.en-US-eeePC.tar.bz2`.

For Celtx to work, it is necessary to remove the `scrim` package or, on more recent Netbooks, the replacement `gcin` package. Type the following command:

```
sudo apt-get remove xandros-scrim
```

Or

```
sudo apt-get remove xandros-gcin
```

If the latter does not work, try just the following:

```
sudo apt-get remove gcin
```

What just happened?

Celtx is now installed on a Netbook.

New iPad and iPhone Apps

As this book goes to press, Celtx has just released a new **app (application)** for the Apple iPad tablet computer and also an app for the popular iPhone Smartphone (the latter is free). The first may be purchased through the The App Store, visit `http://celtx.com/mobile.html` for details on both purchase and how to use these add-ons.

This allows us to work on Celtx scripts on the iPad or iPhone and sync them with Celtx on our home computers or laptop.

Testing Celtx

Okay, time to see if this baby will get off the ground! Of course it will. Fasten your seatbelts, please.

In addition to checking out the various features of Celtx, we'll also do some more optional installation chores that need doing from inside Celtx.

Time for action – starting it up

Launching Celtx in any of the four operating systems (Windows, Mac, Linux, and eeePC) is simply a matter of double-clicking on the movie clapper icon, which is shown in the following screenshot:

We Linux guys may need to create a launcher icon in GNOME or KDE to get the movie clapper. In my case, I have Celtx on two Ubuntu servers, a Windows XP laptop, a Vista machine, and two more XP machines. It works flawlessly on all of them.

Creating a launcher, by the way, varies depending on your flavor of Linux. For example, in Ubuntu, left click on the desktop, click on **Create Launcher**, and follow the directions.

What just happened?

Okay, we've double-clicked on the movie clapper and next we see a splash screen. it's the same on all systems and looks similar to the following screenshot:

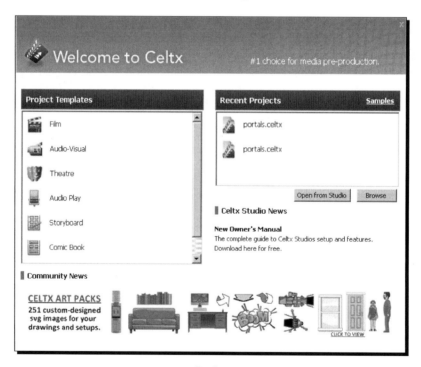

On the left, we have the major types of projects Celtx excels at, which are as follows:

- Film
- Audio-Visual
- Theatre (stage plays)
- Audio Play (everything from radio plays to podcast scripts)
- Storyboard (so you can visually plan projects)
- Comic Book (where we can write graphic novels and other good stuff)

On the right are your current projects. In this case, **Portals** is one of my scripts in progress, which we'll be using as an example. There are two copies of it because it's on two machines as a backup.

The remainder of material at the bottom of the splash page consists of links to the Celtx Studio service and the other things they sell to support Celtx, all optional. This latter information is loaded from the Internet. If it's not visible, you'll need to activate your Internet connection. To get the full power of Celtx, it must have Internet access.

Let's do just a little more installation work before we go wild and have some fun exploring Celtx. Here's why.

Time for action – establishing an Internet connection

Celtx, more than most software, needs a connection to the Internet for several important reasons, including formatting and getting tools. We need to make sure that is in place.

First, let's open an empty project. Just click on **Film** on the Celtx splash page under **Project Templates** to open one up and it will look like the following screenshot:

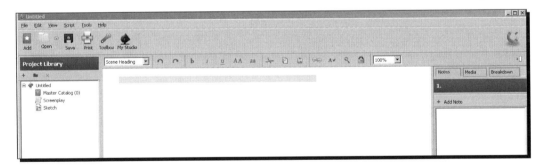

Click on **Tools**, and then click on **Options**. This gives us a dialog box that those of us who use Firefox should recognize! That's because it's the same as Firefox's, as Celtx uses the Mozilla's software as one of its underlying engines. We want to check the Network options, which are shown in the following screenshot:

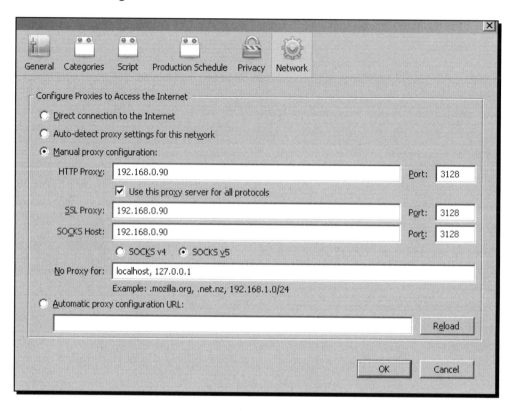

If you have a direct connection to the Internet, you're done and in fine shape. If you need a proxy to connect to the Internet, as I do, then you need to enter the information for your proxy server. This will be the same configuration as is in either Firefox, Internet Explorer, Safari, or whatever browser you use to surf the web. It's crucial that Celtx can see the web.

What just happened?

The full power of Celtx is available through your Internet connection.

Adding dictionaries to the spellchecker

Additional dictionaries are available for the spellchecker. These are needed if you want to, for example, write in more than one language and proof them all. For the basic American English installation, the right dictionary is already in place.

If you seriously want to sell scripts, spellchecking and other proofing is absolutely critical. Nothing will get your script tossed without being read faster than having a script with a bunch of typos in it.

Here's how to add dictionaries, so we can do that all-important spellchecking.

Time for action – getting and adding dictionaries

The following procedure also works for getting other tools:

1. Open Celtx with any project or create a new one (what we just did earlier).
2. Click on the menu option **Tools**, then **Toolbox**.
3. A new dialog box appears. Click on the **Get Celtx Tools** button at its bottom.
4. This opens the Celtx Special Offers page. Click on **Dictionaries** in the left column.
5. A page for spellcheck Dictionaries opens, as shown in the following screenshot:

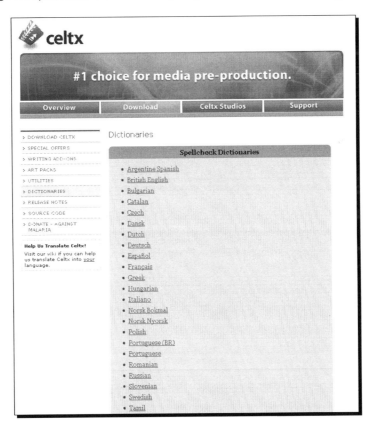

6. Click on the dictionary you want. You will be asked by the application to download the file (Celtx should be open on your computer). The dictionary will download and appear in your toolbox (the dialog box you opened). You can select more dictionaries at this time or exit and restart Celtx to begin using the dictionary that we just downloaded.

What just happened?

Spell checking is now available in the languages for which we downloaded dictionaries. They're free, so add as many languages as you write in.

Celtx's six biggies—its types of projects

If all Celtx did was format screenplays, it would still be a wonderful tool. However, Celtx is more. As is stated on the Celtx website (`http://celtx.com`), "Celtx is the world's first fully integrated software for pre-production and collaboration of film, theatre, radio, AV, and comics." That is a lot!

So, let's get a brief introduction here to the six major project areas of Celtx. Throughout the rest of this book, we'll look at these areas in detail.

Film

Film projects are screenplays for movies and television shows. Screenplays have very rigid format requirements. The names of characters must start a certain number of spaces from the left margin. Dialog has its own starting point. Top, bottom, left, and right margins all must be exact. The typeface must absolutely, positively, definitely be Courier 12 point.

For reasons—both traditional and practical, Hollywood producers, agents, and managers have zero tolerance policies on any variance from accepted script standards.

Now you could calculate all these things manually. As a matter of fact, back in the mid 80's when I made my few sales to movie producers, I used a primitive word processing program and did that formatting manually. It was a major pain.

Celtx gives you all you need to write professional level screenplays from Day One.

Here's the short course as an intro. Open a Film project (again, on the splash page, click on **Film**). Look at the little window just to the right of **Project Library**, the one with the word **Scene Heading** in it. Click on the down arrow to the right of **Action**. We have eight choices. For now, we will ignore **Transition** and **Shot**, as those are not used in **spec** screenplays (spec screenplays being scripts written on "speculation" as opposed to being assigned). The other six give you everything needed to write a screenplay that could sell to a major motion picture director.

As mentioned, we'll be using my script "Portals" as an example. This is what the script is about (a one sentence summary called a **logline** (more about those in *Chapter 7*) is used to interest agents and producers in reading your script).

Logline: An engineer's invention instantly teleports people thousands of miles but he must battle to save himself and his friends from greedy corporations and panicked governments determined not to become obsolete.

The following screenshot shows how the script looks as it is being written in Celtx's Film project:

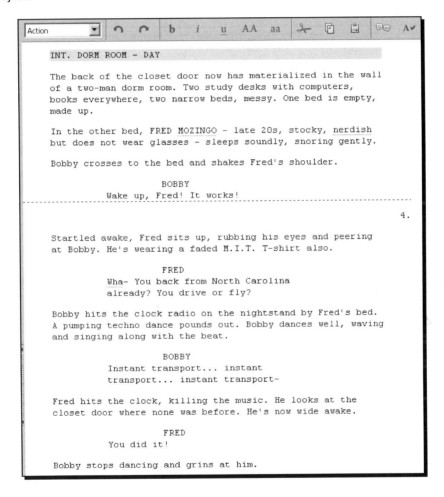

This is easy to accomplish by selecting **Action** from the drop-down. Similarly, you can select **Character** and put in the speaker's name, or select **Dialog** and type what they say. However, the real magic comes when we hit the **Typeset/PDF** button at the bottom of the screen and get a PDF file ready for saving and printing, or just e-mailing (the more normal thing these days) to an agent or producer, and which looks similar to the following screenshot (remember, we got to have an Internet connection for this to work):

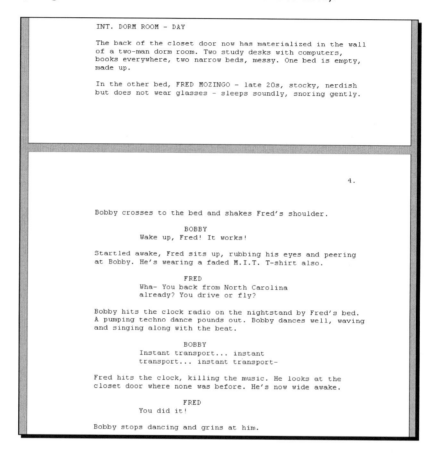

Of course, if we are writing this script for an independent producer or ourselves to produce, we can add scene numbers, transitions, types of shots, and a lot of other stuff forbidden in spec scripts. We discuss more about all this and show you how it works with some good tips as we move on through this book.

Audio-Visual

Okay, let's close the Film project and restart Celtx to get the splash screen (although you can have several projects open at once, if you like). Click on **Audio-Visual**.

What? It doesn't look very different from the Film project we just opened, does it?

Well, the big difference is in that little magic box just to the right of Project **Library** again. Click on the down arrow. Now we find only five choices: **Scene Heading**, **Shot**, **Character**, **Dialog**, and **Parenthetical**. This is because audio-visual presentations are different from the storytelling of a movie. Audio-visual could be anything from a script for a slide show, to a documentary video, to a commercial for TV. The printed format is different as well, as we can see in the following screenshot:

VIDEO	AUDIO
Bill standing by the bulldozer.	BILL This is Bill of Honest Bill's Used Bulldozers. We got us a real cream puff here. This baby was only used by a little old lady on Sundays to build a road through the Rocky Mountains.

Theatre

Now, let's open a Theatre project. (Yep, Celtx uses the British or, in this case, Canadian spelling, eh?) Go to our magic box. The big difference is **Stage Direction**. Also, the output format for a standard stage play differs from that of a film or audio-visual production.

Celtx conforms to the two most accepted play formats—American format and "Classic" or European format. When the play is written, the screen looks like a screenplay, but when it's typeset, the format is changed to whichever option we choose.

Audio Play

An Audio Play project could be a radio play, a podcast, a speech, or any other production consisting solely of sound. Open up a new Audio Play project and check out the selections in that box. Headings such as **Sound**, **Voice**, and **Music** give us clues as to what type of script we will be writing in this type of project.

This format conforms to BBC Radio Drama guidelines in its formatting and is pretty much the only standard which has been clearly defined in the audio world.

Comic Book

Open a Comic Book project. Check the magic box. We find selections such as **Page**, **Panel**, **Caption**, and **Balloon Type**. The things we need to do are write and format a standard comic book script.

Storyboard

Finally, in our tour of the six types of major projects Celtx handles, we come to the Storyboard. Let's open a Storyboard project.

Whoa! Look at the following screenshot; there's something that looks different:

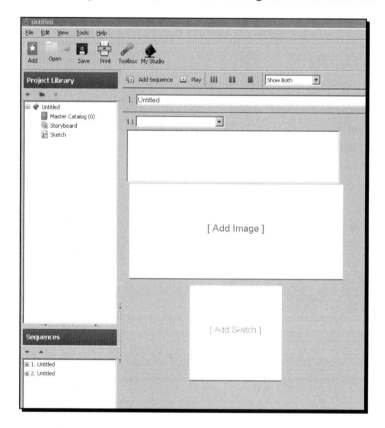

The Storyboard project is a powerful and extensive method of visually planning complete productions. For example, if you're producing an independent film, you can plan every single shot in it.

Okay, we've now had a brief introduction to the six major types of Celtx projects and will be moving on to greater detail in the following chapters.

Summary

In this chapter, we learned how to install Celtx on four different types of operating systems.

Specifically, we covered the very basic requirements for running Celtx on Windows, Mac OS X, Linux, and eeePC (Netbooks), how to download and install Celtx on *your* system, and we did a quick tour of the six powerful types of Celtx projects.

Now that we've installed Celtx and learned how to get around in it, let's move on to learning how to write scripts in Celtx. That's coming up next!

2
All those Wonderful Writing Features

Celtx does more than just practically write your script for you (well, it's not that easy, some creative effort is required on our part, but this software makes scripting much easier). This chapter gives us the VIP overview and a tour of Celtx's powerful writing features.

To simplify, it's about assistants.

In this chapter, we will:

- See how Celtx assists us in developing important parts of our story such as props, characters, and thirty-six other production categories.

- Experience the ways in which Celtx takes care of stuff that otherwise slows the writing process down, such as intuitive formatting and easy shortcuts.

- Learn to "write once, use many" with Celtx's Adapt feature.

- Visit the power of the **Typeset feature**, which automatically formats our scripts to industry standards, whether going to paper or to a PDF file (Portable Document Format), which, more and more, is becoming the way agents, managers, and producers want to receive finished scripts.

- Play with the reversible color-coded electronic Index Cards. You flip the card on the screen to type notes and color-code them to follow plot lines. You can also drag-and-drop them to move scenes around.

Learn how Celtx can track revisions for us.

◆ Use the **Template Engine** to create and save new project types. While Celtx provides you with the industry standard formats mentioned above, you are not limited to them.

By the end of this chapter, we will have a good grasp of all the preceding features and more that Celtx packs into itself to help us write.

Writing with character and mastering the Master Catalog

Celtx assists in developing important parts of our story such as characters, props, and thirty-six other predefined production categories.

As this old writer learned decades ago, stories are about people. So, we'll jump ahead this once (at least) and look at how Celtx helps create and then track characters and other categories needed in production. Having defined characters makes writing scripts a great deal easier.

Now is a good time to emphasize that while this book is a beginner's guide to learning and using Celtx, it also features many tips about creating scripts and what to do with them after they are written.

 Before starting a script, create the major characters by giving them brief biographical histories and motivations to be in the story (like why he or she would risk their lives instead of just running away). Do these for both the good guys and the bad guys; even bad guys need a reason to do what they do.

Now, let's look at some examples of using Celtx to track people, animals, props, and other items in our movies.

Of the several aids to writing built into Celtx, the **Master Catalog** is one of the more powerful features that track information about characters for us along with other useful categories.

 This book is for both folks writing spec scripts (scripts on "speculation", that is, not assigned or paid for up front), and shooting scripts by those involved in actual production of a movie, play, comic book, or other projects which Celtx handles so well.

In a shooting script, a lot more detail is called for and the Master Catalog tracks props, vehicles, extras, livestock (a cowboy got to have his horse), and all the other stuff a producer and/or director need to know. For a spec script, do not worry about tracking anything except characters for ease in writing. Agents who sell and producers who buy do not want that kind of detail. They will kick back scripts that have it. Just give them the story.

Okay, let's get to it.

Start Celtx and, on the "Welcome to Celtx" Splash Page, and under **Project Templates**, click on **Film**. An empty project for writing a motion picture screenplay appears. We explore creating projects and saving projects in detail in *Chapter 5*, but you may want to save this project if, as we go through the following example, you create characters you want to keep.

Time for action – saving a project

1. Click on **File**, and then click on **Save Project** or just use *Ctrl+S*.

2. The dialog (similar to the following screenshot) pops up. In the input box next to **File Name** at the bottom, change **Untitled** to your desired title. Click on the **Save** button.

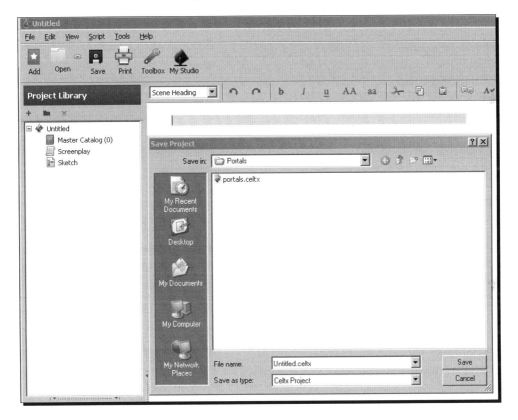

What just happened?

The project is now saved and we are ready to continue.

Okay, let's continue. In the **Project Library** box on the left, double-click on **Master Catalog**. In the following example, I have my script-in-progress **Portals**:

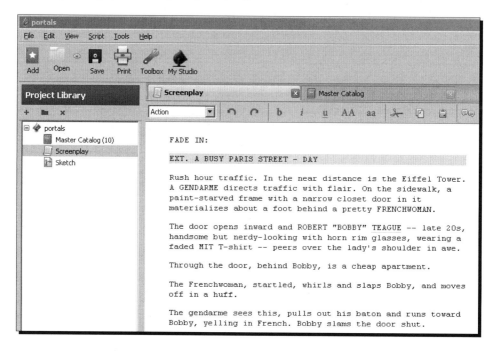

Being up to page 42 already on my script, there are ten characters in the **Master Catalog**. It looks like the following screenshot:

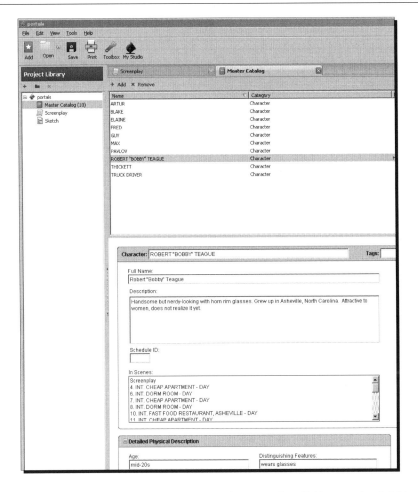

Yours, being a new script, is empty. Create a new character by clicking on the **Add** button, located just below the **Screenplay**. This latter button, if clicked, returns you to the screenplay view. Clicking on the **Master Catalog** button gives you the characters and other categories listed for this project. See how easy it will be to refer to your characters as you write.

The **Add** button gives us the **Add Item...** dialog box. Out of the thirty-six choices (and more custom categories may be added as needed), choose **Character** and type the character's name in the **Name:** box. Characters will also automatically appear in the Master Catalog as we create them in a script by assigning dialog to them. The **Add Item...** dialog box looks like the following screenshot:

Click on the **OK** button and a form to enter data about your character appears (the character's name is already in place because it was just entered). To the right of the name is **Tags**, which can be anything identifying the character—hero, villain, zombie, nuclear scientist, or whatever.

The **Media** block can include a sketch or photo of the character in costume or even a video clip! **Schedule ID:** is used in shooting scripts.

The **In Scenes:** block is neat. Celtx fills that out automatically. Wherever that character speaks in the script or any place that you manually insert the character, Celtx notes it, as shown in the following screenshot:

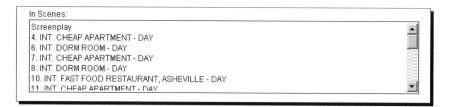

Again, while writing a script when a new attribute for that character occurs to you, just click on the **Master Catalog** button above your script, make the entry, and click on the **Screenplay** tab to return right to the place you were pounding out the script. It's called the creative process, dude, and Celtx has your back on it.

Have a go hero

So take a few minutes and create some characters, filling out physical description, motivation, and the character's background. If we know what he or she or it (got to love them aliens) are all about, such as their history (where they went to school, where they were raised, what their parents did for a living, and so on), and what their motivations in life are, it's easy to write them into a story. We know these "people" and how they will react when the going gets tough.

Tracking people, animals, props, and so on

If you write only spec scripts, it might be okay to skip over the rest of this section. However, what if you get an assignment to turn a spec script into a shooting script? Yeah, baby! It happens!

So, in writing a shooting script, the director and producer and all kinds of other people will want various items tracked. Making movies burns money fast, so it's incredibly important (if there is a trained animal, for example, in our movie) that Blaze the Wonder Horse is on the set ready for his close up in whatever scenes he appears in. Tag Blaze under the **Animals** category and **Master Catalog** keeps track of his appearances.

Let's look at just how easy Celtx makes tracking stuff. In the opening scene of "Portals" (see below), a narrow closet door appears on a Paris sidewalk and also materializes in several other scenes. In filming the movie (in a shooting script), it needs to be on set for each scene. Here's another example of tracking a prop:

```
EXT. A BUSY PARIS STREET - DAY

Rush hour traffic. In the near distance is the Eiffel Tower.
A GENDARME directs traffic with flair. On the sidewalk, a
paint-starved frame with a narrow closet door in it
materializes about a foot behind a pretty FRENCHWOMAN.
```

The door is an important prop in this script; so right in the description, we hold down the left mouse button and select those three words, **narrow closet door**. The words are highlighted in the preceding screenshot.

Look over to the far-right column in the **Screenplay** view and click on the **Breakdown** tab if it is not already selected. Click on **Props** (because a door and frame would be a prop). You will see the name of this prop is already in place, so just click on **Add** and it appears in the list in the bottom window of the right-most column, as shown in the following screenshot:

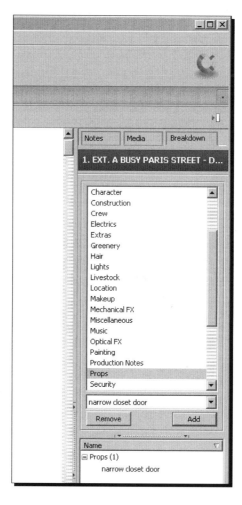

Now, when we visit **Master Category**, we find the "narrow closet door" listed as a prop.

But what if we need a category or even lots of categories not in one of the currently thirty-six defined ones?

Time for action – adding manual catalogs

Carry out the following steps for adding manual catalogs:

1. Click on the main **Add** button.

2. Click on **Catalog**.

3. In the **Select a catalog type** menu list, scroll down and click on **Manual Catalog**.

4. Type the name of your new category in the **Name:** block.

5. Click on **OK**.

The new category now appears in the Project Library, as shown in the following screenshot (we've added **Food** as the category):

Now, an extra step is required. You can tag foods (as in our example) in the script, but you will need to save it as one of the predefined categories. Let's say we have apples and oranges as part of the plot. We save them as **Props**.

Go to **Master Catalog** and you'll see apples and oranges listed as **Props**. Select these by clicking on them (holding down *Ctrl* for PC or the *Command* key on Mac lets you select more than one at a time). Drag these selection(s) to **Food**. Double click on **Food** and we find our food props now listed. Single click on one of these and blocks appear where various details may be entered, just like it did with characters as we saw earlier.

What just happened?

In the **Scenes Used In:** block, Celtx now tracks the scenes in which these items are used. We can add any number of Manual Catalogs needed in this manner. Unlike characters, props must always be put into the catalog manually. Currently, there is no automatic insertion of any elements in the catalog, but speaking characters.

So the Master Catalog lets us both develop and track (in an ongoing creative manner) characters and thirty-five other predefined categories. The Manual Catalog feature gives us the option of adding literally hundreds of other automatically tracked categories. Are we starting to see the power of Celtx already? Yes. We are.

Need an assistant?

It's always good to get someone doing the little things, so that we can concentrate on rolling out words. Celtx jumps in, taking care of stuff that otherwise slows us down, stuff such as intuitive formatting. It's like having a staff of production assistants in a box. For example, type a character name, hit the *Enter* key, and automatically go into the dialog mode without having to select it.

We also get auto-completion of names and scene headings, handy shortcuts, page breaks and pagination, scene numbers, dual dialog, scene management, scratchpad, embedded notes, title page generation, and spellchecking.

Let's play with the time-saving "assistants" listed in the preceding two paragraphs.

Time for action – intuitive formatting

Intuitive formatting basically is what Celtx does to keep our fingers moving. The less we have to think about formatting, the easier to keep the old creative juices flowing and the story building.

Open a new film project (all examples also work in the other types of script projects) and look at the example script that I've started below. Follow along by typing it, and we'll see some examples of Celtx doing intuitive formatting for us.

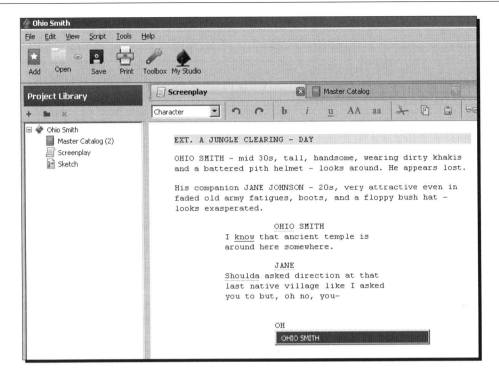

We met the drop-down menu box just over the big script window in *Chapter 1*. We learned there how important it is in five of Celtx's "six biggies", defining the elements that go into Film, Audio-Visual, Theatre, Audio-Play, and Comic Book projects (Story Board is the sixth type).

Elements such as **Scene Heading**, **Character**, and **Dialog** are the very basics of a script. Get their format right and our script looks (and darn well is) professional. Celtx works hard at doing formatting for us unobtrusively.

Okay, let's analyze what happens when writing the little example script above.

When we open a new **Film** project (that is, start a new screenplay), the choice in the dialog box is **Scene Heading**. Scripts start with a scene heading (actually, two screen headings but we'll get into that in *Chapter 7* when we start a script for real).

So, all we have to do now is click in the big script window and type our scene heading.

```
ext. a jungle clearing - day
```

Type in lowercase, as shown above, and hit *Enter*.

What just happened?

Wow! Celtx turned it into all caps. That's because industry standard formatting for scene headings is all caps and this is our first introduction to Celtx's intuitive formatting. Again, for this to work, we must have **Scene Heading** showing in the drop-down menu window.

Note the little element window now. It reads **Action**. The action element is used for description and, yes, actions. Celtx knows this most likely comes next, so type in the first two lines of action.

```
OHIO SMITH - mid 30s, tall, handsome, wearing dirty khakis and a
battered pith helmet - looks around. He appears lost.
```

> Always capitalize the names of characters the first time they appear in a scene and describe them. That's a basic convention that agents and producers expect and look for in scripts.

Continuing, when you hit *Enter* at the end of the first action paragraph, the element window continues showing **Action**. This is because Celtx thinks we are likely to add more actions, as we do in introducing the delectable Jane Johnson.

Now, a manual formatting step is required. Click on the arrow beside **Action** in the events menu window and choose **Character** by clicking on it.

Note the blinking cursor in the script has moved over some spaces. It's now at the right place to enter a character's name. Type:

```
ohio smith
```

Again, we do not have to touch the caps keys. Celtx automatically puts character names where the names appear above the dialog in all caps, as that is standard script formatting (in action from now on, just capitalize names normally after the first time they've appeared).

Look at the events menu window again. It now shows **Dialog** because, having entered a Character element, Celtx knows speech or at least a grunt comes next.

We finish Ohio's dialog by pressing *Enter* and the elements window shows **Character** since usually someone answers. We type:

```
jane
```

Celtx puts it in all caps and we type Jane's reply and Celtx asks for another character name. Well, we just know Ohio's got a retort coming and he speaks next but, having already entered his name once as a character, Celtx knows him and just typing the first two letters of his name causes a blue box (see the preceding figure) to come up with the full name in it. Click on the full name and it is entered for you.

While typing out, `Ohio Smith` might not seem all that bad; what if the character's name is `Daivajna Varāhamihira` (a famous Indian astronomer who lived 506-587)? Right, count on Celtx to remember the spelling of that so we don't have to!

Auto-Complete also works for scene headings. With the elements window showing **Scene Heading**, type `ext.` and Celtx puts it in all caps (the right format) and pops up a list (see the following screenshot) of the previous scenes. Click on one of these or type in a new scene heading, which will be in the list the next time we start an external or outside scene.

Another set of shortcuts is in the small box to the lower-right of the main script window (see the following screenshot). There we find the name of all the characters who have a dialog in the current scene, that is, the one we've inserted the little I-beam editing cursor. Clicking on a character's name in the list in the box will open up the information about that character from the Master Catalog.

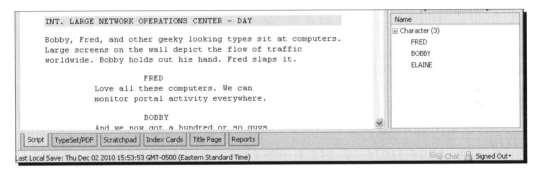

Easy Shortcuts

While we're looking at formatting elements, which in Celtx are the basic building blocks of a script, now's a good time for us to learn some handy shortcuts that also speed up writing.

There are, as a refresher from *Chapter 1*, eight formatting elements in Celtx's **Film** project: Screen Heading, Action, Character, Dialog, Parenthetical, Transition, Shot, and Text. In a spec script, only the first six are used. In a shooting script, we add in Transition (how one scene moves into another) and Shot (camera setup such as close-up, wide, and so on). Text has some important uses, which we'll see later.

First, let's look at changing an existing formatting element (reformatting). Say we want to change a snippet of dialog to action. Simply place the cursor anywhere in the dialog and select **Action** in the events window. In this manner, we can reformat any of the eight types of elements to any of the others.

Now, here's a big problem that Celtx solves to accelerate our writing. It's both cumbersome and distracting having to lift your eyes from your place in the screenplay, look at the elements window, drop-down the menu, and choose an element.

In the previous section, we saw some of the automatic ways in which Celtx helps us in choosing format elements. If you type in a scene heading, the element window now shows **Action**. Knowing this, we can just keep typing without looking up at the elements window.

However, when the actions and descriptions are written and we want a character to start talking, we have to look up and choose **Character** from the drop-down menu, right?

Nope.

Celtx has an easy shortcut. Just hit the *Tab* key and type in the character name. Then hit *Enter* and the Dialog element becomes active. Hit *Enter* at the end of a character's speech and you are in **Character** again, ready for someone to respond.

At the end of the last character's speech, hit *Enter* twice and we are in **Action**.

Are we ready to start the next scene? At the end of a dialog, hit *Enter* three times and you are in **Scene Heading**. At the end of the action, hit *Enter* twice.

Get accustomed to these simple shortcuts and we can pound out perfectly formatted scenes, one after the other, in a white hot fury of creativity without once looking up. Is that cool or what?

But that's not all; there are more shortcuts. The following table, for example, shows you keyboard shortcuts for all the elements in the Film project:

Keys	Element
Ctrl+1	Scene Heading
Ctrl+2	Action
Ctrl+3	Character
Ctrl+4	Dialog
Ctrl+5	Parenthetical
Ctrl+6	Transition
Ctrl+7	Shot
Ctrl+8	Text

As discussed earlier, the *Tab* and *Enter* keys provide shortcuts for switching from one formatting element to another. For a handy-dandy table of all the combinations of these shortcuts, see `http://wiki.celtx.com`.

The Celtx Wiki (Celtx's online manual) is a bit outdated, leaving a place for a book like... well... this one, eh? Still, there's lot of good information there and on the `http://celtx.com` site in general. Overall, it's a great resource for using and keeping up with changes in Celtx.

One more shortcut, if we have selected the wrong formatting element, hitting the *Shift+Tab* key combination allows us to rotate through the formats until we have the format element we want.

Page breaks and pagination

Page breaks are simply where one page ends and another begins. Celtx automatically puts the script standard fifty-four lines per page and inserts page breaks automatically.

Celtx also makes sure that there are no **widows** or **orphans**. A widow is the last line of a paragraph appearing alone at the top of the next page. An orphan is the first line of a paragraph alone at the bottom of a page with the rest of the paragraph on the next page. Script format being all about maximum readability, widows and orphans are frowned upon.

Again, page breaks and widow and orphan control are automated by Celtx.

Pagination (the building of pages) is also all done for you. However, in the default state when you create a new project, your scripts are continuous and while paginated when printed out, you can't see where the page breaks. Should you want to, just look on the very top menu line of the screen, click on **Script**, and then click on **Format Options**. In the **Format Options** dialog box (shown in the following screenshot), check the pagination box and then press the **OK** button:

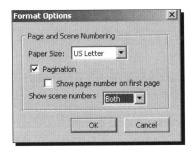

Now your script will show the page breaks, as depicted in the following screenshot:

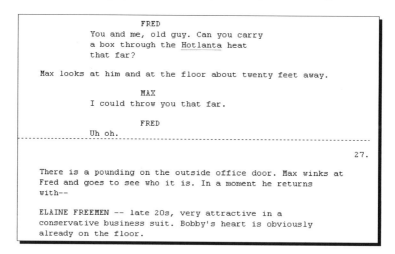

Later in this chapter, we'll see how to build PDFs and print script pages.

Let's take note again here that the on-screen pagination isn't always the same as in the PDF—on screen, Celtx will never split a paragraph where it will split it (with the appropriate "CONTINUED"s) in the TypeSet PDF.

Time for action – numbering scenes

Carry out the following steps:

1. In the **Format Options** dialog box (previous page) where we turned on pagination, we can also turn on scene numbers.

2. To do it, in the **Show scene numbers** drop-down menu, choose **Both** (scene numbers on both sides), **Left**, or **Right**. Scene numbers appear as we see in the following screenshot:

```
20  EXT. I-85 NEAR CHARLOTTE - DAY                              20

    The Charlotte skyline rises above I-85 as a car passes with
    three large men in it.

    SUPERIMPOSE: I-85 near Charlotte, North Carolina

21  INT. CAR, I-85 - DAY                                        21

    Three burly Russians in cheap suits. PAVLOV - 30s, blond
    -drives. VLAD - 40s, dark - sits in front. ARTUR - 20s,
    eager - is in back.

                        ARTUR
                Captain, Americans pay us to kill
                their own?

                        PAVLOV
                Da.

                        ARTUR
                Love America. Such opportunity.

22  INT. CHEAP APARTMENT - DAY                                  22

    Bobby puts his trash into a bag and wads it up. Then sighs.
```

What just happened?

Celtx now numbers the scenes for us, keeping track and revising those numbers if we add or delete scences.

Of course, we only turn on scene numbers in shooting scripts, never in a spec script. Doing so will mark the script as amateurish and it probably won't get read. Yes, they are that picky. Most script readers stop at the first mistake and scene numbers in anything but a shooting script is a mistake.

Dual dialogue

Dual dialogue shows quick interplay between two or more characters. To set up dual dialogue, select the dialog and character's names and click on the little speech balloon icon, shown at the upper-right in the following screenshot (the same icon appears next to character names indicating dual dialogue format):

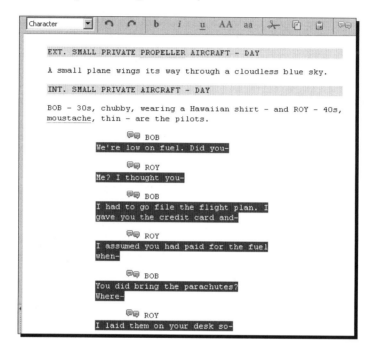

When printed (done by clicking on the **TypeSet/PDF** button at the bottom of your screen), Celtx gives us a nicely formatted dual dialogue, as shown in the following screenshot:

```
EXT. SMALL PRIVATE PROPELLER AIRCRAFT - DAY

A small plane wings its way through a cloudless blue sky.


INT. SMALL PRIVATE AIRCRAFT - DAY

BOB - 30s, chubby, wearing a Hawaiian shirt - and ROY - 40s,
moustache, thin - are the pilots.
          BOB                          ROY
We're low on fuel. Did you-      Me? I thought you-


          BOB                          ROY
I had to go file the flight      I assumed you had paid for
plan. I gave you the credit      the fuel when-
card and-


          BOB                          ROY
You did bring the                I laid them on your desk
parachutes? Where-               so-
```

Scene management

We saw earlier how **Characters** and thirty-five other predefined categories are tracked in the Master Catalog, even showing us which scenes a character or prop appears in. Well, Scenes themselves are tracked and Celtx assists us in easily managing them in various powerful ways.

On the right lower part of the scripts screen (the main screen in all Celtx projects except **Storyboard**), we see the **Scenes** box. In the following screenshot, we have depicted the scenes in "Portals." You can grab the right edge of the box by moving the mouse cursor across until it turns into a double-headed arrow, then press the left mouse button and pull to widen or narrow. I've widened mine, so that we can see the entire scene titles.

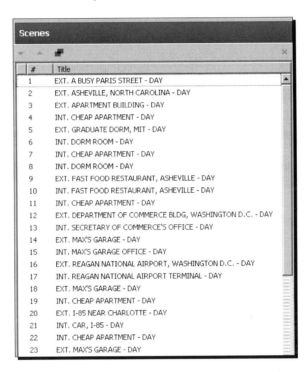

Several actions can be done using this list of scenes. First, move the mouse cursor to the name of a scene and double-click on it. Look over in the large script window and the script will now be at that scene. So navigation around your script using this feature is easy and fast.

Deleting scenes

Now, move the cursor over a scene title and click the left mouse button once. The following mini dialog box pops up:

This gives us three choices. **Go To** we already know about; that's the same as we did by double-clicking on a scene title above. **Delete** is obvious; it deletes the scene from the script. Be careful with this choice. Make sure you really want to get rid of that scene permanently. A better choice would be **Send to Scratchpad**. This option cuts the scene, but we still have access to it (we'll see how the **Scratchpad** works coming up next and how to get stuff into and out of it).

Moving scenes

As we write, sometimes it becomes obvious to us that an already written scene works better in another area of the story. Instead of deleting the scene where it now is and rewriting it where we think it should be, it saves work just to move the scene. Celtx lets us do this easily, keeping track of our changes for renumbering, and so on. Here's how we do it.

Move the mouse cursor over a scene name in the **Scene** box and hold down the left mouse button. Doing this allows us to drag the scene up or down. An underscore bar appears under scene numbers. Releasing the left mouse button inserts the entire scene (no matter how many pages it might be) where the underscore is now.

So, Celtx's power lets you shuffle around scenes and reformats the entire script automatically.

Time for action – using the Scratchpad

The **Scratchpad** is a handy place to keep notes and another of Celtx's writing assistants. I have the outline of "Portals" in mine for easy referral.

1. To open, click on the **Scratchpad** tab at the bottom of your screen and the scratchpad appears over the bottom of the script window, as shown in the following screenshot:

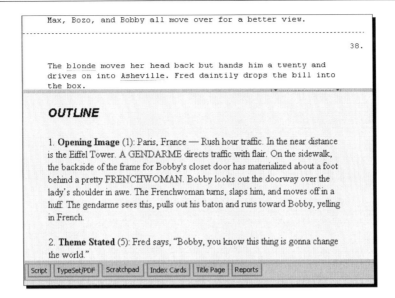

```
Max, Bozo, and Bobby all move over for a better view.
--------------------------------------------------------
                                                    38.

The blonde moves her head back but hands him a twenty and
drives on into Asheville. Fred daintily drops the bill into
the box.
```

OUTLINE

1. **Opening Image** (1): Paris, France — Rush hour traffic. In the near distance is the Eiffel Tower. A GENDARME directs traffic with flair. On the sidewalk, the backside of the frame for Bobby's closet door has materialized about a foot behind a pretty FRENCHWOMAN. Bobby looks out the doorway over the lady's shoulder in awe. The Frenchwoman turns, slaps him, and moves off in a huff. The gendarme sees this, pulls out his baton and runs toward Bobby, yelling in French.

2. **Theme Stated** (5): Fred says, "Bobby, you know this thing is gonna change the world."

| Script | TypeSet/PDF | Scratchpad | Index Cards | Title Page | Reports |

Before writing any script, it's smart to outline it first. Having a roadmap prevents a lot of wrong turns and meandering around aimlessly.

2. If you click one of the other tabs (**Script**, **Typeset/PDF**, and so on), the scratchpad hides itself until the next time it's needed. While open, move the mouse cursor over its top edge, press the left button, and drag it to make it larger if needed. The next time the scratchpad is opened, that size will be remembered.

Another use of the scratchpad would be to save bits of dialog or other information. There are two ways to do this. In the script editing window, we can select text (see the following screenshot) and then right click to bring up the Script Editor Context Menu (the small pop up menu below).

3. Click on **Send to Scratchpad** to remove the text and put it in the scratchpad. Click on **Copy** to leave it in place.

4.   Then, at the bottom of your screen, click on the **Scratchpad** tab, move the cursor in the scratchpad to where you want the text copied, and press *Ctrl+V* to paste it in place.

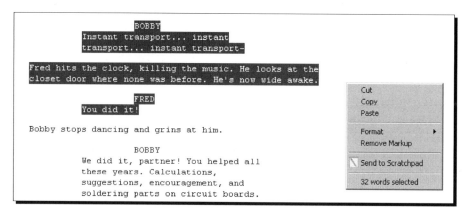

What just happened?

We've now saved that snippet of dialog to the **Scratchpad**.

The size of information you keep in the scratchpad is limited only by your hard disk size. The scratchpad is unique to each project.

Embedded notes

The scratchpad feature discussed earlier, might be thought of as a legal pad or notebook; we can have page upon page of information but nothing is tied to a specific point in the project. Now embedded notes are more like those yellow sticky notes. We jot something down on the pad, rip off the note, and stick it at a certain place.

The following figure is an example. Look at Fred's dialog at the very bottom. There is a little note icon next to the dialog. This symbol does not print but it alerts us to the fact that an embedded note has been stuck there. Double-clicking on the icon shows the note, as shown in the following screenshot, on the upper right. Notice that it is time and date stamped depending on when it was added:

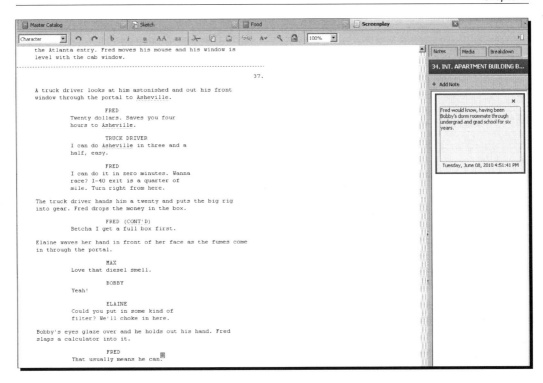

Time for action – adding embedded notes to a script

Carry out the following steps:

1. Move the mouse cursor to the place in the script where an embeddable note is to be added, and click.

2. Move the cursor up to the three tabs (**Notes**, **Media**, and **Breakdown**) in the right sidebar of the screen. A flashing vertical line remains at the place where the note is to be inserted.

3. Click on the **Notes** tab, then click on **+ Add Note**. A yellow "sticky note" appears. As other embeddable notes are added, there will be additional yellow notes in the box.

4. Type in the text content for the note. The notes are of a fixed size but you can add more text than shows with a scroll bar automatically appearing, so that the entire note can easily be read.

What just happened?

The small note icon shown in the preceding figure will also be in place now. Embedded notes are retrieved either by double-clicking on the small icon in the script, or by clicking on the **Notes** button at the top of the right sidebar of the screen.

Title Page generation

Celtx automatically creates a title page for our projects, but we need to fill it out. To open the title page, click on the **Title Page** tab at the bottom of the script window and the following screenshot shows what we get:

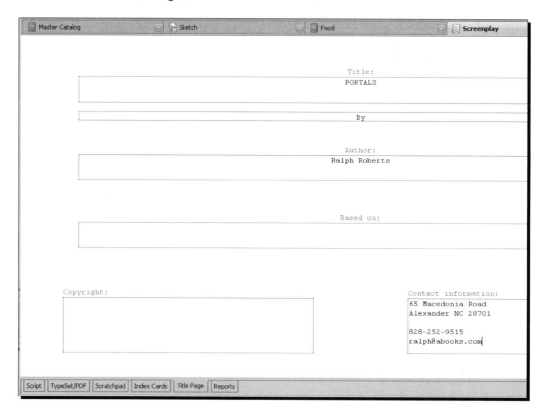

A title page is pretty much self-explanatory

1. Fill in the **Title** of your script (use all caps).

2. Under **Author**, put your name and the names of any co-authors.

   ❑ In the **Based on**: field, fill this out only if the script is based on a book or other literary work. In my case, "Portals" is an original work.

❏ Do not enter anything at all under copyright for a spec script. You'll want to have your script copyrighted or registered with an organization like the Writers Guild of America (WGA) but do not put it here. This is the way agents and producers expect to see a title page and not adhering to that convention makes one look amateurish. There are times when you'll want to use this feature, but they will always be clear. For example, some screenwriting competitions require WGA registration for entry, and the registration number can be included here. Do not include this information unless you are specifically asked for it.

❏ Finally, add your contact information. The address you see in the preceding screenshot is my real contact information. "Portals", although it's used as an example in this book, is an actual script for sale. Always, in trying to market your scripts, make sure producers, agents, and managers know where to contact you.

Once your script is completed, protect it. One of the most common ways is by getting a Writers Guild of America West WGA number. At `http://www.wgawregistry.org/webrss/`, you can register your script online for $20 US and get a number immediately.

One more thing, there is a known bug in the way Celtx (at least through Version 2.71) generates the title page (and this is only on the title page). The top three blocks are sometimes off center, depending on whether there is an odd or even number of letters and spaces. Many people might not notice but me, as I always want my scripts to look perfect, it irks.

So, here's a workaround until the centering bug is fixed. Insert the cursor behind (to the right) the text you want to center. On a PC keyboard, hold down the *Alt* key and in the numeric keypad (not the numbers along the top of the letter keys) type `0160`. That key combination is *Alt+0160*, which inserts a non-breaking or hard space. Insert, however many of these, it takes to center the title and byline to your satisfaction. See the following screenshot for the difference (left = before and right = after). (Also adding extra normal spaces might work, depending on your machine's set up):

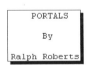

A subtle difference, but for a two or three hundred thousand dollar sale, we want to make a little effort, eh? Which brings us to the next effort we had better be doing, *fixing spelling errors*.

Spellchecking

Nothing turns off a reader faster than spelling errors, typos, and mistakes in grammar. We simply cannot get by with those in a screenplay being marketed to Hollywood, Bollywood, or any other professional buyer of scripts. Proof, proof, and proof again before sending any script out.

Here's an old writers proofing tip. Read your script aloud! Read every single page, every single word out loud. You'll catch errors overlooked for weeks this way. It's well worth the effort and should be an ironclad rule to do before any script goes out the door. It's also good to get people to read it aloud for you. Sometimes you find errors easier that way.

Celtx helps us with spelling. As we saw in *Chapter 1*, dictionaries are available in several languages and easily installed. Celtx comes with a U.S. English dictionary in place.

To start the spellchecker, click where the checking is to start in the script, a flashing vertical bar appears. Then, on the Editor Menu, just above the script window, click on the button that has the letter **A** followed by a check mark (see the following screenshot, the button is just above the title of the pop-up **Check Spelling** dialog box).

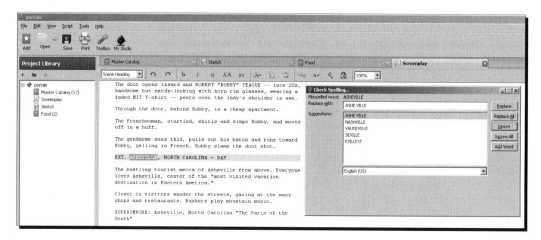

Celtx finds the first word not in the dictionary, in this case, **ASHEVILLE**, and highlights it. We now look at the buttons on the right of the dialog box, which show our options. We can replace it with one of the suggested spellings such as **ASHE VILLE** or **NASHVILLE** by selecting our choice and clicking on **Replace** for just that one instance or **Replace All** to always make that change.

Clicking on **Ignore** causes Celtx to ignore this one instance of the word, and **Ignore All** to not mention it from now on in this script.

The correct response, **ASHEVILLE** is spelled correctly and used several times in the script, would be the **Add Word** button, which causes Celtx to learn the word.

Celtx's spell checking feature is wonderful; use it often, and it will make you and your scripts look good.

When proofing, watch for "spellcheck errors", words spelled correctly but used incorrectly. For example, a character saying "I beet his butt" instead of "I beat his butt" or "Did you loose the key?" instead of "Did you lose the key." No spellchecker catches those kinds of mistakes.

Inline Spellchecking

On the very top menu line of the screen, click on **Tools** and then **Inline Spellchecking** to turn this feature on. Now misspelled or unrecognized words in our script will be underlined in red. Right clicking on the work brings up a context menu with suggestions for the word, giving you a chance to immediately correct it, as shown in the following screenshot:

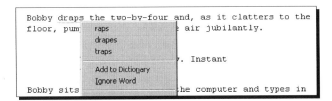

Write once, use many

That's always been one of my goals as a longtime professional writer, to use it as many times as I could. Celtx's Adapt feature does exactly that. You can, with one click, change formatting on your screenplay to a stage play or a comic book or any of the other formats which Celtx knows (and you can add additional formats as needed). That's pretty powerful.

Okay, I decide "Portals" would make a good comic also. To convert or adapt (in Celtx parlance), click on **Script** (top menu, see the following screenshot) and then select **Adapt To**. Then choose **Comic Book**:

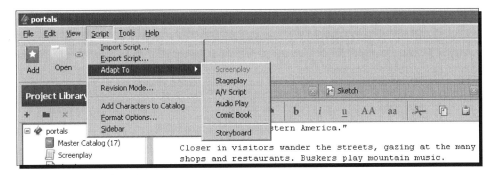

```
Page 1    EXT. A BUSY PARIS STREET - DAY

   Panel 1   Rush hour traffic. In the near distance is the
             Eiffel Tower. A GENDARME directs traffic with
             flair. On the sidewalk, a paint-starved frame with
             a narrow closet door in it materializes about a
             foot behind a pretty FRENCHWOMAN.

   Panel 2   The door opens inward and ROBERT "BOBBY" TEAGUE --
             late 20s, handsome but nerdy-looking with horn rim
             glasses, wearing a faded MIT T-shirt -- peers over
             the lady's shoulder in awe.

   Panel 3   Through the door, behind Bobby, is a cheap
             apartment.

   Panel 4   The Frenchwoman, startled, whirls and slaps Bobby,
             and moves off in a huff.
```

Do a **Save As** and we have "Portals" now as both a Film project and a Comic Book project. I'll need to go through and add balloon types and a few other things, but everything is already in the correct industry standard comic book format.

Time for action – getting the script out of your computer

PDF or Portable Document Format, developed by Adobe Systems, is the standard format these days for transmitting or printing out screenplays and other types of scripts. Celtx formats your scripts in industry standard formats (that is, for a movie screenplay, stage play, audio-visual script, and so on) and creates a PDF file of the result. However, this is done in an interesting way.

To keep Celtx's footprint (use of resources on your computer) small, formatting is actually done out on the web. This means, when it is time to format, an Internet connection must be live. Celtx sends your script to a server out there somewhere (we don't care where), turns it into a PDF, and returns it to your computer (without saving anything out there, by the way).

For Linux and other tech heads among us (I wave both hands excitedly), this conversion is accomplished using XSL (Extensible Stylesheet Language) and LaTeX (my long-time and far away favorite open source typesetting language) on a big iron server out there in the Internet cloud. Never mind the techie stuff. The short of it is that in this manner, Celtx gives us more power than our own computer can and keeps our local software lean but powerful and, above all, free.

Let's see how we create PDFs and print our scripts. At the very bottom of the big script window, we have the following tabs:

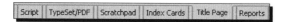

After making sure that we have an Internet connection, we click on **TypeSet/PDF**. After usually a very brief pause, even for a 110-page standard spec screenplay, the formatted script is returned to our computer and appears in the script window.

What just happened?

The PDF may now be printed or saved for use with programs like the free Adobe Reader. We can also e-mail out saved PDFs to agents, managers, and/or producers when requested. A returned script in PDF format is shown in the following screenshot:

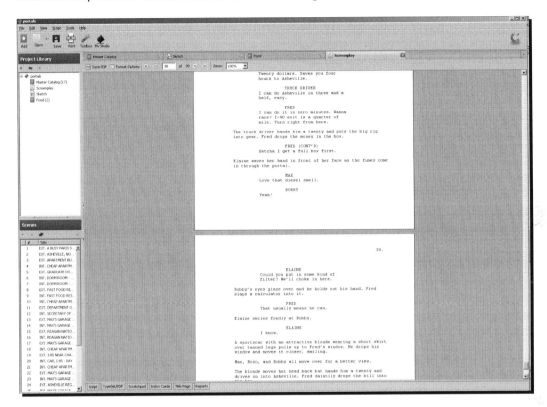

From this point, we could print our script by clicking on the **Print** button at the top right of the screen. However, one more step is needed to give us an actual PDF file, one that we can print from or e-mail to an agent or producer.

Just above the formatted script in the large script window, there is a **Save PDF** button, which is shown in the following screenshot:

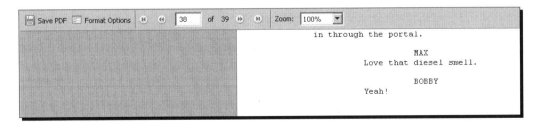

Click on the **Save PDF** button. The Save As dialog box that pops up allows us to select a name and a location to save our PDF file. Then click on **Save**. A blue progress bar appears at the bottom of the screen as the PDF file is created. On completion of this operation, we now have a PDF ready for use.

To view or print this new PDF, we must have software that handles PDF files installed on our computer. The best (and it's free) is Adobe Reader. Download it for free at:

`http://www.adobe.com`

Let's look at one more item relating to creating PDFs. Just to the left of the **Save PDF** button, we have the **Format Options** button, as shown in the following screenshot:

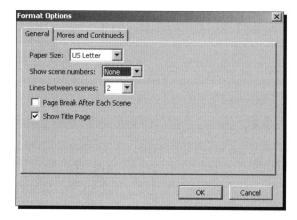

We can use the Format Options dialog box (which has two tabs, as shown in the preceding screenshot) to change format options for our script and it will automatically reformat. Please note, the settings in the two figures are the proper ones for a spec screenplay.

Finally, to the left of the **Format Options** button, we find navigation aids to move through the pages of our script and a zoom feature to help us see it better.

Using Index Cards

Included in Celtx are reversible color-coded Index Cards, yet another type of assistant making your job as scriptwriter easier. Celtx ties these cards to the proper place in your script and puts the scene heading and first 40 or so words of the scene on this electronic "card." You flip the card on the screen to type notes and color code them to follow plot lines. You can also drag and drop them to move scenes around.

What does that mean? Something truly powerful! Let's see for ourselves.

At the bottom of the script window, click on the **Index Cards** tab, as shown in the following screenshot:

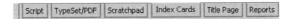

The script window is now full of blank cards; the numbers on the cards correspond to the scene numbers in our script.

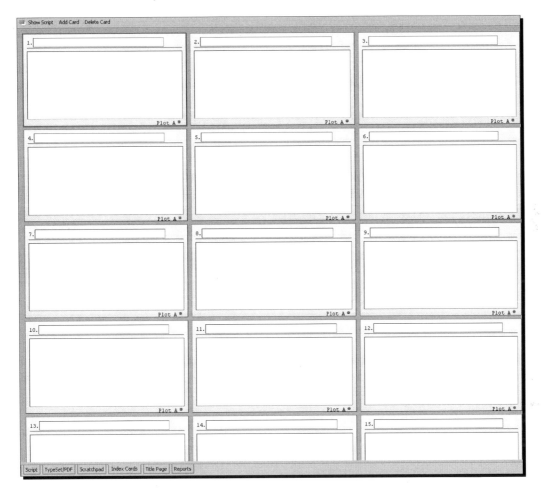

This "side" of the cards may be thought of as the "back" (and is for our notes). Ah, then what's on the front? Click on the **Show Script** button just above the top row of cards. Blap! The cards flip over and we have every single scene in the script with the heading and the first few lines of the scene (the button's label changes to **Show Notes**. Click on it to flip back to notes).

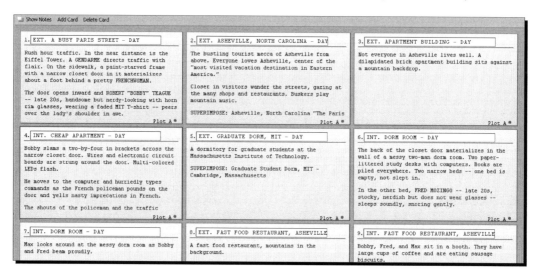

Clicking on the **Show Notes** button flips the card back over, so that we can make notes about a scene.

Notice down in the extreme right hand corner of each card where it has **Plot A**. Click on this and we get the **Pick a Colour** dialog box (the developers of Celtx are headquartered in Newfoundland, Canada, so they use "colour" instead of "color"). This box allows us to color-code (or ever colour-code) the index cards. Thus we can more easily follow the threads of the different plots. More on this in a moment.

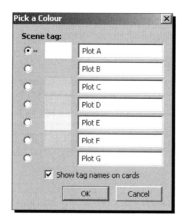

Now, move the mouse over the cards. A set of crossed double arrows appears (see the following screenshot, it's different on Mac being a hand instead of an arrow). Hold down the left mouse button and that card can be dragged to another location. Remember, earlier in this chapter when we learned scene management using the Scenes window over on the lower left of the Celtx script screen? We dragged the scene heading up and down and it moved the entire scene in the script. Well, shuffling these cards also moves the entire scene in the script!

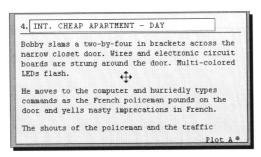

Moving scenes around by moving these Index Cards is really a big deal, but beyond the scope of this book to explain. Let me suggest here a classic book about screenwriting, *Save the Cat* by the late and great *Blake Snyder*. It's still in print and readily available at an inexpensive price. In this book, Blake shows how we manually use Index Cards in rows to plot movies. The Index Cards feature in Celtx is a computerized facsimile of this process integrated into your scriptwriting software; that's why it's exciting and useful.

Revision Mode

Celtx excels at tracking changes in our scripts. This is especially important for a shooting script in production. To turn on the revision mode on the top menu bar (top of the Celtx screen), click on **Script**, and then click on **Revision Mode....** The **Revision Options** dialog box pops up over the script, as shown in the following screenshot:

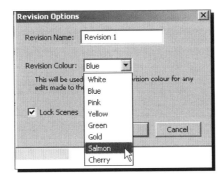

In the dialog box, you can enter the name of the revision and choose a color. Save the project under a new name, so that previous versions will still be available. Now when changes are made, they are shown in the script in the color that we chose for this revision name (Salmon).

Once the first revision has been made, a revision tool bar appears just above the script as shown in the following screenshot:

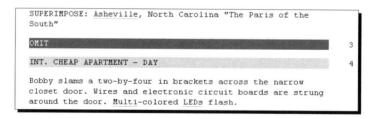

Clicking on the green button with the white cross in it creates a new revision. The Revision Options box pops up again and we can change the color and name of the revision. However, be sure to save the new revision under a new name to preserve the previous revision.

To the right of the revision name in the revision tool bar above is the color selector. We can change the color of the current revision and all edits made after that will be in the new color.

The small window with **Right #** in it lets you change the way scene numbers are shown. Remember, in shooting scripts we have scene numbers. The choices are right, left, and fix. The **Fix** choice lets us set the scene numbers, so that they don't change if we add or remove scenes.

In the last small window we see **All Marks**, which is the default and shows all revisions made in this and any previous revisions. Other choices are **Current Marks**, which shows changes made only in this revision, and **Hide Marks** which hides all the colored changes.

Finally (see the following screenshot), the last icon to the left on the revision tool bar hides whatever scene the cursor is in, putting the word **OMIT** in place of the entire scene:

When we build a PDF of the script, the fact that lines have changed is indicated by the industry standard inclusion of an asterisk (*) in the right margin of the page, as shown in the following screenshot:

```
Through the door, behind Bobby, is a really cheap apartment.        *

The gorgeous Frenchwoman, startled, whirls and slaps Bobby,         *
and moves off in in a really irked manner.                         *
```

Finally, we can reset (lose) all the revisions and revert to the original script by (in Script mode) clicking on the **Script** button at the top toolbar, and then clicking on **Reset Revision Mode...**. Again, this will clear all revisions, so be sure it's the right thing to do.

It is common practice in larger productions to print revisions on colored paper, so the director, actors, and others involved on the set knows a change has occurred. Sometimes there are so many changes that they run out of colors and have to cycle through again. Such is the magic of making movies.

Time for action – adding new project types with the Template Engine

While Celtx provides us the five standard industry formats, Film, Audio-Visual, Theatre, Audio Play, and Comic Books, we are not limited to them. In case, a different or non-standard format is needed, we can create and save them using the template engine feature.

To create a new template, open Celtx in the one of the five formats discussed previously. Click on the **File** button on the top menu bar, and then click on **Create Template...**. A Save Project dialog box appears. Enter the name and save it.

The name of the new template appears as a project type in the list on the splash page as Celtx starts and only opens the documents we want (that is, those created using that template).

To make that a bit clearer, we open a standard format (any of the ones provided), make the changes to the format we want, and then save it as a new template that we can use over and over again.

Summary

In this chapter, we met a number of assistants, which Celtx provides to handle drudge work and keep our creativity flowing. Specifically, we learned about tracking characters, plots, and thirty-six other production categories. Also we saw how to make use of intuitive formatting and easy shortcuts.

We explored the power of "write once, use many" with Celtx's Adapt feature and built PDFs of our scripts with the TypeSet feature.

Using the reversible color-coded electronic Index Cards made following plots and changing scenes around a breeze, as was letting Celtx track revisions for us. We learned how using the Template Engine lets us create new project types.

Coming up next, we'll learn about storyboarding, part of several strong aids in Celtx to pre-visualize how our movie or other production will look (this can save you a lot of time in writing coherent scripts).

3
Visualizing Productions Ahead of Time

In this chapter, we explore how Celtx lets us use sketching (drawing a quick thumbnail of a scene), built-in storyboarding techniques (more elaborate visualization), and also attaching media files (pictures or descriptions of costumes, for example, an audio file showing how a bit of dialog should really sound, or even video clips). This lets us plan our production (movies, audio-visual presentations, stage plays, or whatever) before even writing the script. We can save immense amounts of money and effort by knowing what will happen before reaching the time where expensive people and equipment are standing around.

If you just write scripts, you won't need the features in this and the next chapter, Getting Organized. However, Indie (independent) producers, folks actually making movies, putting together audio visual shows, or creating documentaries will find these tools of immense value and here we look at visualizing all this good stuff (pun, as ever, intended).

Besides, even if we are just writing a script, visualization techniques can make that a lot easier as well. Knowing where we are going is wonderful in helping us get there, eh?

In this chapter, we will learn the following:

- ◆ Sketching: Sketches let us diagram camera, light, character and prop placement, and the other items that we need to visually plan the setup of a scene for filming.

- ◆ Storyboarding: Celtx helps us build storyboards using external clipart or photos and included icons to give a visual representation of our script. We can do storyboards before writing a script, or afterwards, to help turn the script into a film or video.

◆ Add media files: Media files (photos, graphics, videos) may be attached to any of the thirty-six production categories, including wardrobe, props, and locations.

By the end of this chapter, we'll be well familiar with why and how to use these visualization features in Celtx.

Sketching

Celtx's Sketch Tool allows us to easily visualize ideas and shot setups by adding our drawings of them to projects. Sketches can be separate items in the Project Library (or in folders within the library) or added to a project's Storyboard (more on that in the next section of this chapter).

The Sketch Tool comes with pre-loaded icons for people, cameras, and lights, which we can drag and drop into our sketches, making them look more polished. The icons are **SVG** images (**Scalable Vector Graphics**), which allow us to make them as large as we like without losing any quality in the image. The `http://celtx.com` site makes additional icons available (**Art Packs**) at low costs (example: $2.99 for 23 icons).

Also provided in the Sketch tool are tools for drawing lines, arrows, shapes, and for adding text labels. Just to avoid confusion, let me tell you that there is nothing like pens or erasers or other free drawing features. We'll use various drag-and-drop icons and any of us, artistic talent or not, can turn out very professional-looking storyboards in no time at all.

 Celtx Projects are containers which hold items such as scripts, index cards, reports, schedules, storyboards, prop lists, and more including sketches.

Time for action – starting a new sketch

We have two ways of creating a new Sketch, which are as follows:

1. First, open a project (new or already in progress) and look in the **Project Library** in the upper-left quadrant of the Celtx screen. **Sketch** is included by default, as shown in the following screenshot:

2. The following steps show the second method for creating a new sketch:

   ❏ Click on **File** at the very upper-left of the Celtx main window

   ❏ On the drop-down menu, choose **Add Item...**

   ❏ Click on **Sketch** and then click on **OK**, as shown in the following screenshot:

What just happened?

The new Sketch is added to the Project Library window. If one was already there (likely since it is by default), you now have two with the same name. No problem; simply right-click on one of them, choose **Rename**, and change its name. We can also delete or duplicate a Sketch this way.

To open the main **Sketch Tool** window from anywhere in a Celtx project, double-click on the name of the **Sketch** in the **Project Library**.

In the case of a new **Sketch** created through the **Add Item** dialog box, as shown in the preceding section, it will already be open and ready for use. That is, the main window covering most of the center of the Celtx screen is where we sketch. Double-clicking on **Screenplay** or any other item in the **Project Library** window navigates us to that item and away from our **Sketch**. It is saved automatically.

The following screenshot shows how the **Sketch Tool** looks when opened:

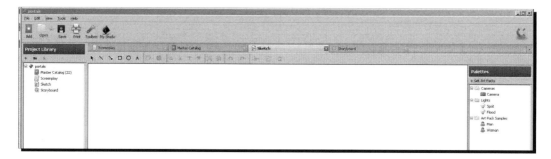

Sketch Tool toolbar

Along the top of the middle window (the **Sketch Tool** window), we have a toolbar. In the preceding screenshot, most of these tools are grayed out. They become fully visible when conditions are met for their use.

Let's take a tour. The following screenshot shows the sketch toolbar in its entirety:

Now, let's explore these tools individually and see what they do. In addition to the tool bar (shown in the preceding screenshot), I'll include an image of each individual tool as well:

   ◆   **Select tool**: The first tool from the left is for selecting items in the sketch. There's nothing to select yet, so let's click on the second tool from the left. The select tool is shown in the following screenshot:

- **The diagonal line**: It is the second tool from the left and it draws a line. Move the cursor (now a cross) to the point where the line begins, hold down the left mouse button, and drag out the line, releasing the mouse button at its ending point. The diagonal line is shown in the following screenshot:

- **Line tool**: Click on the first tool above. The mouse cursor becomes a hollow arrow on a PC but remains a black arrow on the Mac. Select the line we drew by clicking on it (a little hard for a line) or holding down the left mouse button and drawing a box all the way around the line (easier). When the mouse button is released, we know the line is selected because it has a dotted blue line around it and two small gray circles or "handles" at either end. Once the item is selected, just hold down the left mouse button and it can be moved anywhere in the **Sketch Tool** window.

  Select either of the handles by moving the cursor arrow over it and pressing the left mouse button. We can now move that end of the line all over the place and it stays wherever the button is released; it's the same for the other end of the line.

  While the line is selected, just hit the *Delete* key to erase it. This also works in the same way for all the other elements.

- **Arrow Tool**: The third tool from the left (the diagonal arrow) works exactly like the line tool, except there's an arrowhead on one end. It's a useful drawing tool for pointing to something in our diagrams or using as a spear if it's that kind of movie, eh? The arrow tool is shown in the following screenshot:

- **Box and Circle Tools**: The fourth tool (the box) draws a box or rectangle and the fifth (the circle) a circle or oval. Clicking on the select tool (the first tool on the left) and using its cursor to click inside of a square or circle selects it. There are two little gray circles which allow us to manipulate the figure just as we did with the line above. The box tool is shown in the following screenshot:

And the circle tool is shown in the following screenshot:

◆ **Text Tool**: Suppose we want to label a line, arrow, box, or circle, we can use the sixth tool, that is, the little letter "A", which is shown in the following screenshot:

Draw a box and click on the **A**. The mouse cursor is now an "I-beam". Click in the box. A mini-dialog box appears, as shown in the following screenshot:

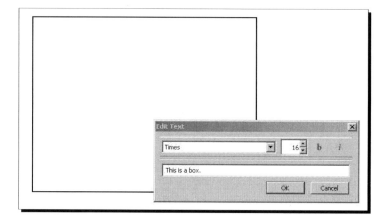

This **Edit Text** box allows the selection of the font, size, bold, italic, and provides a place to type in the label, such as the stirring **This is a box**. Click on **OK** and the label is in the box, as shown in the following screenshot:

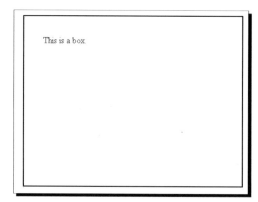

If we need to edit an existing label, click on the select tool, double-click on the text, the **Edit Text** mini-dialog box comes up, and you can edit the text.

Keeping the labeled box as an example, we're ready to visit the next two tools, namely, the empty circle and his brother the solid circle, both of which are grayed out at the moment. Let's wake them up.

◆ **Stroke and Fill Tools**: Click on the select tool and then click inside the box. These two tools turn blue and allow us access to them. These are shown in the following screenshot:

The empty circle controls the color of the **stroke** (that's the outline of the item, such as our box) and the solid circle, the **fill** (the inside color of the item). Note that there is a small arrow on the right side of each circle. Click on the one next to the solid (fill) circle. A color selection box drops down; choose a color by clicking on it. The box now has that color inside it as a fill, as shown in the following screenshot:

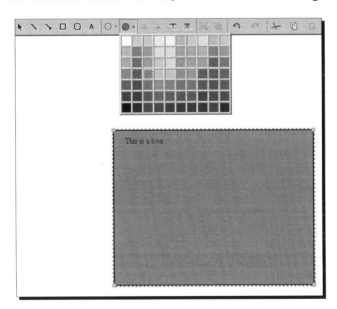

If you want to change the stroke and/or fill colors, just click on the stroke or fill tool to drop-down the selection box again.

Moving on, add another box (or circle, whatever) and move it. Use the select tool, hold down the *Shift* key, click on the new box, and move it over the original box.

◆ **Layer Tools**: Okay, we now have one item on top of another. Sometimes that's inconvenient in a scene diagram and we need to reverse the order (move one or more items up a layer or more). With the top box selected, look at the toolbar. The next four icons to the right of the stroke and fill circles are now "lit up" (no longer grayed out). The layer tools are shown in the following screenshot:

These are, in the order, lower to bottom, lower, raise, and raise to top. In other words, the selected box would be lowered to the bottom-most layer, lowered one layer, raised one layer, or jumped all the way to the top-most layer.

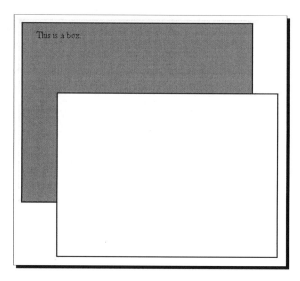

◆ **Group and Ungroup**: Now, to save a few million electrons, let's use the same two boxes again. Select the one on top, hold down the *Shift* key, and both boxes are now selected. We can move them together, for example. However, note that the next icon to the right is now no longer gray (it's now two blue boxes, one over the other and four smaller black ones). This is the group tool, which is shown in the following screenshot:

Clicking on it groups or bonds the selected items together. This, of course, lights up the next icon on the toolbar, the (wait for it) ungroup tool, which restores independence to grouped items.

- ◆ **Undo and Redo Tools**: The next two toolbar icons, the curved arrows, are undo and redo tools. They reverse an action to the previous state or restore an item to its next state (if there is one, that is, "undo" and "redo"). These tools are shown in the following screenshot:

- ◆ **Cut, Copy, and Paste Tools**: The last three tools on the **Sketch Tool** window toolbar are the cut, copy, and paste tools, as shown in the following screenshot:

    Cutting removes an item but retains it on the clipboard, copying leaves the item and also puts a copy of it on the clipboard, while paste puts the item from the clipboard back into the sketch.

Now, we come to the fun part, icons! As in "yes, icon do a professional-looking sketch." (Sorry, couldn't resist.)

Icons for a professional look

Celtx provides icons, giving our sketches a polished professional look (neat, artistic, follows industry entertainment conventions) while requiring little or no artistic ability. The **Palettes** windows, found on the right side of the main **Sketch Tool** window, list available icons.

The default installation of Celtx includes a very limited number of icons, one camera, two kinds of lights, and a top-down view of a man and a woman. Celtx, of course, is open source software and thus free (a price I can afford). However, one of the ways in which its sponsoring developer, a Canadian company, Greyfirst Corp. in St. John's, Newfoundland, makes money is by selling add-ons to the program, one type being additional icons in the form of Art Packs. In the following screenshot, if we click on the **+ Get Art Packs** link, a webpage opens where one can order Art Packs and other add-ons at quite reasonable prices:

A personal statement here: the *only payment* I receive for writing this book comes in the form of royalties, a commission from the sale of each book. You, the readers (thanks), are my only source of income. So, while I won't go out of my way in giving free advertisement for the commercial add-ons of Celtx, they will be mentioned where explanation benefits us, the final users of this wonderful software. Any purchase is totally your decision.

Now, to use an icon in a sketch, let's start with the camera. Open a new sketch by double-clicking on **Sketch** in the **Project Library** window or **Add Item** from the main File menu. In the **Palettes** window, move the mouse cursor over **Camera** and hold down the left mouse button while dragging the camera icon into the main **Sketch Tool** window. It looks like the following screenshot:

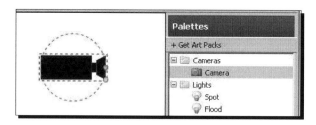

Manipulating icons: When any icon is dragged into the main window of the **Sketch Tool** (and anytime that icon is selected by clicking on it with the select tool cursor described earlier) it has a dotted circle around it (as shown in the preceding screenshot) and two small solid circles (violet on top, olive below). Clicking on the violet circle and holding down the left mouse button while dragging allows rotation of the icon. Releasing the button stops rotation and leaves the icon in that orientation.

Clicking on the olive circle (the lower one) and holding down the left mouse button and dragging allow resizing the icon, either larger or smaller. As these icons, like the lines, arrows, boxes, and circles we discussed earlier in this chapter are also **SVG (Scalable Vector Graphics)**, we can have them as large as desired with no pixilation or other distortion.

Using the **Sketch Tool** toolbar and the supplied icons, we can rapidly and easily draw professional looking diagrams like the scene shown in the following screenshot, which shows two lights, the camera, the talent, arrows showing their movement in the scene, and the props:

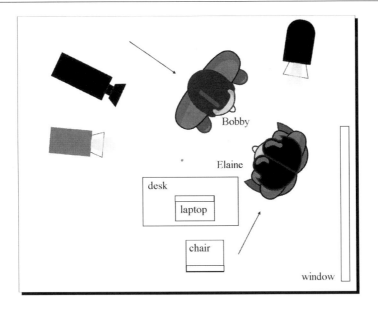

Again, additional icons may be purchased from the `http://celtx.com` website. For example, the following screenshot shows the twenty-three icons available in **Art Pack 1**:

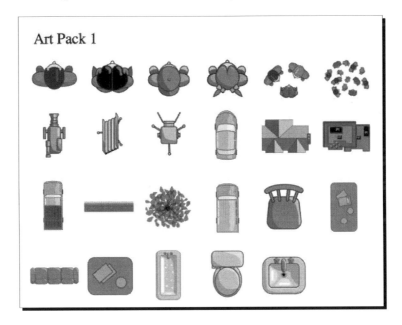

Saving a finished Sketch

Now is a good time for us to take a moment and discuss the limitations of the Sketch Tool. This feature provides a fast way of whipping up a scene diagram from inside a Celtx project. It does not replace an outside drawing program nor give us the functionality of something like Adobe Illustrator, but it is quite powerful and very handy. By the way, we can use external media files in Celtx and we'll do just that in both of the remaining sections of this chapter.

Another limitation concerns saving sketches. There's no way of exporting the sketch as an external image such as .jpg or .bmp. In fact, even saving within the Celtx project is automated. Do the following to see what I mean:

1. In a Celtx project, double-click on **Sketch** in the **Project Library** to start a sketch.

2. Draw something.

3. Double-click on **Screenplay**. Then double-click on **Sketch**. The drawing is still there.

4. Save the Celtx project, exit, and open it again. Double-click on **Sketch**. Drawing's still there!

We can even use **Add Item** from the File menu (a shortcut is the little plus symbol beneath the **Project Library** title) and add another Sketch (same name) to the **Project Library** and even draw a new sketch in it. Of course, having different drawings with the same name is hardly utilitarian, so here's how we really save a sketch.

Time for action – saving and organizing Sketches

Carry out the following steps to rename a Sketch:

1. Right-click on **Sketch**.

2. On the drop-down menu, left-click on **Rename...**.

3. Name the drawing something unique and descriptive, such as **Scene 5**.

We can accumulate all our sketches in the **Project Library** window, but for a long project that can really get cluttered. We can "neaten" things up by creating folders and grouping sketches (or anything else). To do that, carry out the following steps:

1. Right-click on **Sketch**.

2. Left-click on the little file folder icon just below the **Project Library** title. In the **Add Folder...** mini dialog box (see the following screenshot), give the new folder (or subdirectory) a name, and then click on **OK**.

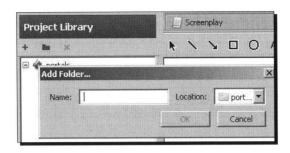

3. When the folder appears in the **Project Directory** window, we can simply select (individually or in groups) sketches and drag-and-drop them into the folder.

What just happened?

Using folders, we organized sketches (made them easier to find again) and reduced clutter by having less items in the main **Project Library** window.

Storyboarding

The **Sketch Tool** is indeed useful, but Celtx provides an even more powerful way of visualizing scenes. Let's look at storyboarding now.

Storyboards are a series of illustrations (sketches) and images shown in sequence to pre-visualize (graphically plan) a motion picture, animation, documentary, interactive website, or any other type of the many productions that can be scripted in Celtx. Essentially, like a large comic (as in a comic book) of the film, storyboards help directors, cinematographers, or videographers (people who run the cameras), clients, or anyone one else involved in a project, visualize the scenes and find potential problems ahead of time.

Even if we are only writing a spec script, it helps us describe how the plot plays out if we have a series of visualizations, namely, a Storyboard.

The storyboard format, which is widely used today and incorporated into Celtx, was first developed at the Walt Disney studios in the 1930s. One of the first major feature films to be storyboarded was the classic *Gone with the Wind* in 1939. Storyboarding is important and helpful in the creative process. Instead of pinning drawings all over the walls, like the first storyboards, Celtx lets us do it right inside our project.

Time for action – storyboarding

Let's dive right in to storyboarding. On the Splash dialog box that appears when we open Celtx, there's a list of recent projects, as shown in the following screenshot:

Click on **Samples** in the upper-right corner and we now have a list of several sample projects, which come included in Celtx when it's downloaded and installed. Double-click on the top one, the complete script of the **Wonderful Wizard of Oz**, as shown in the following screenshot:

As shown in the following screenshot, the Storyboard screen depicts a drawing of each shot:

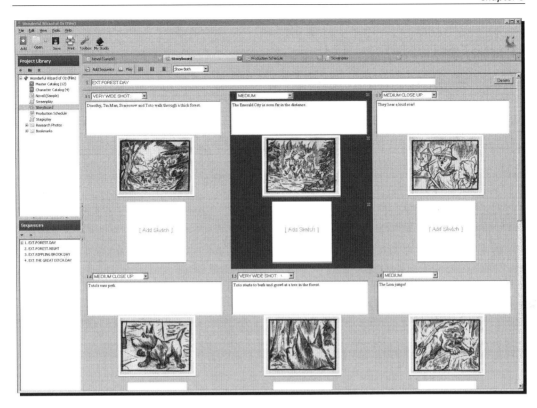

In Scene 1 of the **Wonderful Wizard of Oz**, we find 19 different shots, each with a drawing showing its setup. I'll show you how to get drawings and photographs placed on a Storyboard in just a moment. First, we'll examine the parts of a shot (one camera setup, there often are several per scene).

Look at the first shot on the preceding screenshot. By default, it is numbered as shot **1.1** because it's the first scene. The second shot in that scene is **1.2**, the third **1.3**, and so forth. Scene 2's shots are 2.1, 2.2, 2.3, and so on.

Each shot has the following four items:

1. The type of shot such as **VERY WIDE SHOT**, **MEDIUM**, **OVER THE SHOULDER**, and so on. Clicking on the arrow button next to **VERY WIDE SHOT**, as shown in scene 1 and a drop-down menu in the preceding screenshot, gives us the choice of eighteen standard shots. If a special shot not on that list is needed, simply note that fact in the following text entry box.

2. The Description entry box allows notes about the shot to be entered.

3. The **Add Image** box lets us insert scanned drawings (the ones in this Storyboard come from simple .jpg files).

4. And finally, the **Add Sketch** box. Remember sketches? Yep, we just learned about those, now we'll see how to get them into our Storyboards.

What just happened?

We found out that Storyboards boil down to being no more than a series of drawings serving as a shorthand dry run of our projects and, also, an easy way to interest and wow investors or other types of clients. *Storyboards are a great tool.*

Storyboard controls

The tools to create our storyboards, as in all Celtx projects, live along the top of the main section of the screen. The following screenshot presents a closer view:

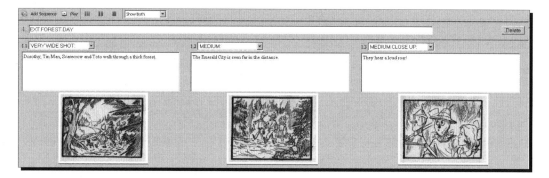

We'll look at **Add Sequence** first. A sequence here is simply a series of one or more shots, basically a scene. If we're doing a comic book, the shots would be pages. And, yes, while it may surprise some, comics lend themselves to storyboarding quite well, allowing us to determine the placement of balloons, characters, and play around with the overall look and story before committing lines to paper in drawing the comic pages.

So, clicking on **Add Sequence** adds a blank but numbered scene. We fill in the title of the new scene and the other components such as drawings, photos, other media files, and sketches.

Now, here's a neat feature, speaking of wowing someone. After our storyboard is done, we can play it as an automatic slide show by clicking on the **Play** button, which brings up a flash player, similar to the one shown in the following screenshot. Experiment with that. Movement gives a sense of how the completed movie or any other project will play out.

Going back to our storyboard toolbar, the next three buttons—the three bars, two bars, and single block buttons—cause the shots to be displayed three across, two across, or just one per line. The buttons look like the following screenshot and, again, are found at the top of the main storyboard window.

The **Show Both** drop-down menu displays both media files and sketches, or we can opt to **Show Images** or **Show Sketches**.

Okay, drop down to the scene title line. Each scene title has a **Delete** button on the far right which allows deletion of the scene, including all shots in it. Be careful.

In the window that has the shots for each scene, at the bottom-far right we have an **Add Shot** button. This, not surprisingly, adds a new blank shot behind the last shot in the scene.

To delete a shot (if the sequence has two or more), click on the shot to select it and then click on the **X** icon at the top right of the shot and it will go away, as shown in the following screenshot:

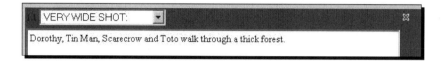

Generating scenes automatically

If we already have a completed script or even one in progress, there's no need to manually create scenes for our Storyboard. Simply use the **Add Item** feature (remember the little **+** symbol shortcut under the **Project Library** window title) from inside your script project, as shown in the following screenshot:

After selecting **Storyboard** from the preceding screenshot and then clicking on **OK**, we get the following screenshot:

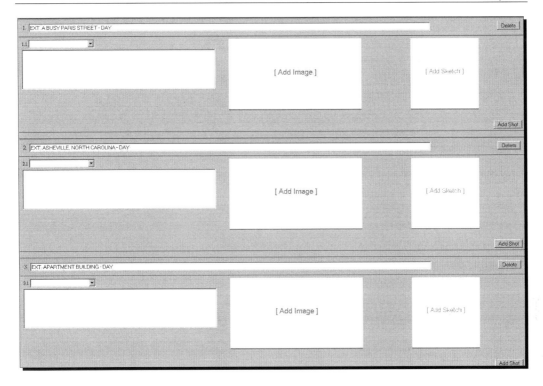

 An even easier shortcut is that big blue **Add** button, just under File on the extreme upper-left of the Celtx screen.

Be sure that you associate the new Storyboard item with your script using the drop-down menu labeled **Script:** at the bottom of the **Add Item** dialog box.

Celtx generates a Storyboard that has all our scenes already in place (such as the one above my script Portals. All we need to do now is add shots, media files, and/or Sketches.

Now, let's have a look at the window at the bottom-left of the screen, namely, the one below the **Project Library** window. When we're in a script window (such as **Screenplay**), this window is labeled **Scenes**. We learned in *Chapter 2, All those wonderful Writing Features* about the **Scenes** block or window and how we could move scenes around, delete them, copy them, and/or send them to the **Scratchpad**.

On the Storyboard screen, this block is labeled **Sequences** and shows each sequence in our Storyboard. Like in the Scenes block, we can move the sequences around, shuffling their order as we like in order to look at different ways of structuring our production. Here's how the **Sequences** window looks:

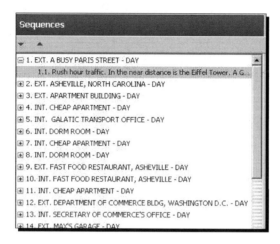

We can use this block as a navigation aid. Clicking once selects the sequence or individual shot. Double-clicking takes us to it on the screen.

There are two major differences we need to be aware of. First, you can't delete or send Storyboard sequences to the **Scratchpad**. (You can delete a sequence by using the **Delete** button on the sequence title line in the storyboard window.) And most importantly, changing the order of the sequences *does not* change the order of scenes in the script, nor vice versa. This is so we can experiment in the Storyboard without messing up our script.

Adding Sketches to a Storyboard

In the section on Sketches, I did one of scene five; Bobby meets Elaine in the offices of Galactic Transport. Bobby comes through the door and Elaine gets up and comes around her desk to fondly greet him. That sketch is still in the Project Library, labeled as **Scene 5**.

To get the Sketch (or any Sketch) into our storyboard, refer to the following section.

Time for action – moving a Sketch to a Storyboard

1. Open the Sketch to be moved by double-clicking on it in the **Project Library** window.

2. Use the select tool and draw around everything in the Sketch. Every item will now have blue dotted lines around it.

3. Click on the **Edit** menu at the very top left of the Celtx screen and then click on **Copy**, or just type *Ctrl+C*.

4. Double click on Storyboard in the **Project Library** window.

5. Click in the **Add Sketch** box in Scene 5 of the Storyboard; it opens a blank Sketch screen just like the one we just copied from.

6. Do it the easy way, press *Ctrl+V* to paste the sketch. Return to the Storyboard view and it's there!

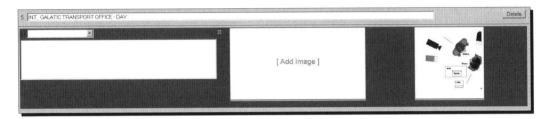

Double-click on Sketches embedded in storyboards to open a Sketch Tool window and see them at full size again. To delete a Sketch, click on the small **X** icon next to the image (it shows up in the two and three wide views).

What just happened?

We just learned how to insert our Sketches into a Storyboard.

Adding image files to a Storyboard

The **Add Image** box in shots, as we saw in the Oz Storyboard, lets us add drawings or (as follows) even photographs. Standard `.jpg` or `.bmp` files work fine.

Click in the **Add Image** box to bring up an **Add Media** dialog box (shown in the next screenshot). Basically, if we can see it, we can add it. The Storyboard is restricted to images but, coming up in the last section in this chapter, we'll play with adding video and audio files as well. As an example, the following screenshot shows the directory in which I am accumulating images for this chapter:

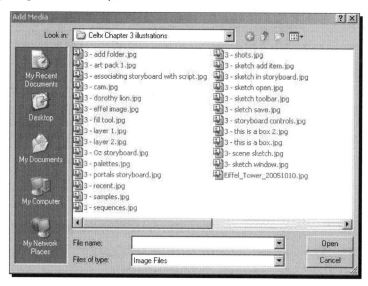

To delete an image, click on the small **X** icon next to the image in the Storyboard.

Nor are we limited to inserting just one image at a time. In the **Add Media** dialog box (get it by clicking on **Add Image** in any shot on the Storyboard), we can select a series of images by holding the *Shift* key or a bunch of individual ones (separated list) by holding down the *Ctrl* key, as shown in the following screenshot:

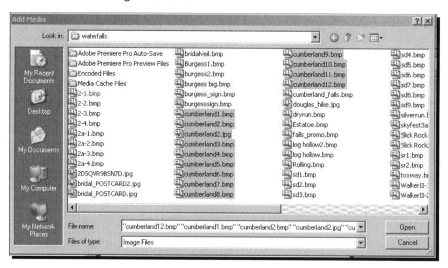

The selected files are batch imported as shots, numbered, and the title of the image put in the description box, as shown in the following screenshot:

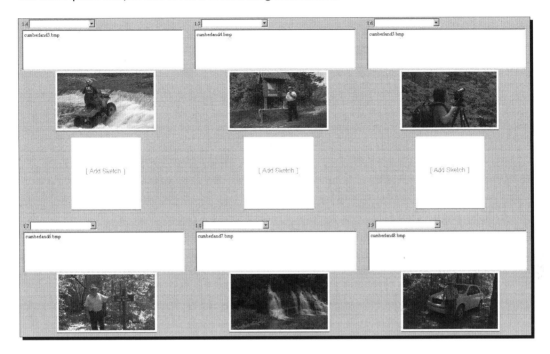

We can now title them and add sketches, if needed. This group of pictures, by the way, is from a series of documentary films that my wife, Pat, and I produce and sell on `Amazon.com` as "Waterfalls of the Southern Highlands." Where we live, in the mountains of Western North Carolina, there are literally hundreds of waterfalls within a forty-mile radius of our house. We've done over a hundred but are just getting started good. Celtx is already helping me in Storyboarding and writing documentary scripts for these and the other series we produce.

On now to adding not only drawings and images but also videos and audio files to our Celtx projects!

Time for action – adding media files

In *Chapter 2*, we learned that we could insert notes into a script (see the little note icon next to Ohio Smith's name in the following screenshot):

> OHIO SMITH
> I know that ancient temple is
> around here somewhere.

Clicking on the note icon brings up the note, showing it in the right-most column of the Celtx script screen. We click the **Notes** tab to both add and read notes. Now, what's the name of the tab next to **Notes**? **Media**! See it in the following screenshot:

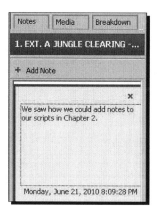

Insert a vertical bar in a script by moving the I-beam mouse cursor to the desired point and left-clicking. In this case, I've click after **temple** in the short Ohio Smith example. Now go over to the right column of the Celtx screen and click on the **Media** tab. We get a screen similar to the following screenshot:

The white writing that we see on the black background in the preceding screenshot shows the scene title. The **+** icon below the scene title lets us add an image or other media file and the **x** icon deletes it.

Now, I want to add a picture of an ancient temple just as a reference after the word "temple" in the script. First, I need the picture, so here's a fantastically useful feature. I type the words "jungle temple" in the text box, hit the blue **G** (a Google icon), and BLAP, Google gives me more than 1,670,000 photos of jungle temples to choose from, as shown in the following screenshot (it helps an awful darn lot to be connected to the Internet when one tries this):

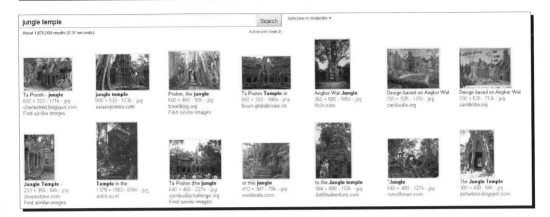

Cool beans! So I pick out one, download it, and use the little + icon to add it to the Ohio Smith project, as shown in the following screenshot:

And now, as shown in the following screenshot, a picture icon is attached to **temple**:

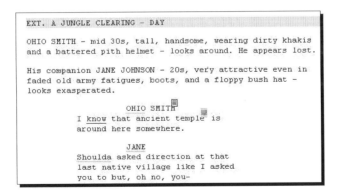

Double-clicking on the little icon causes the thumbnail on the left to be displayed in the right-hand column. It's still small and hard to see, but just double-click on it and the image appears full size in whatever image viewer is installed as the default viewer on your computer.

Save yourself hassles from copyright lawyers if using photos from the Internet for commercial purposes. In the case of **Google Images**, use **Advanced Search** and click on **labeled for commercial reuse**. This returns only those photos that are okay to reproduce without written permission and/or some kind of royalty payment.

Now, I want a little ambience sound to set the mood, so I clicked after "native village" and added the "Scary Wind" audio file from my rather large library of royalty-free music and sound effects. I can click on the icon and hear the audio, as shown in the following screenshot:

We aren't limited to just pictures and sound; Celtx will also let you embed video clips. How would we actually use these things? The following are some examples:

- Use a recorder to record production or writing notes while out and about and embed those into the script for reference
- Add photos of places, props, actors
- Shoot a video of a filming location and embed it, so that details of prop, character placement, and so on can be worked out by seeing where they go

Now, finally, time to embed some video. Again, choose a place in the script by inserting a vertical bar after moving the I-beam mouse cursor to the desired point and left-clicking. Now, with the **Media** tab clicked, hit the little **+** icon and choose the video to add. If you can see it in the **Add Media** dialog box, Celtx will probably handle it well. Let's see what we see.

As shown in the following screenshot, I've included an mp4 file in Portals. It happens to be HD (High Definition) at 1280 x 780 pixels. This is one of my exercises in creating special effects in film. I was throwing a ping pong ball and, through movie magic and a little help from Adobe After Effects, getting the ball into the cup every time. However, that got boring, so I started having the balls explode when they entered the cup. Hey, you've got to have some kind of break from writing computer books, eh?

Okay; that covers inserting media inside scripts, but remember those thirty-six categories of items we explored in *Chapter 2*? The ones Celtx tracks for you in the Master Catalog? Well, guess what? Yep, you can attach media files to every character, prop, animal, and so on, namely, every single category there is that Celtx tracks.

To add media, click on the **Master Catalog** in the **Project Library**, then on the item you want to attach a photograph, drawing, audio file, or video to. In the following screenshot, we put a photograph on Bobby's character page (Bobby is the hero of Portals):

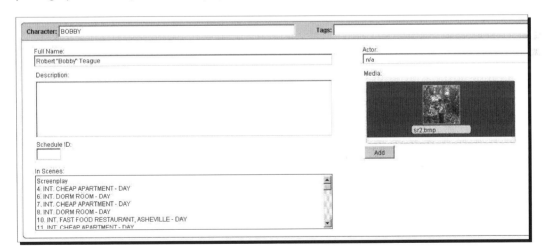

Click on the **Add** button below the media box and follow the same procedure that we followed when we added media files inside scripts.

What just happened?

As we've just experienced, Celtx gives us a lot of power in visualizing productions by letting us embed actual photos, drawings, even videos of actors, props, locations, or whatever right in the script itself!

Summary

In this chapter, we saw ways of visualizing productions ahead of time. Specifically, we learned about using diagrams to visually plan the setup of a scene for filming, and also, the utility of employing external drawings and images to create a visual representation of our script.

Finally, we added media files (photos, graphics, and videos) that we found can be inserted in scripts and attached to any of the thirty-six production categories, including wardrobe, props, and locations.

Now, it's time to get organized! And we'll do just that in *Chapter 4, Tools for Getting Organized* which, just now, is coming over the horizon.

Tools for Getting Organized

Now let's look at how Celtx assists us in organizing scripts, storyboards, and text files for easy retrieval when needed, and also production scheduling (another expensive software package; however, we don't have to buy it, thanks to the generosity of Celtx and open source).

In this chapter, we will cover the following topics:

- **Project Library**: The Project Library has lots of virtual shelving and we'll look at all the things that we can store on those shelves, from scripts and storyboards to even actors and actresses and all sorts of props.

- **Scheduling, call sheets, and shooting reports**: Celtx gives us a "Just in Time" scheduling feature, letting producers manage the production of projects in real time. For example, open a schedule based on your script, drag and drop scenes into the calendar, and Celtx builds a shooting schedule. We can then customize as needed into shooting reports, which include lists of the actors, props, and costumes required for that scene. Call sheets are also generated, so that actors and crew know when and where to show up for the day's filming.

- **Inter-project document management**: Got a list of props for one project you'd like to use in another? No problem, drag and drop documents from one Project Library to another. A very powerful and timesaving feature.

- **Toolbox**: While Celtx comes with tons of tools built in, the Toolbox feature allows for the creation of customized tools (or perhaps more likely for most of us, downloading additional tools). This section shows how that is accomplished.

By the end of this chapter, we will be able to schedule production activities and generate reports based on our scripts using the scheduling features in Celtx. We'll also have the ability to move documents between projects, and understand how to create or add custom tools.

Project Library

As we saw in *Chapter 1, Obtaining and Installing Celtx* that Celtx comes with seven predefined project templates, which are as follows:

- **Film**
- **Audio-Visual**
- **Theatre**
- **Audio Play**
- **Storyboard**
- **Comic Book**
- **Text** (hiding down in the scrolling menu on the Splash Page, as shown in the following screenshot)

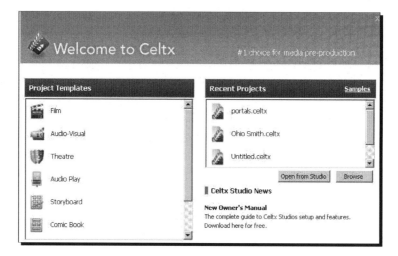

We also saw, in that same chapter, how new project templates are created and added. We click on whichever type of project we're working on, for example, **Film** to start a feature movie screenplay.

When we open any project—new or saved—we find the **Project Library** on the left side (see the following screenshot, which shows the included sample project that comes with Celtx, the *Wonderful Wizard of Oz*):

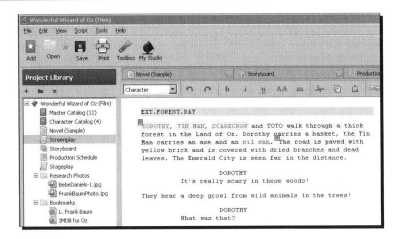

Looking in the **Project Library** window (to the left side of the preceding screenshot), we begin to get an idea of all the things that can be stored with our scripts (and the high-dollar commercial script writing programs do not offer this kind of power). In fact, it's possible to have literally thousands of items stored in each and every Celtx project you have.

Just in this brief sample project's **Project Library**, we see the **Master Catalog** with twelve items (actors, sounds, props, location, scene details, and so on—we learned about the Master Catalog in *Chapter 2, All those Wonderful Writing Features*), a **Character Catalog** with four characters (Dorothy, Tin Man, Lion, and Scarecrow), a portion of the original novel by Frank Baum, the **Screenplay** (or at least the part included in this sample), a **Storyboard** (we saw that in *Chapter 3, Visualizing Productions Ahead of Time*), **Production Schedule**, **Stageplay** (another script), a folder of photographs, and a folder of bookmarks (web links).

By the way, the *Wonderful Wizard of Oz* refers to the 1914 silent movie. Several versions of this story, based on the series of Oz books by L. Frank Baum, have been made over the years, the most well-known being *The Wizard of Oz* (1938) with Judy Garland as Dorothy (who so famously said "...we're not in Kansas any more").

Okay, back to the Project Library. The **Project Library** window (or sidebar), again, is in the upper left corner of the Celtx screen. Just below the window's title, we have the three control buttons, as shown in the following screenshot:

Time for action – adding Items

Clicking on the small **+** (plus) icon brings up the **Add Item...** dialog box, as shown in the following screenshot:

The top item we can add is **Script**. Note that in the right part of the dialog box, we can choose *which kind of script*. This is one heck of an important concept. We opened a **Film** project, which gives us a way to write feature movie scripts that Celtx formats in the industry standard way for such scripts. We did not open a **Theatre** (Stageplay) project or a **Comic Book** project or any other kind.

Okay, drum roll please, here it comes, that important concept: but we can add any kind of script to this Film project and it will format properly depending on the type, that is, comic books as comic books, A/V scripts as A/V scripts, and so on. This action adds additional scripts (of the type we selected) into the **Project Library**.

We can have any number of scripts in any combination in any type of Celtx project. Four comic book scripts, an A/V script, and three audio plays, for example. We can have whatever we need. In short, any type of Celtx project is a container that will hold all sorts of stuff including other scripts and storyboards.

- ◆ **Scripts**: To add a new script of any kind, select the type by clicking on the circle to the left of the script type name and then, down in the Item Details section, rename the script if desired. The next selection down lets you specify a subfolder of the Project Library should the item belong there instead of on the main lists. To finish, click on the **OK** button at the bottom of the dialog box.

◆ **Storyboards, Sketches, Catalogs, and Production Schedules**: Referring back to the previous screenshot—the **Add Item...** dialog box—the next three items we've already discussed in the preceding chapters. **Storyboard** and **Sketch** were discussed in *Chapter 3*, and **Catalog** in *Chapter 2*, however, we'll meet **Production Schedule** in the next section of this chapter.

◆ **Bookmarks**: Web links (bookmarks) may be added to the **Project Library** (or its subfolders) by clicking on the **Bookmark** choice in **Add Item...**as shown in the following screenshot:

There are many useful links for any project. These could include sources of useful research about the story, online resumes of actors, and scads of other stuff found on the Internet which might require checking again. In the preceding screenshot, I'm bookmarking the main Celtx website as an example.

◆ **Calendar**: This powerful item provides a calendar function which tracks two kinds of dates: events (things that are happening) and tasks (things we got to do). To add a calendar to a project, click on either the **Add** button at the top left of the Celtx screen (with the white star in it) or on the + icon below the title of the **Project Library** window, then click on **Calendar**. When the **Add Items...** dialog box pops up, we can name our calendar and choose whether it goes in the main **Project Library** window or one of its subfolders. Click on **OK** to continue.

The new calendar opens initially in the main part of the Celtx screen and, afterwards, we open it by double clicking on the name of the calendar in the **Projects Library**. The following screenshot shows a calendar with an event in the process of being edited; tasks appear in the left hand column (beneath the **Project Library** window, one is there already):

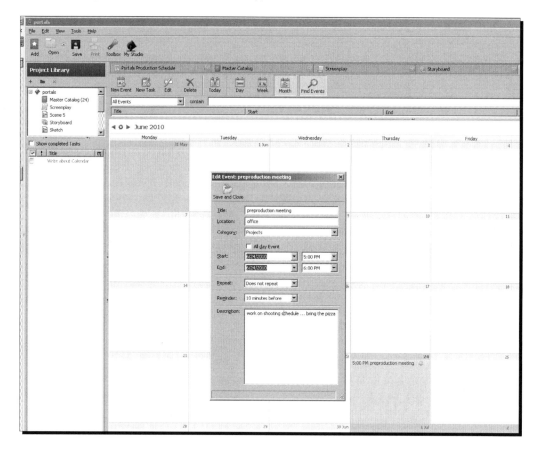

The calendar toolbar (shown in the following screenshot) lets us (left to right) add a new event, add a new task, edit a selected event or task, delete a selected event or task, show events for today, show events for a selected day (defaults to today's date), show events for the week, and for the month, and finally also lets us search events. The next line now lets us (using the drop-down menu) choose the type of event or even a search term:

The Celtx **Calendar** item is a powerful adjunct to our projects and well worth playing with and learning.

◆ **File**: Next we have the add **File** selection. A file can be *any file* on your computer! As long as that file is associated with some program on your computer (such as a Word file or an Excel spreadsheet or an Adobe Photoshop .psd file). Just double-clicking on the file name in the **Project Library** window causes it to open on top of the Celtx window. The following screenshot shows how it looks when a file is being selected (with minor variances in cosmetics for Macintosh and Linux systems). Just click on the **Browse** button to the lower left of the **Add Item...** dialog box (obscured in this figure but it is there), and the **Choose a file dialog** box appears as shown:

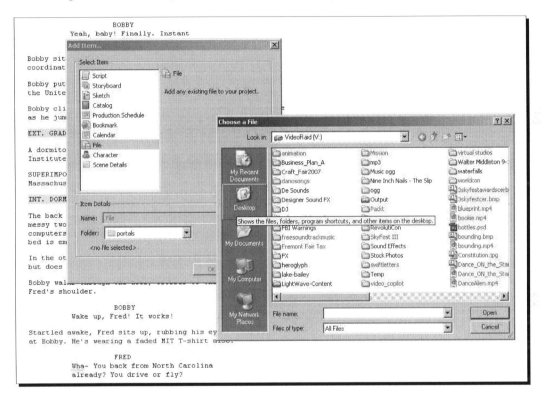

In fact, the following screenshot shows adding a file from one of my Linux systems (Ubuntu 10.04). It looks a little different, but works exactly the same:

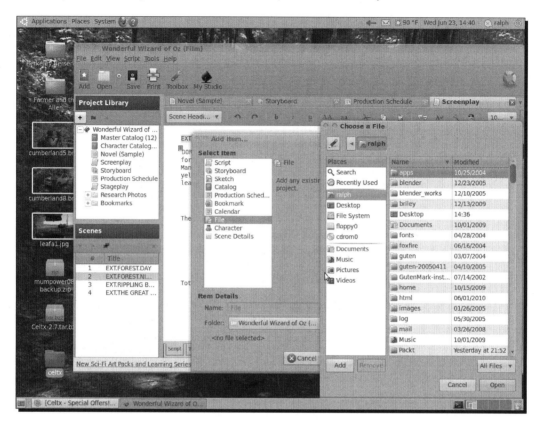

A file retains its system name but you can choose, in the **Folder:** mini window, whether to have the file link in a subfolder of the **Project Library** window for better organization and less clutter. (How we create folders is coming right up).

◆ **Character**: We explored this in *Chapter 2*. Creating a new character here adds him/her, or it, to the **Master Catalog** (this would be for a character not already in our script, since those are added automatically).

◆ **Scene Details**: The final item choice, **Scene Details**, we have not met before and is quite useful. We have two choices here—we can click on an existing scene name or (down in the **Name:** box in the next figure) create a name for a forthcoming or potential scene. Click on **OK** and the new scene details item is added automatically to the **Master Catalog**, as shown in the following screenshot:

Scene details number themselves among the many items Celtx tracks for us. Add a scene details item and then look in the **Master Catalog** (just double-click on it in the **Project Directory** window). Find the item in the list and click (single-click) on it. We now have a form where all sorts of information may be added about the scene and we can even attach media files just like we learned to do in *Chapter 3*.

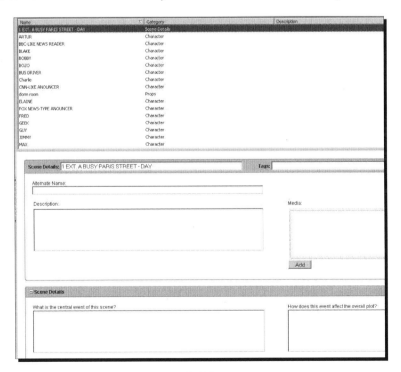

We'll talk more about all the hundreds and thousands of things Celtx tracks for us later in this chapter. I've written this already and will do so several more times. None of the expensive commercial software screenwriting packages (I paid for one before finding Celtx), and I do mean none of them, have the incredible power and completeness of Celtx. Did I mention Celtx is free?

What just happened?

We learned how to add all ten items on the **Add Item...** menu.

Time for action – adding a folder

Okay, having thousands of files, links, and items as noted in the previous section can clutter the **Project Window** up. Imagine having a thousand items in that window and having to scroll though all those to find one. No problem, we can easily create subfolders, which have subfolders, which also have subfolders, and on and on. Glorious organization!

To create a subfolder, carry out the following steps:

1. Click on the file folder icon, which is located just under the **Project Library** title, between the **Add Item** button and the grayed out **x** of the delete function, as shown in the following screenshot:

The **Add Folder...** mini dialog box pops up, as shown in the following screenshot, like a rabbit from its hole:

2. We enter the title of our new folder in the **Name:** text entry box.

3. In the **Location:** box, we find the name of our current project, which corresponds to the root folder of the **Projects Library**, as shown in the first screenshot of this section.

4. Clicking on this box's drop-down menu shows existing subfolders. Choosing one of those would make our new folder a subfolder of that subfolder and we can nest folders as deep as we like.

What's the utility of subfolders? In my case, while writing this book, I find myself with my Portal's project often open but needing to refer to a previous chapter to make sure this point or that has not already been covered. I just double-click on the chapter name and it opens in Word. Clicking on the little – (minus) icon next to the folder icon and title **CELTX FOR BEGINNERS** (refer the first screenshot of this section) collapses the subfolder until needed again, decluttering the main **Project Library** window.

What just happened?

We now have seen how to add subfolders, which allows us to organize our files. As a project grows in complexity over perhaps several months, this becomes more and more beneficial to us and saves time in finding a file or type file quickly.

Time for action – deleting items

To delete an item from the **Project Library**, left-click on it, then look at the line of three icons just below the window's title (refer to the first screenshot of the previous section). The little **x** icon is no longer grayed out. Click on it and a **Delete Item** mini dialog box gives us one last chance to repent. Click on **OK** to really delete the file, or **Cancel** if it gets a last minute reprieve.

Warning: There is no recycle bin. Once you've deleted an item, it's gone. Of course, this is where all of us here have regularly backed up our projects and can always copy an item we've mistakenly killed back into the current project.

 Always keep regular backups of your projects. This habit can save you lots of work since you don't have to recreate accidentally erased or corrupted projects.

What just happened?

We now can delete items and know to have good backups, in case we delete something we really needed to keep.

Scheduling, call sheets, and shooting reports

In the real world of film, stage, radio, A/V, and so on production, writers turn in scripts and production people, manually or using expensive scheduling software, try to turn it into a shooting schedule. Celtx makes all this easy by combining all these processes into one package. As scripts are rewritten (there are *always* script rewrites), Celtx tracks those changes and updates schedules, call sheets, and shooting reports.

If a small indie film maker, documentary producer, stage theater manager, or anyone else putting on any kind of production with a low budget and few people does not love Celtx, it's only because they don't know about it yet. Give them this book for their birthday, eh?

Time for action – scheduling

Celtx offers "Just in Time" scheduling, meaning that we can work on our project right up to the time of scheduling for the shoot.

So, let's build a shooting schedule. Let's assume I wanted to film Portals myself instead of selling it to Hollywood for big bucks. I would need such a schedule. You guys can help. With the project open, we bring up the **Add Item...** dialog box just like we learned earlier in this chapter. Select **Production Schedule** from the list, as shown in the following screenshot:

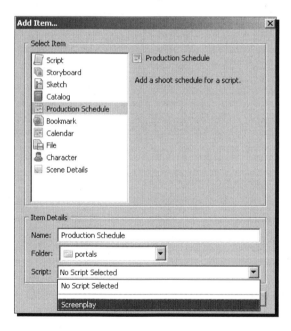

Looking at the bottom part of the dialog box, we can use **Name:** to name our schedule, **Folder:** to place it in a subfolder, and **Script:** to associate it with our screenplay.

We can then customize as needed into shooting reports, which include lists of the actors, props, and costumes required for that scene. Call sheets also are generated, so that actors and crew know when and where to show up for the day's filming. The latter is very important since we want Celtx to track our changes and automate the process for us as much as possible. The new production schedule opens in the main window and looks like the following screenshot:

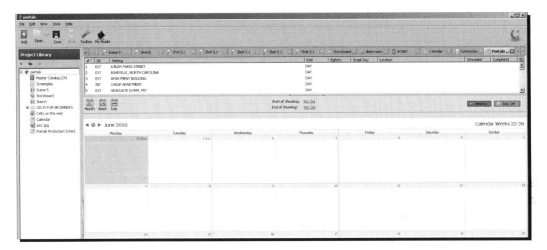

We can also call it back up any time it is needed by double clicking on its title in the **Project Library** window.

Note that a list of scenes is already in the top window of the schedule. Great, now we're ready. The first task is, setting the start and end dates of our shoot. If it's this month, we're fine. However, let's say our filming starts the second week in July and runs for three weeks. Not long to shoot a feature movie but it's all we, micro budget indie guys like me, can afford.

Click on the right arrow next to **June 2010** (in the example, your date will be later, eh?) and the month will advance to July. Now click on **Start of Shooting** (center top of the main screen). In the Shoot Days box, adjust the start and end months (in our case, both will be July). Now we start the second week and end on the 25th.

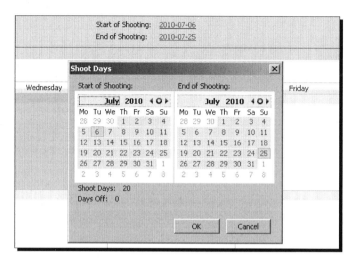

With the start and end of the shoot defined, it's merely a matter of clicking on a scene and dragging it to the day of filming. The standard time for a scene is two hours. However, this is easy to change. Double-click on the scene in the calendar and we get the **Edit Event** box, which allows us to change times and add comments.

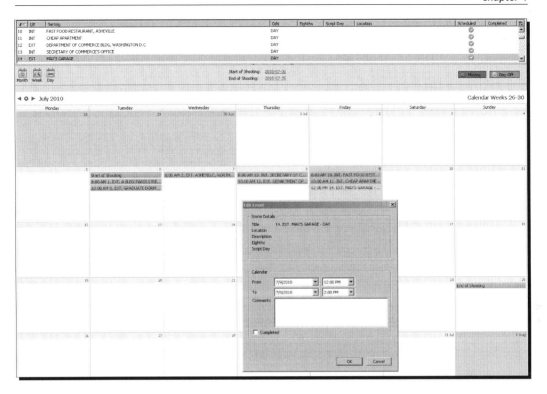

Notice in the **Edit Event** dialog box that **Location**, **Description**, **Eighths**, and **Script Day** have no information. We can enter this information by clicking on the scene title, as shown in the following screenshot, or by adding a **Scene Details** item to our **Master Catalog**, as we saw earlier in this chapter:

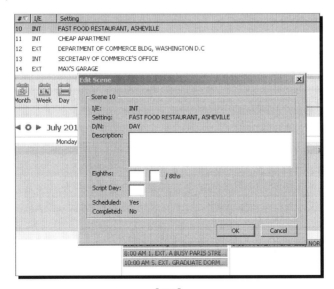

We can add a description in the **Description** box. The lower two entry boxes—**Eighths** and **Script Day**—are script-related. **Eighths** is a traditional measurement of a script for shooting purposes, which is measured by dividing each page into eight pieces (about one inch each). A scene that takes up one page and two-eighths of the next page would be entered as 1 in the larger box and a 2 in the smaller **/8ths** box. Screen day is the day in the script's story when the action happens, such as the *third* day. So enter a 3.

Two other things of note about our main **Production Schedule** window, we should know. In the scene window, when a scene is scheduled, a green circle with a white check mark appears in the **Scheduled** column to help make sure we film all scenes. Secondly, on the upper right of this window, there are a violet **Moving** icon and a green **Day Off** icon. These may be dragged into your schedule as appropriate.

 Scenes do not have to be scheduled in order. Group them by similarity, location, or any other factor that minimizes cost and effort.

What else? Ah, yes. Those three icons just above the date in the **Production Schedule** window are nice for helping us view our schedule in different ways. Clicking on them shows the schedule respectively by month, week, and day. These views are interactive. For example, if you wanted to add an event at 10:45 or 4:30, you can drag within the hour (easier to see this in the week or day views) and create a place for it. Play with this, it's cool.

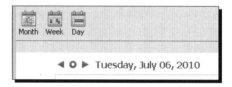

What just happened?

We've learned Celtx's scheduling facilities. For indie producers, documentary film makers, and anyone else doing production instead of just writing scripts, this feature lets you track all the many things that go into a successful and efficient production and have them happen at the right time.

Time for action – customizing schedule options

If the defaults for time per scene, length of day, or days in the workweek are not to our liking, we can customize schedule options. In the very topmost menu bar on the Celtx screen, click on **Tools**, then **Options**, then **Production Schedule**. (On a Mac it's **Celtx** then **Preferences** then **Production Schedule**). In the following dialog box we can edit the defaults:

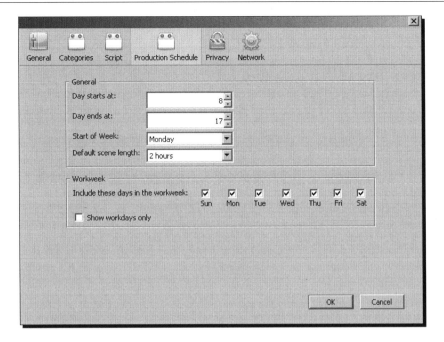

What just happened?

Customizing scheduling defaults, as we just did, is easy.

Time for action – call sheets, shooting schedules, and other reports

At the bottom of the **Production Schedule** Window, we have a **Reports** tab. Click on it to get reports generated by Celtx using our scheduling information. These reports are **Month** (monthly schedules ready to be printed), **Week** (a breakdown of scenes and other events for each week), **One Line Schedule** (a list of scenes per day with descriptions, day or night, eighths, and cast), **Shooting Schedule** (shows on what day each scene is to be shot and the cast), **Call Sheet** (call sheets inform actors, extras, and crews where they need to be and when), and **Scene Summary** (shows unscheduled, scheduled, and completed scenes).

The following screenshot shows part of a **Shooting Schedule**. To get the other reports, click on the name of the report in the **Reports** box, lower left.

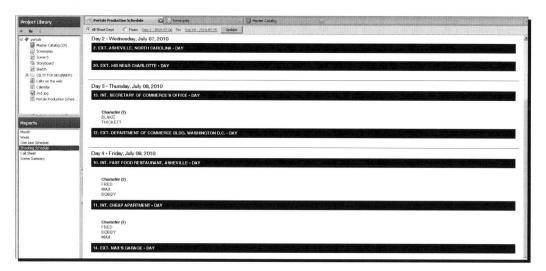

To sum it up: we enter things about scheduling in the **Production Schedule**. We output specific types of reports, based on the information we enter or Celtx generates automatically from tracking all those items in the **Master Catalog** and other items in the **Project Library**, in the **Reports** window. Celtx makes it all easy to learn and even easier to use.

What just happened?

We've just mastered generating call sheets, shooting schedules, and other reports. These documents help the producer and all the involved parties. Printouts are distributed in order to bring together productions with the right items and people at the right place when needed.

Inter-project document management

Okay, we know by now that a Celtx project has the capacity to contain hundreds or thousands of items. However, what if there's something in another project we would like to have in our current project? That's what inter-project document management is all about, moving stuff between projects.

It's incredibly easy. Celtx has that small footprint I was so enthusiastic about in the Preface. This means it's easy to run another version of Celtx over the current one and to, thus, have two projects open at once. Do that and move one slightly offset as I have in the following screenshot:

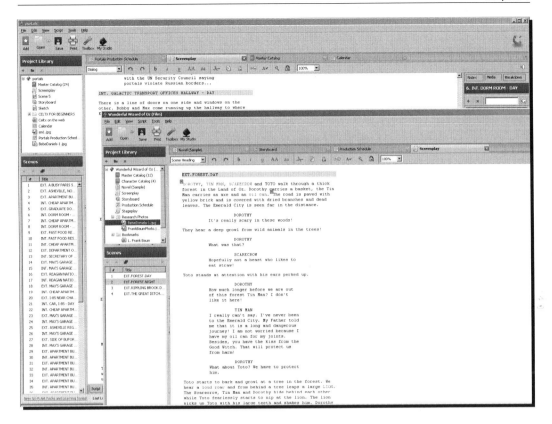

Now comes the hard part. Oh! Wait. There is no hard part. Just click on the item in the top Celtx that we want to move, let's say the .jpg photo of Bebe Daniels. Hold down the left mouse button and drag it into the other project's **Project Library**. That's it! We can copy anything or all in one project's **Project Library** almost instantly in this manner.

Who, you ask, is Bebe Daniels? She played Dorothy in the *Wonderful Wizard of Oz* movie, the 1914 version of that classic story. The following screenshot shows the photo of her we just moved. You have it, too—it comes in the Oz sample project when Celtx is installed:

Toolbox

While Celtx comes with tons of tools, the Toolbox feature allows creation of customized tools (or perhaps more likely for most of us, downloading additional tools). To open the **Toolbox**, click on the wrench icon on the top toolbar of the main Celtx screen, as shown in the following screenshot:

The Toolbox dialog box that opens is empty as shown in the following screenshot:

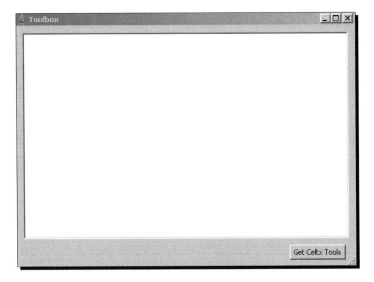

Clicking on the **Get Celtx Tools** button opens up a page on the Celtx website offering a number of commercial tools for purchase. Want some free tools? Click on **Utilities** on the left of that webpage and the following screen appears:

To install, click on the tool desired, then restart Celtx.

Summary

We've now had a good look at what a project is (a container of a whole lot of stuff), scheduling production activities, generating reports based on our scripts, how to copy items from one project to another, and adding tools to the Toolbox.

Now, we begin tooling up for some real hot and heavy scriptwriting!

5
Tooling Up for Scriptwriting

This chapter shows the basic menus and tools provided by Celtx to make our writing experience much easier by providing things which remove drudgery. Celtx frees us so that we can be creative!

In this chapter, we will cover:

- **File menu**: Using the File menu options, we can open or create new projects, save our projects (really important), and carry out other operations.

- **Edit menu**: Using the Edit menu, we can undo, redo, cut, copy, paste, make global changes and replacements, and more.

- **View menu**: Using the View menu, we can adjust the look of the shortcut toolbar as needed.

- **Script menu**: Using the Script menu, we can export, import, adapt type (such as changing Film to Audio Play, and so on), change page format (A4 to Letter, and so forth), and more.

- **Tools menu**: Using the Tools menu, we can check spelling, inline spelling, preferences, and more.

- **Help menu**: The Help menu provides us with the various methods of obtaining help and tutorials online.

- **Top buttons**: Add, Open, Save, Print, Toolbox, My Studio—all demystified.

- **Project Library**: Catalogs, scripts, and other documents—open whatever you need, and we'll look at how to use them.

- **Scenes**: Navigate easily through your scripts using this handy feature.

- **Editor toolbar**: The name for often-used tools for each type of editor. Includes a drop-down selection for the various elements such as Scene Heading, Action, Character, and Dialog (all industry standard script elements, automatically formatted for you). Also Undo, Redo, Bold, Italic, Underline, Cut, Paste, Dual Dialog, Text Lock, sizing the view, and more.

- **Bottom buttons**: Script, TypeSet/PDF, Scratchpad, Index Cards, Title Page, Reports—all very useful and here's the way they work.

- **Customizing your workspace**: We can adjust the look and feel of the screen to what suits you best.

By the end of this chapter, you will have increased your speed using the on-screen tools, which Celtx provides for screenplay formatting and editing, and important related actions including saving your work, global searches and changes, and more—which we'll learn about in *Chapter 7, Writing Movies with Celtx*.

The File menu

There are seventeen items (all related to file operations) on the **File** menu; let's briefly look at each choice and learn about them. We start at the very upper left of the Celtx screen (in all projects) with the first selection on the top menu line—**File**. Click on **File** and Celtx gives us the menu, which is shown in the following screenshot:

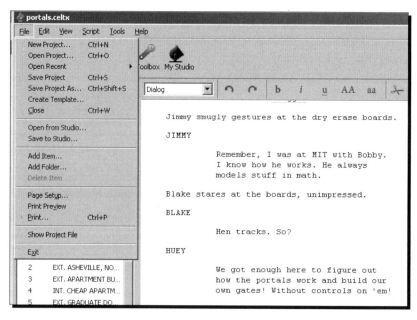

The **File** menu may be thought of as a sort of "front door" where we go to bring things into or send them out of Celtx, or pass through to enter another project.

Time for action – starting a new project

At the top of the menu, as shown in the preceding screenshot, the first item—**New Project**—allows us to create new projects. Click on it and we get the **Create a Project** dialog box, as shown in the following screenshot:

We click on the type of new project to create, unless you've created custom projects as described in *Chapter 1, Obtaining and Installing Celtx*. Those choices are **Film**, **Audio-Visual**, **Theatre** (Canadian spelling, eh?), **Audio Play**, **Storyboard**, **Comic Book**, and **Text**. The new project then opens, but the old project does not close; it's still there underneath the new project, as we see in the following screenshot. It's possible to have several Celtx projects open at once (the only limit being the amount of working memory in your computer):

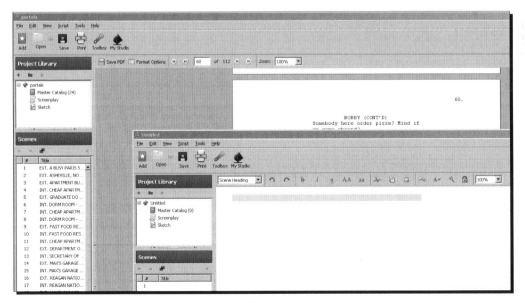

On a Windows-based computer, use the key combination of *Alt+Tab* to rotate around through open programs.

A shortcut is the key combination *Ctrl+N*, which also gives us the **Create a Project** dialog box.

What just happened?

We have now a new project container (it can have many different kind of files as we shall see throughout this book), but it specifically has a new empty script (or storybook, or text file) of the type we choose, such as **Film**, **Audio-Visual**, **Audio Play**, **Storyboard**, **Comic Book**, or **Text**.

Time for action – opening an existing project

Clicking on the second choice on the **File** menu—**Open Project**—lets us retrieve projects already in progress. The **Open a Celtx Project** dialog box materializes (like the gates in Portals, my screenplay I'm using for examples). The next illustration is in Windows XP, but you get a similar one in Windows 7, Vista, Mac, and on Linux systems. If the old file is not in the directory shown, navigate up and around your hard disk(s) in the standard way of opening any file in any program. When the project name you want appears (Celtx project names all have the `.celtx` extension, as shown in the following screenshot), double-click on that name (or icon) to open:

Just to be thorough, the following screenshot is an icon view of the same files as in the preceding screenshot:

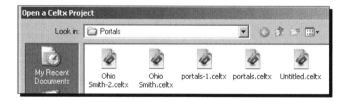

The actual look depends on the type of operating system, of course, as Celtx uses that for file operations. This is another example of Celtx avoiding bloat by not duplicating already existing routines that are already embedded in your operating system.

Rather than opening the **File** menu, we can also use *Ctrl+O* as a shortcut. This gives us the **Open a Celtx Project** dialog box the same as we get while clicking on **File** and then **Open Project**, but is only one step instead of two.

Time for action – opening and saving recent projects

Third down on the **File** menu, Celtx tracks the projects we've had open. Clicking on **Open Recent** presents a list of the most recently opened projects, as shown in the following screenshot:

Click on one of these titles and that project opens (just like creating a new project or finding an old one) on top of the current project.

There is no shortcut for this menu selection.

Time for action – saving early and often

Selecting **Save Project** on the **File** menu, or using the *Ctrl+S* shortcut, saves our current project. I contend that this is the most important selection on any menu, in any software we might run, at any time, on any computer! Programs exist to assist us in accomplishing work—saving that work keeps us from having to do it over and over. Personally, it really, really irks me when I'm forced to recreate some very good writing just because I forgot to save it. Save early, save often!

There, I just saved the Word file I'm writing this chapter in.

Time for action – saving a project under another name

Just saving our current file is not enough insurance. Good backup procedure (a series of steps making sure we never lose anything) calls for more than one copy of important projects. The **Save Project As** (*Ctrl+Shift+S*) **File** menu choice plays an important role in insuring we never lose all that hard effort that we put into writing scripts in Celtx (or the work we do in any other program). Here's an example of what I do while writing a screenplay in Celtx:

1. Several times a page, I hit *Ctrl+S* to save. This is a simple, fast action that quickly becomes habit (a good habit), takes no time at all, and does not interrupt your creative flow. It protects you from losing work because of power blips and computer crashes (the infamous "Blue Screen of Death" on Windows machines, for example).

2. A few times during each writing session, I will save the script under another name, such as `portals7-14-10` (using the date in the title). This is a two step process. Save as, and then reopen the original file. I leave these dated files and have a set of "rolling" versions in case I should want to revert back for some reason (scripts become living beings, sometimes you have to discipline them back on track).

3. At the end of each writing session, I do the following:
   - Copy the files over to another computer (or you can use another directory if you just have one computer).
   - E-mail the regular file plus the daily backup file to my Gmail account. I highly recommend this latter practice. It's easy to get a free offsite account on Hot Mail, Gmail, and so on. So if, God forbid, your house burns down or a meteorite hits your hard drive, you still have a copy of your work out there on the Internet. Does this sound paranoid? Lose six months of work just one time and you'll say "no".

Save Project and **Save Project As** are two of our very best buddies in the whole enormous universe. Let's buy them a beer sometime—they work hard to protect our work.

Time for action – creating new project types

In the last part of *Chapter 2, All those Wonderful Writing Features*, we learned about using Celtx's Template Engine to create additional project types (other types than the included ones such as **Film, Theatre, Audio Play**, and so on). The **Create Template...** selection on the **File** menu is the first step in this process. Open an existing project type such as **Film**, modify it to your needs, and use **Create Template...** to save it. The new project type will now appear as a choice on the Splash page when we open Celtx.

Time for action – closing a project

This is an easy one. Clicking on **Close** on the **File** menu (or using the *Ctrl+W* shortcut), shuts down the current copy of Celtx (you can have several running at one time). If changes have been made since the last save, Celtx will let us know we need to click on **Save**, and then it continues to close, as shown in the following screenshot:

Time for action – closing tabs and windows

Oh, but... wait. Times change! Once we begin using a project (writing a script, adding items, and so on) the single **Close** option on the menu is replaced by two new selections, as shown in the following screenshot:

These selections (the bottom two in the preceding illustration) are **Close Tab**, with the same *Ctrl+W* shortcut as **Close** and **Close Window**, which has a *Crtl+Shift+W* keyboard shortcut.

Once we have content, the **Close** option needs to be (and is) more sophisticated. Look at the following screenshot as an example:

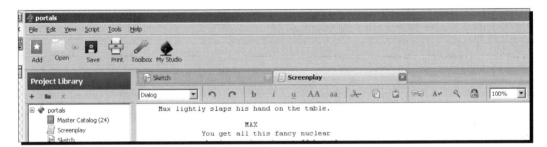

In the main script window, we have a **Screenplay** (which is active) and (underneath) a **Sketch**. We can switch to viewing the Sketch by clicking on the **Sketch** tab.

 By right clicking on item names in the **Project Library** windows, such as **Screenplay** and **Sketch**, we can change them from generic to specific like Portals and *Scene 12 Setup*. These names will then appear on the tabs.

Now, press *Ctrl+W* and the active tab closes. It's possible to have numerous tabs open in Celtx's main script window. Each time we do a *Ctrl+W* or choose **Close Tab** on the **File** menu, a tab closes. We can also use the small **x** icon on the right side of each tab to close that tab. As the last tab closes, Celtx closes because we've got nothing open to work on anymore. When we restart Celtx, the tabs we had opened are remembered and restored unless you've saved the project during this process. In the latter case, only the tabs left after the save will be restored.

Close Window or its shortcut, *Ctrl+Shift+W*, now works the same as the **Close** selection did before it got replaced—Celtx closes, first asking (if we have not saved since the last change) if we want to save the project.

Time for action – opening and saving a project stored on Celtx studio

The company that oversees development of Celtx makes revenue (nothing wrong with that) to support its work by offering commercial add-ons. We've met the Art Packs already (additional icons for storyboards). The **Open from Studio...** choice on the **File** menu is for opening projects stored on the online **Studio** service. For a monthly subscription fee of $4.99 (US) you can:

◆ Securely store all your Celtx projects plus those of others you designate, such as co-writers or people in your production company (up to five with the basic account)

◆ Keep a backup and history of all your versions (an automated way of doing what we discussed earlier in the *Saving a project under another name* section)

◆ Share your projects with others and/or manage a team's workflow

◆ Engage in live online chats with other Studio users

The following is a screenshot from a sample **Studio** account showing subseats (other users on your account, all of whom you can control and monitor). This book deals primarily with the open source parts of Celtx. For more information on the Celtx Studio service, please visit `http://studio.celtx.com/` to determine if you would like to have this service (and it's not a bad idea):

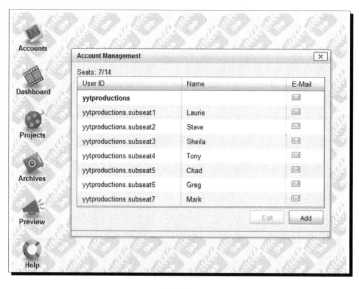

Saving a project to Celtx Studio

If we can save our projects online to **Studio** (assuming we have an account), then we must be able to put them there in the first place. The next selection down on the **File** menu is **Save to Studio...** and clicking on it brings up the dialog box as shown in the following screenshot:

Enter the **Username** and **Password** for a Celtx Studio Account and click on **OK**.

Time for action – add Item, add Folder, delete Item

Look at the following screenshot to see where we are on the **File** menu:

Add Item..., **Add Folder...**, and **Delete Item** have already been covered in detail. We first came across **Add Item...** in *Chapter 2* and again in *Chapter 4* along with **Add Folder...** and **Delete Item**.

To refresh our memory, clicking on **Add Item...** brings up the **Add Item...** dialog box depicted in the following screenshot:

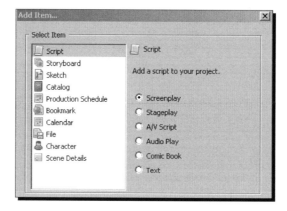

We can then add these items (**Script**, **Storyboard**, **Sketch**, and so on) to our current Celtx project. Another way of adding items is by clicking on the blue box with the white star in it, which is the **Add** button, just below the **File** menu in the upper left of the Celtx window. A third way is by clicking on the plus icon just below the **Project Library** title. Celtx is quite flexible and often offers us more than one way to accomplish tasks.

Newly created items appear in the **Project Library** window.

Folders—created with the **Add Folder...** menu item—as we saw in *Chapter 4*, are subdirectories (and sub-sub, and so on) in the **Project Library** which remove clutter and help us better track the hundreds of items that can and most likely will accumulate in complex projects, such as feature films. As with items, folders may also be created with the blue **Add** button or also with the small folder icon beneath the **Project Library** window title.

The **Delete Item** selection on the **File** menu is normally grayed-out (inactive). It becomes active when we select an item to be deleted in the **Project Library** window. Clicking on **Delete Item** (after selecting an item in the **Project Library**) gives us the **Delete Item** mini dialog, as shown in the following screenshot:

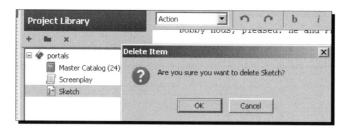

Click on **OK** to delete or **Cancel** to back out.

Okay, that takes care of creating items and folders, and deleting items. What are we missing? Ah, yes, there's no selection on the **File** menu to delete folders? Well... actually... there is. We use the **Delete Item** selection! Simply select a folder instead of an item in the **Project Library** window. Now, click on **Delete Item** on the **File** menu. As can be seen in the following screenshot, we get essentially the same mini dialog box but this one adds the wording ...**This will delete any items it contains**. Folders contain files and other folders which in turn also have files and so forth.

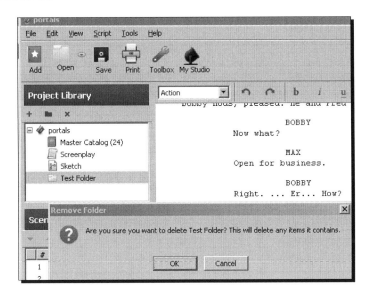

 Before deleting any folder look in it (just click on it) and see if it contains any files or folders you wish to keep.

As usual, there's more than one way of going about any task in Celtx, including deleting both items and folders. In addition to **Delete Item** on the **File** menu, we can also use the small **x** icon below the **Project Library** title. Select the item or folder to be deleted, click on the **x**, and the same mini dialog boxes appear.

Time for action – setting up a page

Clicking the **Page Setup...** selection on the **File** menu brings up the **Page Setup** dialog box which, in turn, has two tabs: **Format & Options** and **Margins & Header/Footer**. The following screenshot shows the first tab, **Format & Options**, which controls how the page looks when it prints locally:

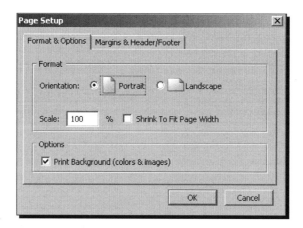

Printing locally means, in this case, using the **Print** selection on the **File** menu (or the *Ctrl+P* shortcut) and printing to a printer that is either attached to our computer or is on a local network. This is meant only for internal use, such as proofing or passing around to others working on the project with you.

Printing globally (creating a final PDF script for distribution to the world) is a completely different process, even if you still plan to print it on a local printer and bind it. We briefly saw this in *Chapter 1* (using the **TypeSet/PDF** tab instead of the **Print** selection). So this section, again, is for printing and proofing use while a project is in progress. The formatting and printing of a script's final version is automatically sent out on the web, converted to PDF in the proper format for whichever type of project we are writing, and then sent back to our computer. This is both a wonderful and a powerful feature, which we will explore later in this chapter.

The first choice on the **Format & Options** tab is **Portrait** or **Landscape**. The larger dimension is vertical in portrait. That is, the page is taller than it is wide. In landscape, the larger dimension is horizontal, so the page is wider than it is tall. This is the same as other programs such as Word, Excel, and so forth. Landscape, in Celtx, is good for printing out storyboards.

Next is **Scale**. The default, **100%**, will print standard margins on the entire page (which we'll set in the next tab). Decreasing the percentage from 100% to a lesser amount shrinks the amount of the page printed on. Checking **Shrink** to fit page width lets us be sure that wide sketches, photos, and so on fit within the margins. Finally on this tab, checking the **Options** box allows background color or images (such as watermarks) to be printed.

The second tab of the **Page Setup** box, **Margins & Header/Footer**, as shown in the following screenshot, controls both the size of margins and what information is printed within:

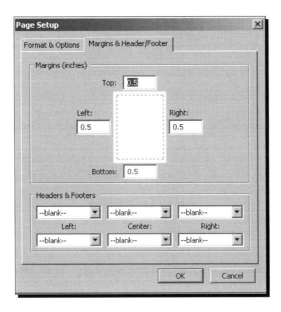

The margins are defined in inches with the default setting being 0.5 (one half) inch on top, bottom, and the left and right sides. We can adjust these to suit our own purposes. For example, we have several lines of information to go in a header (space inside the margin at the top of every page) or footer (space inside the margin at the bottom of every page).

The **Headers & Footers** block on this tab allows us to insert information which prints at the top or bottom of every page. Once more, let me emphasize, this is for local use only. Think of the headers and footers here as akin to those little lines at the top of fax pages with telephone and date on this—this is only for local use but can be quite handy in a group situation.

The three boxes in the top row are for the left, center, and right side fields (places for data) of the header. The bottom three allow information fields to be specified for the left, center, and right sides of the footer or bottom of the page. Again, this information appears on every page in the project both existing and all the ones that will be created in the future.

Each of these blocks has a drop-down menu, as shown in the following screenshot, which is a means of entering data for headers and/or footers:

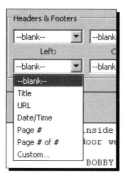

The drop-down menu has the following choices:

◆ **Title**: The title derives from the file name of your script which, by default in a **Film** project is **Screenplay**. That's hardly descriptive. Right click on it in the **Project Library** window and click on **Rename** to change it to something more reflective of the actual title of the script. As we can have more than one script in a project, this is important for clarity.

◆ **URL**: This puts the actual location of the file in whichever of the three header or three footer spaces (left, right, or center) we choose. In the case of working on a local computer, URL automatically puts the path (disk and directory location) of the file.

◆ **Date/Time**: Wait for it, the date and, yep, time as garnered from your computer's internal clock.

◆ **Page #**: Puts the appropriate number of the current page on each page in the script.

◆ **Page # of #**: Prints the number of the current page plus the total number of pages, such as Page 19 of 110.

◆ **Custom**: This lets us type in our own words for a header or footer field. The following is an example of entering custom data; in this case, the script is a "Second Draft." To get the **Custom...** mini dialog, on the drop-down menu, like below in the **Left:** box for the footer, click on the **Custom** selection, enter the data you want, and click on **OK**, as shown in the following screenshot:

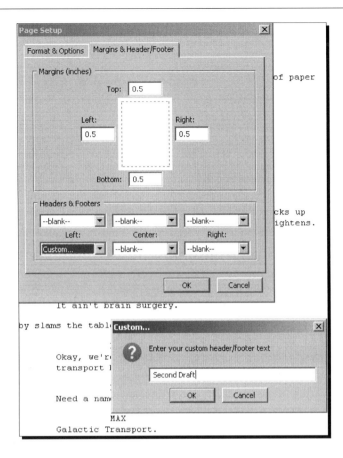

Now it's time to see what this looks like on a (locally) printed page. In the next example illustration, the first field (left) on the header has a custom entry for "Second Draft." In the center is the date and time (which on all pages is when this print job actually started), and on the right is the page number. Note again that it is similar in size and placement to my analogy of the text on the top of a received fax page:

```
Second Draft                        7/16/2010 7:52 PM                        19


        EXT. MAX'S GARAGE - DAY

        Bobby and Fred stand by the two big truck doors. Bobby
        examines the door's edge closely.
                              FRED
                    You can do it, right?
```

As is often the case in Celtx, there is another way to do page setup and we'll see that in our very next selection on the **File** menu.

Time for action – previewing and printing a local print job

Clicking on **Print Preview** on the **File** menu presents us with a preview or "how it will look" for local print jobs. If you have a PDF selected (by clicking on the **TypeSet/PDF** tab at the bottom of the main script window), we find that the **Print Preview** option is grayed out (not active). There's a very important reason for this. The final format version of a Celtx script is controlled by a formatting server out on the Internet to make sure we have exactly an acceptable industry standard format. Local print stuff, we can play around with, but we can't and should not be able to change the final format. More on that later.

Clicking on **Print Preview** turns the main script window (the big window centered in the Celtx screen) into a preview window for our local print jobs, as shown in the following screenshot:

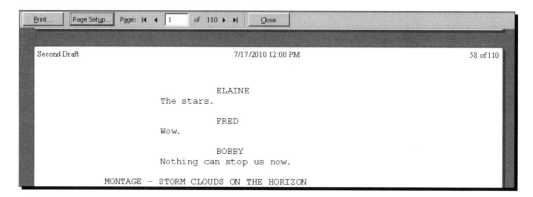

 Note this example has a header, as we learned to create in the section on the **Page Setup...** menu selection.

We can also see the options for **Print Preview** along the top of the window, just above the generated preview page.

- **Print...**: Clicking on this tab brings up the standard print dialog box for your flavor of operating system. Choose the printer and other options offered as you would while printing from any other program.

- **Page Setup...**: As promised, here's another way to do page setup and it pops up the same dialog box with its two tabs as we saw in the earlier section of this chapter. So we could, for example, create our header and footers here or through the **Page Setup...** selection on the **File** menu—both ways give the same result.

Next in the preview controls, we have a way of navigating pages, as shown in the following screenshot:

- Like rewinding an old tape recorder (except a heck of a lot faster), clicking on the bar and left facing arrowhead takes us to the first page. Click on the right facing arrowhead and bar and we're transported to the last page.

- The left facing and right facing arrows move one page per click in that direction.

- The center number is the current page number. We can change this to any page number within the document; hit the *Enter* key, and the preview changes to that page.

- The final tab, **Close**, closes the preview.

Printing a local document

Clicking on the **Print** selection on the **File** menu, just like in the preview window as shown earlier, gives us the standard print dialog box for our operating system. We choose the printer and other options offered to print as with any other program we use.

Time for action – showing the project file

The **Show Project File** is the next to last choice on the **File** menu. Clicking on this selection on the **File** menu opens the folder in which the project lives, such as my directory for Portals, as shown in the following screenshot, which shows all files in the directory, not just the Celtx project or projects:

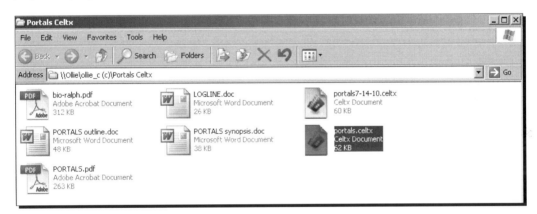

Time for action – exiting

I love the story of the infamous 19th century circus entrepreneur P. T. Barnum (the Barnum in "Barnum & Bailey"). Old P.T. believed in moving the rubes (the public) along if possible. He is said to have posted a sign reading "The Way to the Egress" and people would rush to see the Egress only to find themselves outside the tent and having to pay again to get back in. Egress, of course, is just another word for "exit."

Click on **Exit** on the **File** menu in Celtx and you'll find yourself outside also as Celtx closes down. Being more on your side than circus and carnival hucksters, Celtx makes sure you saved your last changes. Basically, it works exactly the same as the **Close, Close Tab** (as the last tab is closed), and **Close Window** menu selections. This completes the **File** menu, so let's go on to the **Edit** menu.

The Edit menu

The **Edit** menu (which gives us options related to editing) is just to the right of the **File** menu in the upper left-hand corner of the Celtx screen, as shown in the following screenshot:

Clicking on it shows us the menu. The top five selections are inactive but will fire up as we need them. Let's see how that works.

By the way, if you think all 10 of the selections above resemble those on the editing menu of your favorite word processing program, even having the same shortcuts, you're right. No accident that—Celtx has very powerful word processing features built in.

Time for action – undoing a change

The Undo selection works when editing a script, sketch, item, and so on. If our fickle fingers (at least mine are when typing fast) fly furiously into a typo or an action not intended, just click on the **Edit** menu's **Undo** selection and the last action performed will be erased. Better yet, use the shortcut for **Undo**, *Ctrl+Z*. This shortcut works in many other programs also, such as Microsoft's Word word processing software in which I am writing this book. Not that I ever make misteaks... er... mistakes.

Time for action – redoing (restoring) a change

Most of us seldom make mistakes, eh? Sometime we think we've made a mistake but it turns out we were really right. So the Redo selection on the Edit menu restores an undo. The shortcut (as in many other programs) is *Ctrl+Y*.

Time for action – cutting

Choosing **Cut** on the **Edit** menu (while we have text or some other item selected) or using the *Ctrl+X* shortcut, cuts (removes) the text or item. Actually, it's put on our computer's clipboard, so we still have access to it until another item is cut or copied.

Time for action – copying

Using the **Copy** selection on the **Edit** menu or the *Ctrl+C* shortcut also puts the selected text or other items on the clipboard, but it only copies them instead of removing them like **Cut** does.

Time for action – pasting

Pasting text (using the **Paste** menu selection or its shortcut, *Ctrl+V*) or another item, such as an icon in a sketch, inserts (places) that text or item in the tab we are editing, at the point the cursor is. Again, all these editing commands work precisely like many programs you might already be familiar with. This similarity makes learning Celtx a lot easier.

Time for action – selecting it all

Clicking **Select All** on the **Edit** menu, or using the *Ctrl+A* shortcut, selects everything in the tab you are editing. For example—while I started Portals at the same time as I began this book, the script is now complete (and out to market). What can I say, I write scripts faster than computer books.

Anyway, we click anywhere in the script (now 110 pages), type *Ctrl+A*, and all 110 pages are selected (see the following figure). Now we can copy, cut, or delete the entire script. Be careful with this feature, as it's very powerful.

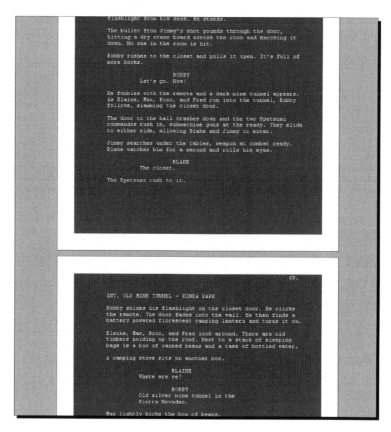

Time for action – finding that which was lost

The bottom block of four selections on the **Edit** menu is Celtx's Detective Bureau. These guys find stuff for us. They are **Find**, **Replace**, **Find Again**, and **Find Previous**, as shown in the following screenshot:

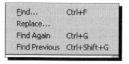

Find and **Replace** use the same dialog box, so there's just one shortcut for both, *Ctrl+F*. The **Find and Replace** dialog box is shown below. It has two tabs, not surprisingly those being **Find** and **Replace**. Let's look at **Find** first.

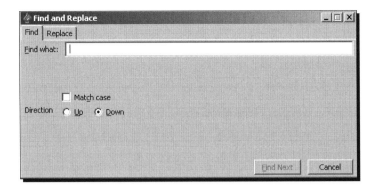

Finding a place or specific wording in a script is as easy as typing a unique part of it into the **Find What:** box. By unique, I simply mean if we're looking for "the green monkey" we'll have a lot better luck searching for at least "the green" instead of "the." Bet you there are a lot more occurrences of "the" in your script than "the green." It's that easy.

Moving down the preceding dialog box, we find some things that help us search. **Match Case**, if checked, causes Celtx to pay attention to upper and lower case as it looks for our search term. For example, if checked (and our search term is "Bubba"), it would find "Bubba" but not "bubba" or bUBBA."

Direction (check either **Up** or **Down**) determines the direction in the script that Celtx searches—**Up** is toward the beginning and **Down** moves toward the end of the document.

The two buttons at the bottom of the dialog box are **Find Next** which moves to the next occurrence of your search term, and **Cancel,** which stops the search. The cursor in our script remains at the last search term found.

Clicking on the **Replace** tab on the **Find and Replace** dialog box adds a second entry box, (see the next screenshot) **Replace with:**. You can also get there by clicking the **Replace** selection found on the **Edit** menu.

Replacing text requires both a search term to find the text and specification of what to replace it with. Here's an example use. We have a character named "Bill Smith" and we want to change it to something more unique, let's say Bill Finklegruberski — that's kind of different. So in the **Find What:** box, enter "Bill Smith" and put "Bill Finklegruberski" in the **Replace with:** box. The **Match Case** and **Direction** choices work the same as in **Find**.

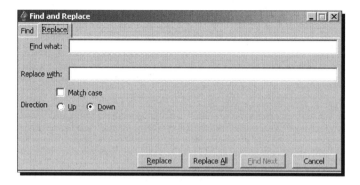

Click on the **Replace** button to replace only the first instance found of "Bill Smith". Click on **Replace All** to change every instance found. To make sure you change every occurrence of a term, go to the beginning of the script and click in front of the very first letter so that the I-beam cursor blinks there. Then **Replace All** in the "down" direction and the entire script will be searched.

Celtx remembers your last search term and settings. So clicking on **Find Again** takes you to the next occurrence of the last search term forward or "down" the document. The shortcut is *Ctrl+G*. **Find Previous** (*Ctrl+Shift+G*) does the same but toward the front of our script.

Now let's look at (pun, as always, intentional) the **View** menu.

The View menu

Celtx's **View** menu currently is only for adjusting the look of toolbars. At this time in Celtx, the second line down (**Add**, **Open**, **Save**, and so on) is the only toolbar affected by the **View** menu. The toolbars are the lines of menus and tools, such as **File**, **Edit**, **View**, **Script**, and so forth. Those are all menus. One line down, **Save** and **Print** are examples of tools. The **View** menu choices shown in the following illustration simply adjust the look of how various menus and tools appear to us:

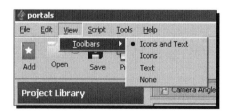

The various options under the the **View** menu are as follows:

- ◆ **Icons and Text**: There's no better way to explain these choices than to show you. The default view is both icons and text, as shown in the following screenshot. Note, on the left, the **Add** button has both an icon, blue box with a white star in it, and the word Add. Clicking on either the icon or the word causes the **Add** menu to drop-down. To the right of that is a file folder icon and the word Open, and so forth for the other choices on this toolbar (which we'll be exploring later in this chapter). That's it for the icons and text view.

- ◆ **Icons**: Click on **Icons** on the Toolbars selection of the **View** menu and we get only icons, as shown in the following screenshot:

- ◆ **Text**: Selecting **Text** yields just the titles as shown in the following screenshot:

- ◆ **None**: The None choice hides the toolbar. This has the advantage of giving you more screen real estate for the main script window (see the following screen capture).

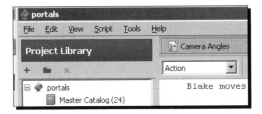

I vote for icons and text but so much for the **View** menu—now we move on to something with more meat on its bones, the **Script** menu.

The Script menu

Celtx is actually pretty logical so, as we are safe to expect, the **Script** menu presents us with ways to work with scripts. The following screenshot shows the **Script** menu:

Importing scripts: Many good reasons exist for importing a script into a Celtx project, and two good ones are as follows:

- It's a script you've written in Word or maybe another scriptwriting program like Final Draft or Moviemaker and now you want it in Celtx because (as we should all be seeing by now) Celtx is mighty powerful.

- You're a producer using Celtx because of its many scheduling and tracking features but the writer of your project did it in another program.

The above and numerous other reasons make having a script import capability in Celtx very useful. By importing scripts, we mean, again, scripts from other programs. Scripts written in a Celtx project are easy to pull over into our current project (as we saw in the section *Inter-project document management* in *Chapter 4*, it's easy).

A script written in another program needs some minor preparation before we import it into Celtx. The script must be exported from the origination software into a text file retaining layout, that is, all the indentation spaces, so that Celtx, during import, can determine what are scene titles, action, character names, and dialog.

For example, in Final Draft, the most widely used screenwriting software, export using the Text with Layout selection. If you have Adobe Acrobat, exporting a PDF script as plain text works well (however, you cannot do this from the free Adobe Reader as it drops the leading spaces and thus the format is jumbled).

Some minor clean up is required, such as fixing dialog breaks in a few places and removing page numbers from a PDF import, but **Import Script...** on the **Script** menu is amazingly accurate and saves tons of retyping in getting scripts into a Celtx project.

To import a proper text file (text with leading spaces), first open a film project (assuming we are bringing in a movie script). Click on **Import Script...** on the **Script** menu and the **Import Text Script** dialog box appears, as seen in the following screenshot, on my computer:

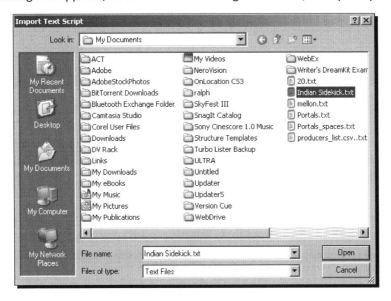

I've selected another of my feature movie scripts—**Indian Sidekick** (the police chief of the Cherokee Indian reservation in the Great Smoky Mountains gets help from a real Indian from India in solving a string of murders).

Click on the **Open** button as shown in the preceding screenshot and the script is imported. Here's what we get:

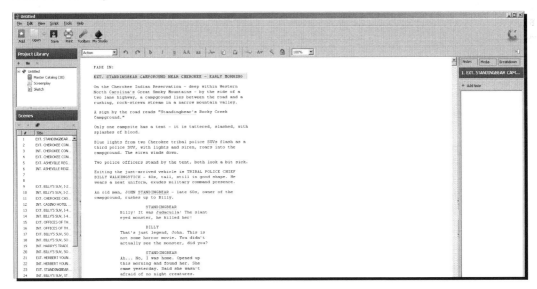

The screenplay is now in Celtx with the right formats for scene titles, action, character names, and dialog. We're ready to, first, save the project then start using it as we like. Such as editing, scheduling, adding storyboards, and all the other great stuff Celtx allows us to accomplish.

Time for action – exporting scripts

What goes in, needs to come back out. Whether we import scripts or type them from scratch, sometimes they need to be exported. The **Export Script...** selection on the **Script** menu lets us send scripts to other programs.

Let's say a producer calls. He's read the PDF script you sent and wants to pay you money and produce the film. Great! However, he wants it in Final Draft because that is what his film company works with (believe it or not, everyone does not yet see Celtx's overwhelming advantages). No problem—with the Celtx project containing the script, open the script in the main window, and click on **Export Script...**. The Export Script dialog box comes up (like the following). Edit the file title in **File name:** if you want something different and click on the **Save** button.

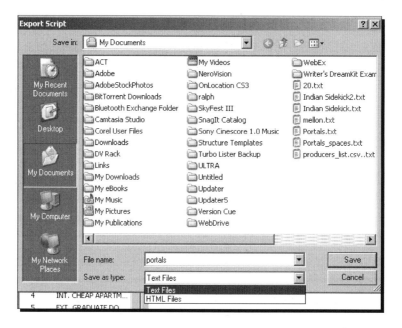

Once the text file is saved, it's ready to be imported into Final Draft or any other software, touched up and sent to the producer who requested it.

Time for Action – adapting to another type of script

The Adapt To selection on the Script menu lets us change the type of script to another. I used one of my favorite adages, "write once, use many" when we first met the adapt feature in *Chapter 2*. Assuming we have a Screenplay open (as we do), on the choices shown in the following screenshot, we see that **Screenplay** is grayed out (we don't need to convert something to the same thing it already is). We can, however convert it to a stage play, an A/V (audio visual) script, an audio play (like a radio program), a comic book, or a storyboard.

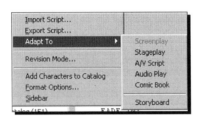

Now I think Portals would make a dandy comic book. With one click, we convert the screenplay to comic format (which looks like the following), ready for a little bit of editing and then submitting to Marvel or whoever:

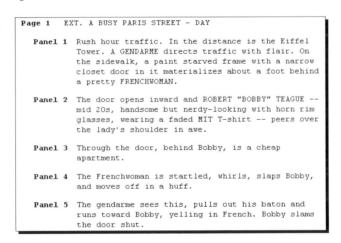

Alternatively, it would make a super stage place. Click. Done.

Also having a storyboard would be useful. Click.

That's how easy it is. Write once, use many.

Converting does not lose any of our previous work. Looking in the Project Library (as below) we see that the screenplay, stage play, comic book, and storyboard are all there. We've lost nothing and gained three more projects with a lot of the work already done on them. Write once, use many. Love it.

Time for action – revising a completed script (and you will)

Clicking on **Revision Mode...** on the Script menu puts our script into Revision Mode, which is especially important if several writers make changes to the script. Revisions are explained in detail in *Chapter 2* in the *Revision Modes* section.

Time for action – updating the Master Catalog

The **Add Characters to Catalog** selection on the **Script** menu is a simple but powerful update utility. For example, open a new Celtx Film project. Now open an older project on top of it as we did in *Inter-Project Document Management* section in *Chapter 4*, where we learned to drag items from project to project. Drag over a script, as I did with Portals. Note that the **Master Catalog** in the **Project Library** has no characters in it. What happened to all our characters?

No problem. Click on **Add Characters to Catalog** and almost instantly Celtx is now tracking our characters for us in the new project (see the following screenshot):

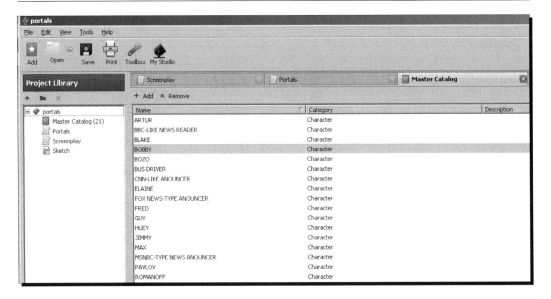

Time for action – using formatting options

Earlier in the chapter we learned about **Page Setup** on the File menu, which controls parameters for local printing. The **Format Options** selection on the **Script** menu has to do with **global printing**, or the information Celtx uses when it goes out on the Internet and formats our script into an industry standard PDF (Portable Document File, the standard for exchanging scripts). The **Paper Size**: box below lets us select US Letter (8.5 x 11 inches) or the European A4 size (8.27 x 11.69 inches) paper. When we use the **TypeSet/PDF** tab at the bottom of the main Celtx screen, the PDF file generated will be for the size of the paper that we specified.

Pagination shows approximate page breaks on our work screen. Actual breaks may be slightly different, but the Celtx servers that do the formatting out on the net ("in the cloud" as the latest jargon calls it) make sure it's done right. Checking **Show page number on first page** changes the default of having no page number on the beginning page.

```
The shouts of the policeman and the traffic sounds cut
out. Bobby goes to the closet, removes the bar, and
cautiously looks inside. Just clothes and an old suitcase.
------------------------------------------------------------
                                                         2.

Bobby drops the two-by-four and, as it clatters to the
floor, pumps his fists in the air jubilantly.

                    BOBBY
          Yeah, baby! Finally. Instant
          transport!
```

Show Scene Numbers, we've seen before. (Remember, do not have scene numbers turned on for spec scripts). Our choices are **None**, **Left**, **Right**, and **Both**. Below, we see **Both** selected with scene numbers on both sides:

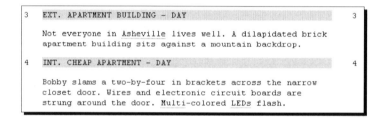

```
3   EXT. APARTMENT BUILDING - DAY                         3

    Not everyone in Asheville lives well. A dilapidated brick
    apartment building sits against a mountain backdrop.

4   INT. CHEAP APARTMENT - DAY                            4

    Bobby slams a two-by-four in brackets across the narrow
    closet door. Wires and electronic circuit boards are
    strung around the door. Multi-colored LEDs flash.
```

Time for action – hiding the Sidebar

The final section on the **Script** menu is **Sidebar**. The Sidebar we've also met before—it's where we add notes, media, and all those items (under **Breakdown**) we want Celtx to track for us, such as actors, props, horses, and so on. Clicking on the **Sidebar** selection hides (giving us more room for the script) and unhides this area.

Okay, that concludes our look at the **Script** menu. Now, we sharpen our tools using the **Tools** menu.

The Tools menu

The **Tools** menu has only four selections—the top two relate to spell checking, which we covered in *Chapter 2*, the toolbox where tools downloaded from online are placed (we'll look at that in a moment), and various options. The **Options...** selection we saw in *Chapter 1*, while setting up an Internet connection for our Celtx (it's critical that Celtx can communicate with the web as we've seen for formatting), but we'll look at it again.

Toolbox

The following screenshot shows how my **Toolbox** (click on **Toolbox** on the **Tools** menu) looks right now—empty. If you've only recently installed Celtx, yours looks the same.

Let's get some tools! To do so, click on the **Get Celtx Tools** button at the bottom of the dialog box shown in the preceding screenshot. Remember, Celtx relies on a web connection being open for several reasons, and downloading tools, art packs, and other goodies into the toolbox is yet another of those reasons.

With a web connection active, clicking on the button just mentioned causes a webpage with "Special Offers!" to open in your browser (the actual web address is `http://www.celtx.com/specialOffers.html`).

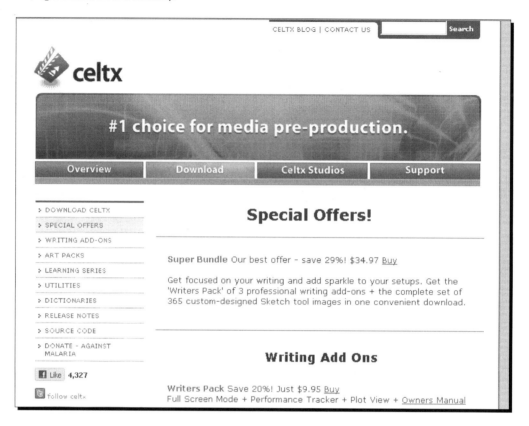

The company that sponsors the development of Celtx, as already noted, has a revenue stream from selling add-ons for Celtx. We (okay me) will actually buy one in a moment but let's first hit the freebies!

On the webpage shown in the preceding screenshot, go down the left column until you find **Utilities** and click on it. On the next page, we are offered five free utilities:

♦ Catalogs CSV Export Tool: Exports Catalog data as a .csv file

♦ Coloured Notes: Color code your script notes

♦ Dialog Numbering: Add a numerical value to each dialog element in your film script

♦ Hide Breakdown Colors: Hide the colored markup in your script

♦ Session Timer : A timer for managing your writing sessions

We might as well get all five, since the price is right. Click on each in turn to download it. The utility will appear in your **Toolbox**, as shown in the following screenshot:

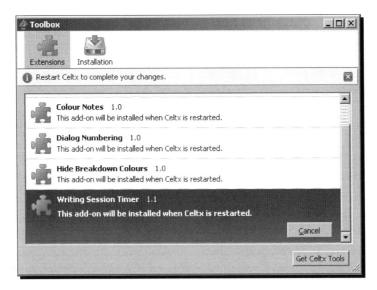

Once all five are downloaded, exit Celtx and restart. Installation for all five is then complete and they are ready for use.

A link to the **Utilities Installation and Usage Guide** is on the same page we download the utilities from. These five tools are small but useful additional features to those that already come with Celtx (the latter being the ones we are learning in this book).

There are a number of art packs (as we saw in *Chapter 3*) and other neat things for sale on the **Special Offers!** webpage. Explore and enjoy. Add-ons for Celtx are reasonably priced and I, for one, am glad to support the continued existence of this great open source software.

Proxy Bug: I need to warn you guys of one possible problem in using the **Toolbox**. When I first tried downloading the utilities just discussed, I got errors and no tools installed. This happened on the several computers here that I have Celtx on (hey, it's free, put it on as many computers as you like). Being under deadline to get this chapter done and turned in, I was flustered. So I went to the Celtx Forums (`http://forums.celtx.com`) and did some research.

If your computer is behind a firewall (and it should be these days), certain types of these protective interfaces between you and the wild and woolly web (www) will not let you download tools. I use a Squid web proxy on an Ubuntu Linux server here and it's definitely one of the ones that cause Celtx to bomb out while trying to copy in tools. A fix is promised for the next release of Celtx.

The temporary solution is to hook your computer to a direct Internet connection (and that's what I did) for at least long enough to download tools (a few seconds per tool). Don't forget to restore your normal connection when finished.

Buying tools and the other offerings: Some neat items are available on the **Special Offers!** The **Writer's Development Kit** for a mere $1.95 caught my eye (and it has some great information in it on loglines and writing a synopsis that I've already found useful). This is shown in the following screenshot:

Order Details

Code	Description	Price
ADLS02	Writer's Development Kit	$1.95
	Subtotal:	$1.95
	GST:	$0.00
	Total:	$1.95
	All prices in U.S. Dollars	

Just click on the item you want and pay for it with PayPal or a credit card. You get a download link that puts it right into Celtx.

A full toolbox is always great to have for unforeseen things like a requirement for variously colored notes, exporting catalogs to spreadsheets, keeping track of your time, or broken pipes in the basement.

Options

The **Options** selection on the **Tools** menu brings up the dialog box similar to the following screenshot, in which we can set various options or preferences:

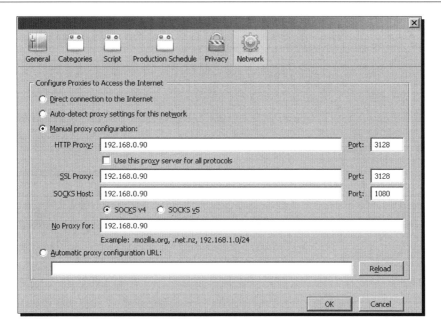

We first came across this in *Establishing an Internet connection* in *Chapter 1*.

We were discussing proxy servers and the bug in downloading tools just mentioned. Here is where you set up for your proxy server. Once more, Celtx needs a connection to the Internet to properly work for us. As this tab has already been covered, let's look at the other **Option** tabs.

The other tabs, left to right, are **General**, **Categories**, **Script**, **Production Schedule**, and **Privacy**:

◆ **General**: The first **Options** tab (Options is selected on the **Tools** menu) is **General**. On this tab you can secure Celtx projects by clicking on **Sign in on Startup** and adding a username and password. The drop-down menu next to **Automatically save project:** lets us set how often Celtx does a save operation (I highly recommend you use this feature; it has saved me from losing work more than once). Finally, if you subscribe to the **Studio** service, you can check or uncheck **Ask me for a comment when saving to the Studio**. Clicking on the **OK** button saves changes to these settings and **Cancel** backs us out with no change.

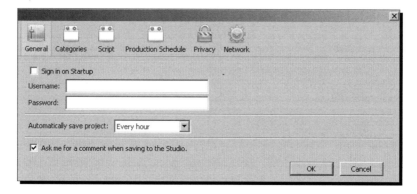

◆ **Categories**: The **Categories** tab is for removing or adding back the items that Celtx tracks for us. It's very simple to use; just click on the item to be removed and then click on the **Remove** button. It will move from the enabled column to the disabled column. To put it back in, click on it to select, then click on the **Add** button and the items will go from the disabled column to the enabled column.

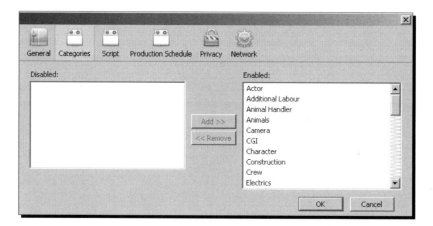

- **Script**: The **Script** tab is for adding new script element words to the standard ones, as shown in the following screenshot:

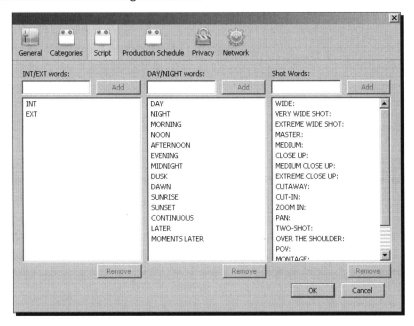

If you write spec scripts, be careful what you add here. Make sure it's something already in use or at least so darn logical you might get away with having it in a script. Exercise care in the latter.

- **Production**: The **Production** tab, which we first visited in *Chapter 4*, lets us specify such things as when the shooting day starts and ends, default scene length, and the workweek. These are all things Celtx will take into account when production schedules get created.

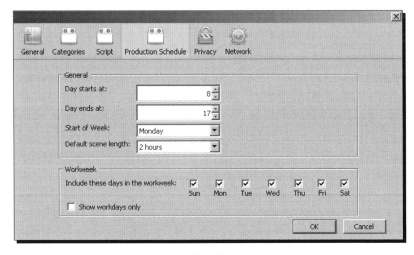

◆ **Privacy**: What? You think you have privacy? Just Google yourself, eh? This tab only has one choice, that is, do you want to be nice and let the development people of Celtx track how many times you use the software? I think this is a good thing. The more of us that are using Celtx out there, the greater encouragement they will have to keep heaping additional goodies into the program.

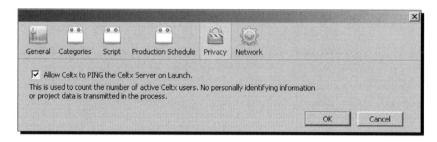

Those are our options and they are good ones. Now, time to call for help.

With a little help from our friends

The last menu on the top menu bar is the **Help** menu (as follows). So, continuing our exploration of the many wonderful tools on the main Celtx screen, here's where we find some help. The following screenshot shows the options under the **Help** tab:

The various options under the **Help** tab are as follows:

◆ **About**: Clicking on **About Celtx** on the **Help** menu gives us the version of Celtx we're running. In my case—as I pound away at my trusty keyboard writing this book in July, 2010—the latest version is 2.7 (released in December, 2009). Other information on this mini dialog box includes a nice movie-style scrolling credits list of folks who worked so hard to bring us Celtx. Let's give a shout out to all those great guys and gals. Thanks!

◆ **Splash Screen**: Clicking on the **Splash Screen** selection brings up the same screen we see when first starting Celtx. It's another way to open a new project— there's always more than one way in Celtx.

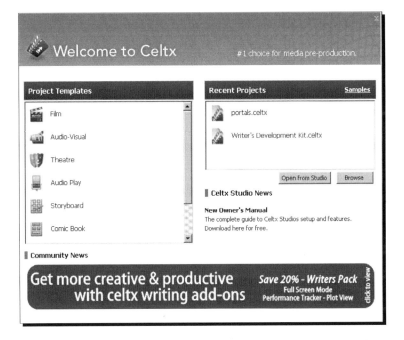

◆ **Online Support**: The **Online Support** selection on the **Help** menu takes us out on the web to **The Celtx Forum**. Reading the posts on the forum keeps us up-to-date and gives interaction with other Celtx users worldwide.

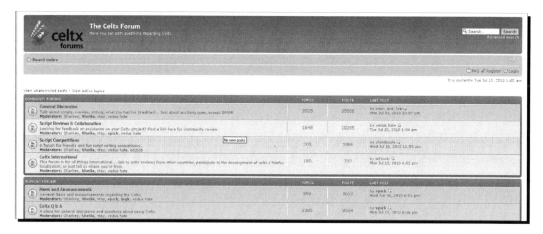

◆ **Celtx Wiki**: The **Celtx Wiki** on the **Help** menu works just like the online encyclopedia, the **Wikipedia**. In fact, it uses the same software. It's the online manual for Celtx and is, alas, a bit out of date. You might want to find a good book with all the latest features of Celtx explained instead. Sort of like... well, okay... exactly like this one.

Still, the Celtx Wiki is a handy quick reference and, to be fair, is being constantly updated.

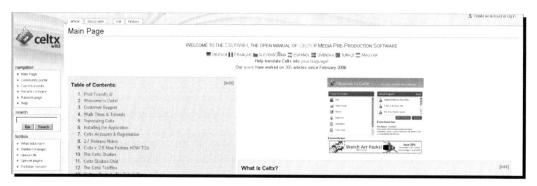

◆ **Video Tutorial**: The **Video Tutorial** selection takes you to the Celtx site and several video tutorials (should be plural on the **Help** menu).

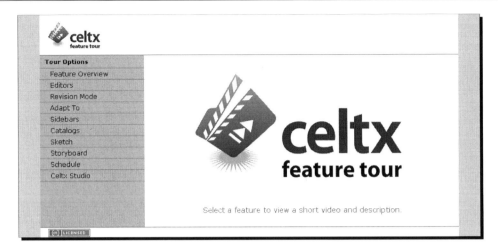

- **Stomping on Bugs**: As with any software in active development one will occasionally finds errors in the operation of Celtx—like the proxy bug we discussed earlier. If you run across a bug (in Celtx that is, not one on the floor) click on the **Report a Bug** selection on the **Help** menu. The **Celtx Report a Bug** forum will open up for you, as shown in the following screenshot:

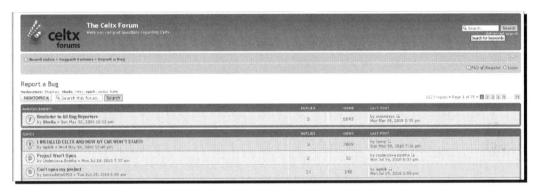

It's also good to check this forum occasionally to stay up to speed on possible problem areas.

◆ **Celtx Account**: This selection on the **Help** menu takes us to the secure **Studio** login page on the Celtx website, which is shown in the following screenshot:

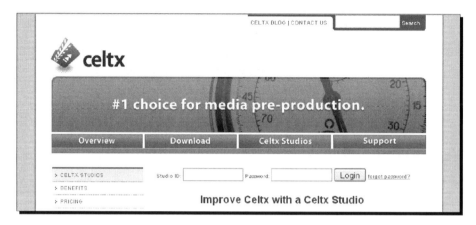

The top buttons

The next row down from the top line of menus (**File**, **Edit**, **View**, **Script**, **Tools**, and **Help**, all of which we have been exploring to this point in the chapter) has several quick hit buttons for various Celtx tools. These tools are **Add**, **Open**, **Save**, **Print**, **Toolbox**, and **My Studio**, as shown in the following screenshot:

These buttons are meant as shortcuts. As we know for a fact now, Celtx has more than one way of doing things. In this chapter, we've already covered what each of these buttons do. The **Add** button is the same as **Add Item** on the **File** menu. The **Open Button** is the same as **Open Project**, and the little doodad beside it (smaller that the other buttons) is **Open Recent**, which gives us a list of recently opened projects.

Save is the same as **Save Project** on the **File** menu, **Print** the same as **Print** on the **File** menu, **Toolbox** the same as **Toolbox** on the **Tools** menu, and **My Studio** the same as **Open from Studio** on the **File** menu. All are just quicker ways of getting to the same place.

The Project Library window

The Project Library is covered in detail in *Chapter 4*. To quickly review, this is where all the items that go into a project or projects get stored. Screenplays, catalogs of characters and props, the other magic of movie making, schedules, photos, bookmarks, folders of folders of folders of documents, notes, research, actor resumes, you name it. It's a truly powerful feature not found in other scriptwriting software.

The Scenes window

The Scenes window of the main Celtx screen is covered in *Chapter 2* in the *Scenes management* section. This gives us a powerful tool to rearrange scenes, navigate the script, and more.

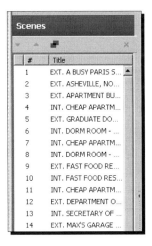

The editor toolbar

The editor toolbar appears on the top of the main script window for each type of project except **Storyboard**. We came across it before in *Chapter 1*, but let's take a quick run through again because you'll use it a lot. We'll go across from left to right, as shown in the following screenshot:

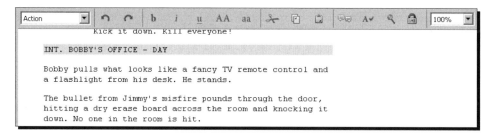

The tools in the editor toolbar are explained as follows:

- The first item on the editor bar is the drop-down script element menu, as shown in the following screenshot:

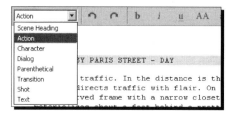

  These elements vary some, depending on the type of project. A **Film** project has different elements than a **Comic Book**. No other screenwriting software has the wide range of possible projects that we can script in Celtx. To insert a Scene Heading or a Character and Dialog, place the I-beam cursor in the script and just click on the element desired on the dropdown menu. There are also shortcuts as we discuss from time to time in this book.

- The next two items, the two curved arrows, are Undo and Redo respectively.

- The **b**, **i**, and **u** icons turn selected text bold, italic, or underline it.

- Clicking on the **AA** and **aa** icons cause selected text to become all uppercase or all lowercase.

- Use the scissors icon to cut selected text (take it out entirely), or the two little pages, one over the other, to copy (get the text on our computer's clipboard but leave it in the script), and the clipboard icon to paste the cut or copied text back into the script where we have placed the I-beam cursor.

- ◆ The two speech balloons icon we've seen before; it gives us dual formatted dialog (side by side to show quick interaction—see the *Dual dialog* section in *Chapter 2*).

- ◆ We can use the **A** with a checkmark beside it to check our spelling.

- ◆ The tiny magnifying glass icon brings up the **Find and Replace** dialog box and is a shortcut to the **Find...** and **Replace...** selections on the **Edit** menu detailed earlier in this chapter.

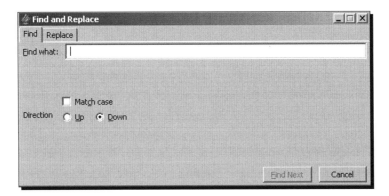

- ◆ Next to last on the editor toolbar, we find a padlock icon. Clicking on the padlock "locks" all the text in the script, so that it cannot accidentally be edited. The editor toolbar is also collapsed, leaving only the search, unlock, and size functions. Clicking on the padlock again restores the editor toolbar and lets us edit the text again.

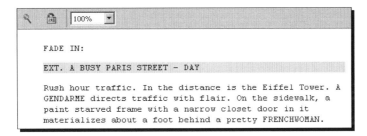

- ◆ The final item on both the full and the collapsed (text locked) editor toolbar is a drop-down menu that changes the size of the text in the script window. This makes it easier to read, but does not affect the font size when printed.

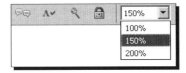

Now, we dive from the top of the Celtx screen down to the bottom. Plop!

The bottom buttons

At the bottom of Celtx's main window, the script window (except when working on a Storyboard) is a row of buttons, as shown in the following screenshot (we've covered all of these already, but a quick review is always good):

- ◆ The **Script** tab or button returns us to the script in progress from any of the other tabs.

- ◆ **TypeSet/PDF** generates a final script (looks like the next screen) ready to be saved as a PDF file and sent to the market or used in a production you or your company is doing. Full details on this process are in the *Getting the script out of your computer* section in *Chapter 2*.

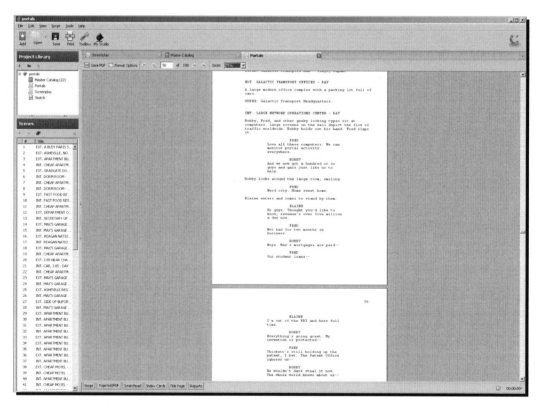

- ◆ Of the other four tabs, **Title Page** helps us construct a title page for our script and the remaining three—**Scratchpad**, **Index Cards**, and **Reports**—are assistants to enhance writing and producing scripts. All are also covered in *Chapter 2*.

Whew! Lots of information so far, but we've now covered all the tools and menus on Celtx's main screen, the stuff you'll be using most in creating all those great scripts and other projects of yours. However, let's look at customizing the look of Celtx.

Have a go hero – create a test script and turn it into a PDF

Seeing results rewards us for learning to use software. The end result from Celtx (if we are writing scripts with it) is a neatly formatted PDF (Adobe Portable Document Format) file which can be printed out or just e-mailed as it is to a producer or agent.

So, hero, have a go at formatting a PDF with Celtx using the **TypeSet/PDF** button we just used. To get a script or part of a script to format you can do the following:

- Use a script you might have already started in Celtx.
- Use one of the sample scripts included with Celtx (on the Splash screen, click on **Samples** and choose the script you'd like to play with here).
- Or, in the main script window, just choose a script element from the drop-down menu, type something in it, choose the next element and do the same, and so on.

Now, hero, make sure your computer is connected to the Internet and click on the **TypeSet/PDF** button. Celtx sends the script out to a server, which formats it into a PDF and returns the file to your computer. You can use the **Save PDF** button at the top of the main screen to put a copy on your hard disk, then print or e-mail it to your brave heart's content.

Customizing the Celtx screen

There are several ways of customizing the Celtx screen to make writing and other work using the software easier and more pleasing to you. One such way, which we just saw a few minutes ago while looking at how the editor toolbar works, is resizing the text in our script. If we can actually see what we write (for those like me who wear glasses) it will probably come out better, eh?

Using **Toolbar** on the **View** menu to remove the row of shortcut buttons at the top of the screen is another way of customizing, in this case to gain more space for the script window.

Yet another is by resizing the various windows that make up the Celtx screen. In the following screenshot, I've widened the **Scenes** window, so that I can read all the scene title text:

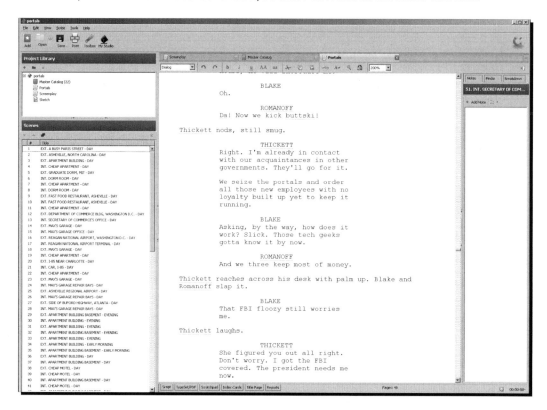

To rearrange the main Celtx screen, move the mouse cursor over the edges of windows until it changes into a horizontal double-headed arrow cursor. In the case of the Scenes window just explained, this would be handy to do while navigating through a script or rearranging scenes, as detailed in *Chapter 2*. If we wanted to consult our Index Cards, we would move the right sidebar border to the left to make that sidebar larger and viewing easier, restoring or even totally collapsing it when finished, so that we can go back to writing on our script with a maximum amount of screen devoted to it.

Additional buttons

In the far upper right of the main Celtx screen, we have a couple of other buttons we should mention. The small arrow/white box icon just above **Breakdown** in the following screenshot collapses the right sidebar and widens the script window:

Click on it again (the arrow has changed directions) to restore the right sidebar.

The round life preserver icon with four red diagonals is not a customization feature but, rather, one of help. Clicking on it causes a Celtx FAQ page to open in our browser.

Pop quiz

1. How do you start a new project?

2. If you had a screenplay that you wanted to adapt into a comic book, how would you change the type of Celtx project?

3. If you are working with Celtx and have a question, how do you find help?

    a. Click on the **Help** menu at the top of Celtx's main window

    b. Visit the Celtx website at `http://celtx.com`

    c. Reread the appropriate section of this book

    d. All of the above

Summary

A lot of small but important details about how to use Celtx are packed into this chapter. Use these things a few times and they will soon be second nature, and you will happily find Celtx enhancing your creativity by making writing easier and faster. To recap, in this chapter we've learned the following menus:

◆ **File menu**: Lets us open or create new projects, save our project (really important), and related operations.

◆ **Edit menu**: Lets us undo, redo, cut, copy, paste, global changes and replacements, and more.

◆ **View menu**: Lets us adjust the look of the shortcut toolbar as needed.

◆ **Script menu**: Lets us export, import, adapt type (such as changing Film to Audio Play, and so on), change page format (A4 to Letter, and so forth), and more.

- **Tools menu**: Lets us check spelling, inline spelling, preferences, and more.

- **Help menu**: Tells us about various methods of obtaining help and tutorials online.

- **Top buttons**: Add, Open, Save, Print, Toolbox, My Studio, all demystified.

- **Project Library**: Catalogs, scripts, and other documents—open whatever you need, and here you will see how to use them.

- **Scenes**: Navigate easily through your scripts using this handy feature.

- **Editor toolbar**: The name for often-used tools for each type of editor. Includes a drop-down selection for the various elements such as Scene Heading, Action, Character, and Dialog (all industry standard script elements, automatically formatted for you). Also, undo, redo, bold, italic, underline, cut, paste, dual dialog, text lock, sizing the view, and more.

- **Bottom buttons**: Script, TypeSet/PDF, Scratchpad, Index Cards, Title Page, Reports—all very useful and here you will see how they work.

- **Customize your workspace**: Adjust the look and feel of the screen to what suits you best.

Now, let's move on and look at some features of Celtx as a final precursor to actually starting the writing of a script, as we will in *Chapter 7*!

6
Advanced Celtx

Here's a more detailed look at some powerful Celtx features.

In this chapter, we will cover the following topics:

- **Multiple projects in a single project container**: Unlike conventional screenwriting software, we can have many files in the same Celtx project, even unrelated scripts, Word files, photos, video clips, and much more. We'll see the incredible power of this feature.

- **Working with multiple project containers**: Thanks to Celtx's small footprint (economical use of our computers' resources); we can have several copies of it open at once. In other words, several projects open, each containing many more projects. This, too, is real power.

- **Importing Scripts in detail**: Tips, hints, kinks, and more in this in-depth look at getting already written scripts into Celtx.

- **Exporting Scripts in detail**: As the entire world does not yet use Celtx (that comes after this book, eh?), here are accurate ways to put our completed scripts out in formats others can use.

By the end of this chapter (and the previous five), we will have a good grasp of how to use various advanced features of Celtx and, even more importantly, when to use them.

Multiple projects in a single project container

When we start Celtx, the Splash screen presents us with the option of creating seven specialized projects, as shown in the following screenshot:

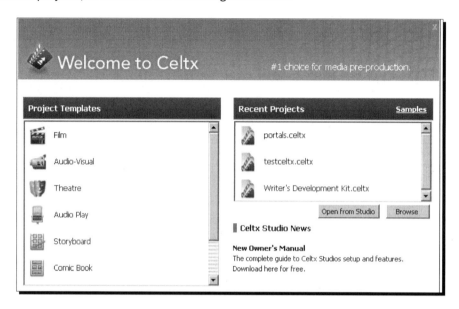

We came across these in *Chapter 1, Obtaining and Installing Celtx*, and, for review, they are: **Film**, **Audio-Visual**, **Theatre** (that good ole Canadian/English spelling, eh?), **Audio Play**, **Storyboard**, **Comic Book**, and **Text**. Also, we can customize and define other types of projects as detailed in *Chapter 2, All those Wonderful Writing Features*. We define and discuss these projects throughout this book and even have separate chapters on most of them.

Also already seen, the difference between projects is the type of script included when the project is created. A Film project's screenplay has different script elements than a Comic Book's script because one describes live action and the other details drawing images on paper. The following screenshots are an example of this difference. The elements of **Screenplay** are as follows:

The following screenshot shows the elements of a Comic Book script:

Big difference, so everyone, myself included, tends to mostly describe Celtx projects by these specific types: **Film**, **Audio-Visual**, **Theatre**, **Audio Play**, **Storyboard**, **Comic Book**, and **Text**. We are, of course, totally wrong.

◆ **Celtx projects are containers**: A Celtx project—as we've seen a number of times already—can contain all sorts of stuff. We can have Word documents, various kinds of scripts, photos, drawings, catalogs of characters, props, and all those 30-some other items. Celtx generates schedules and various other lists. In the **Project Library** window, we—as learned in *Chapter 4, Tools for Getting Organized*—need directories and subdirectories, and subdirectories of subdirectories to manage all the stuff we can have. The **Project Library** is found in the upper left of the Celtx screen

The following screenshot depicts a **Project Library** in a just-created Film project to which has been added every other kind of script that Celtx generates. Nor are we limited to just one project of each type . By right clicking on **Screenplay** or **Comic Book** or **A/V Script**, and so on, we get a mini dialog box, as shown in the following screenshot:

Click on **Rename...** and we can change the name of the script to something closer to its actual title.

Now, we can click on the blue **Add** button (or use the other two ways of adding items we played with in *Chapter 5, Tooling Up for Script Writing*) and include yet another Screenplay script or copy one in progress over from another project.

In this manner, by renaming the previous Screenplay, Comic Book, Audio Play, Text or whatever script, we could have literally hundreds of Scripts, Storyboards, and Text documents in varying types in just one Celtx project. Yes, directories and subdirectories of scripts, and they do not even have to be related to each other.

In short, starting a Film project only means, as a convenience, a Screenplay script is created. The same is true of each of the other choices on the Splash page. Projects, other than the initial type of script, are not specific in any way. We can use them for anything!

♦ **Packing a container full of stuff**: Another use for Celtx is sharing a project. Independent producers, for instance, can put all documents—Scripts, Schedules, Character and Prop lists, and so on—in one Celtx project. Copies of that project can then be e-mailed or put online, including in Celtx Studio, for sharing with others working on the same project. Alternatively, you and a co-writer can share a script in progress, including all research notes and so on.

♦ **Putting our stuff into a project in moderation**: Celtx project are containers. We can load up a single project with as much stuff as we like. It's exceptionally powerful. Just remember to use the organization techniques we learned in *Chapter 4* to avoid clutter. Also, just because we can add 4,000 files or more to a project does not always necessarily mean we need to.

Celtx also lets us have as many projects as we want. Let's get to that next.

Time for action – working with multiple project containers

So, while we might be able to cram every project, we and all our neighbors for a forty mile radius might be working on at any one time, it is not always a good idea. Believe me, if you're involved in the production of a project of any reasonable length, even just writing the script, the research, plot notes, character lists, and much more will grow pretty quickly. So, it's simply good practice to restrict a project container to material relating to a single project.

The good thing is Celtx allows us to stack projects as high as our computers can reach (which is usually darn high). In other words, the only limit is the hard disk space.

While it's not necessary to have more than one project open at a time, we can do it. The following screenshot shows four Celtx projects open on my computer. At the same time Firefox is running, a couple of chapters are open in Word, and a Lightwave animation rendering in the background:

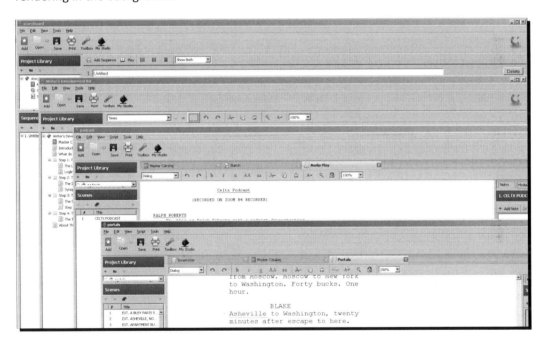

With multiple projects open, as we saw in *Chapter 4*, we can copy items from project to project by a simple *drag and drop*. That is, we put the mouse cursor on the item in the **Project Library** of the project from which we want to copy, hold down the left mouse button, and drag it to the **Project Library** of another project. Release the left mouse button and, blap; we have a copy of the file in the new project.

The following screenshot is an example of that. We've copied an **Additional Labour Catalog** from one project to another. Translating from Canadian to American that would be a Labor catalog, eh? No worries, if you want to change the spelling or name of any library object, just right click on it and choose **Rename**.

There are some limitations in copying from project to project. As we're discussing catalogs, an important exception is the **Master Catalog**. There is only one **Master Catalog** (really a built-in database) per project file in Celtx. We cannot copy it or even delete it (although we can rename it). Click on the **Master Catalog** to select it, then on **Edit** on the top menu line, and we find **Cut**, **Copy**, and **Paste** all grayed out. This is a good thing as this item can contain a lot of information about the project and we certainly do not want to lose it.

However, we can have any number of other useful catalogs (databases) in the **Project Library** window and in as many subdirectories as we care to or need to create.

Multiple projects can save us lots of work. It's always good to use work already done to save time in creating new work—things such as using existing scripts, catalogs, sketches, and so on as templates in new projects. In short, using multiple Celtx projects saves us time and work ("write once, use many"—as I've said before is a great philosophy).

Finally, multiple projects greatly contribute to organization, giving us a big stack of virtual containers, if you will. By having all the files for specific real-world projects in specific project containers, we can easily find what we need, when we need it, and copy it over to our current project.

Now, here's yet another way in which Celtx saves us work.

Importing Scripts in detail

Take me, for example. I'm pretty prolific, always have been. I have a number of decent scripts written in Final Draft. Final Draft is expensive commercial screenwriting software. Final Draft along with Movie Magic, are the "big two" Hollywood-loved scriptwriting programs (albeit Celtx does much more for a whole lot less).

Anyway, I want to move several of these scripts over to Celtx, as it has so many advantages over the high-dollar spreads. One tip I'll share. As Celtx is so good at putting together scripts with catalogs of what's required, schedules, and so on—all contained in a project file—why not offer scripts as a more complete ready-to-film movie package to independent movies producers? The big dogs in Hollywood and Bollywood with their herds of assistants would not be impressed, but Indies always have limited budgets, people, and time. Any help they can get like this would be attractive. Maybe, in addition to Written By, I can also glom onto an Associate Producer credit and the like.

You guys and gals out there reading this book probably have scripts in other formats, too, or will certainly have need to import scripts into Celtx from time to time. Basically, there are four ways to do this—there's the right way, the wrong way, Celtx's way, and my way.

Okay, forget the first two ways. Let's look at Celtx's way first, which we've already seen back in *Chapter 4*. It does work, but with some annoyances that cause extra work.

Using my script written in Final Draft, "The Farmer and the Alien" as an example (even aliens can get in trouble making an old Carolina mountain farmer grow something he doesn't want to grow), let's get it into Celtx. Celtx asks that we first get the script into text format as Celtx can only import text files. Okay but...

The trick to importing scripts into Celtx is having proper spaces. To discern action from character names and dialogs, Celtx relies on how many *leading spaces* (the spaces before the text begins on a line) exist. Final Draft, other scripting programs, word processors like Microsoft Word, and so on will all export their formatted text to a text file, but often drop the leading spaces. This kills any chance Celtx has of understanding and properly formatting the imported script.

Time for action – importing the Celtx way

A limited number of software packages can handle this for us. Looking at the following screen captured from my copy of Final Draft, we first do the import the Celtx way. In Final Draft, we simply click on **File** (up on the top menu bar just like in Celtx), then **Save As**. In the **Save As** dialog box, we ignore **Plain Text** (which would do the standard text export of stripping leading spaces) and instead pick **Text with Layout (*txt)**. This latter choice retains leading spaces.

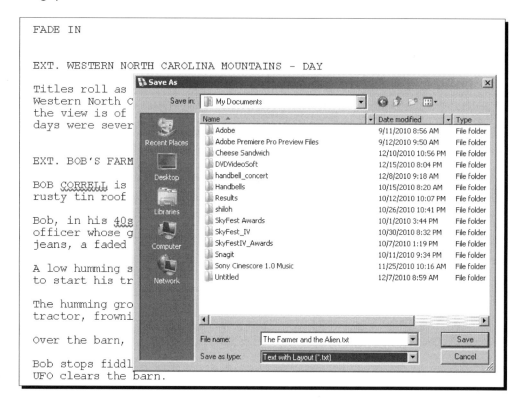

In Celtx, first open a new script of the type you are importing. Otherwise, the imported script will be appended to the bottom of whatever is currently open. Once that's done, click on **Script** (on the top menu bar), select **Import Script...** and we get the **Import Text Script** dialog box as follows:

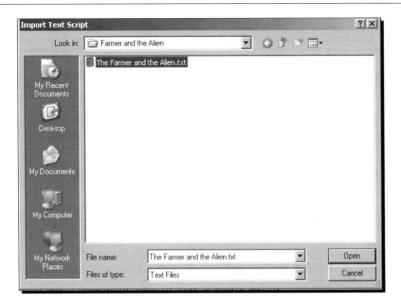

Within a few seconds, the progress indicator (shown in the following screenshot) shows the script as having been converted and read into Celtx:

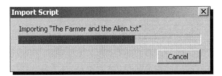

The following screenshot shows a script that has been imported into Celtx:

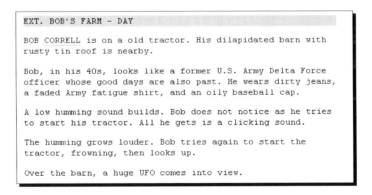

At first glance, everything looks good. The preceding screenshot shows that a script has been imported perfectly. The scene heading is recognized, the action paragraphs look fine. Great... except, when I look at the first dialog down at the bottom of the first page.

So here's my peeve—probably Final Draft's fault but if I accept it, there's a lot of unnecessary editing to do. First, the following screenshot shows how Joe's dialog was imported:

```
Joe is dressed in an expensive three-piece suit and looks
human except for green skin and his head is that of an
alien. Joe steps up to the tractor, and bangs his hand on
its hood.

                    JOE
          Name's Joe. Real piece of junk you
          got here, friend. Remind me after
          this is over. I'll put you on a
          practically new John Deere for next
          to nothing. Papers might be a
          little iffy, but it'll run like a
          champ.
```

However, the following screenshot shows how it should look (that is, not jumbled together):

```
Joe is dressed in an expensive three-piece suit and looks
human except for green skin and his head is that of an alien.
Joe steps up to the tractor, and bangs his hand on its hood.

                    JOE
          Name's Joe. Real piece of junk you
          got here, friend.

          Remind me after this is over. I'll
          put you on a practically new John
          Deere for next to nothing.

          Papers might be a little iffy, but
          it'll run like a champ.
```

A rule in scriptwriting followed by many, including me, is if a piece of dialog runs over four lines, then break it up. This keeps it snappy, easier to read, and helps actors better interpret it the way we write it. To break dialog in both Final Draft and Celtx, we use the *Shift+Enter* key combination to insert two carriage returns (using just *Enter* would cause the second bit of dialog to turn into an action element instead).

Since I've used this technique a number of times in each of my scripts, going through over a hundred pages for each script finding and fixing work already done appeals very little. So, I want a more accurate import and I bet you do too.

Time for action – importing my way

As mentioned earlier, in addition to Celtx's way of importing a script, there is also my way—that is, the method I've developed for script import. Using it, we can export from just about any program that formats scripts—Final Draft, Movie Maker, Word, and so on—and get a text file that will import into Celtx and be converted more accurately to script elements. Print to file!

Printing to file is an old formatting trick we used back in the dawn of personal computing, before PDFs, Postscript, and all the great new stuff came along. It gives us an exact text format including leading spaces (Celtx's conversion process relies heavily on leading spaces).

All we have to do is set up a generic text printer. The exact method of doing this will be in the documentation for your operating system. I've done this on XP and Vista and in Linux on Ubuntu (hint: find a generic text driver for CUPS). Mac users will need to check their manuals.

As an example, in Windows XP, go to **Start | Printers and Faxes**. In the dialog box, select **Add Printer**. For port, choose **FILE: (Print to File)**, as shown in the following screenshot:

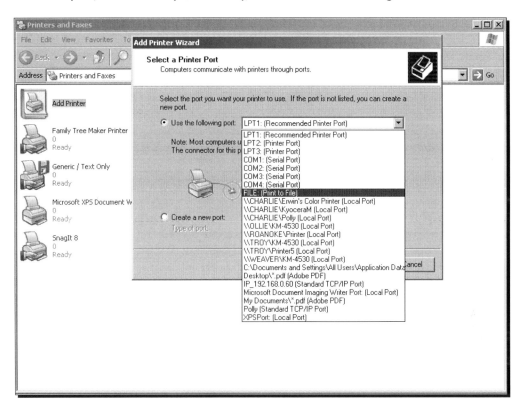

In the next step, choose the **Generic/Text Only** driver, as shown in the following screenshot:

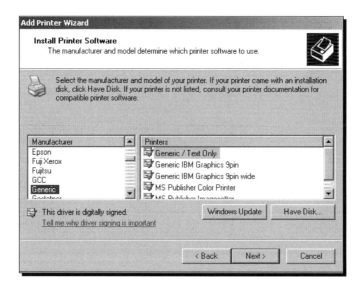

You now have a text file printer in your printer list that is used like any other printer, except the result is plain text with leading spaces in a file, instead of spewing out paper.

Time for action – accurately importing scripts

To import a script accurately (meaning it will be converted by Celtx into the right script elements such as scene Headings, Action, Dialog, and so on) use this technique:

1. In the exporting program (we're using Final Draft as an example) make sure that page numbers and any other header and footer information is turned off. We want only formatted script going to the file. In Final Draft, click on **Tools**, **Options**, **Header/ Footer**. Just uncheck **Header** and **Footer** as shown in the following screenshot, which kills page numbers, and that is all the prep we need:

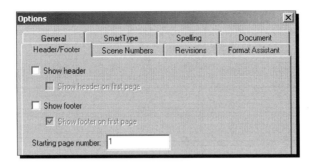

2. Now (still in Final Draft or whatever program) click on **File**, **Print**, and choose your generic text printer, as shown in the following screenshot:

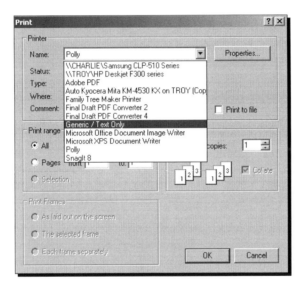

Now, back to Celtx (with an empty **Screenplay** item open). Click on **Script** (top menu bar) and **Import Script…** and select the text file just printed. Celtx does the rest of the work, importing and converting. In my case, looking at the entire script for *The Farmer and the Alien*, I see it's precisely what I wanted (you can see it too, in the following screenshot), a script formatted in Celtx just like it was in Final Draft and ready for me to work on without wasting time cleaning up import errors.

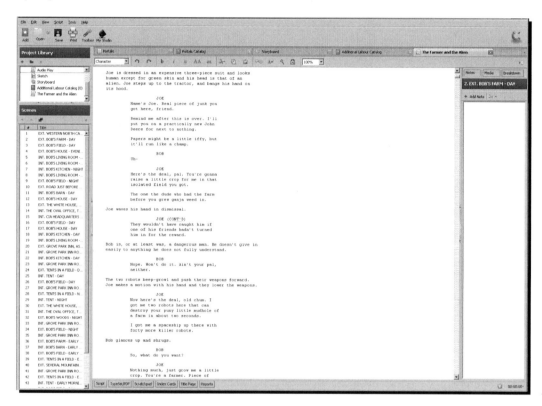

What goes in, of course, must (at least sometimes) come out.

Time for action – exporting Scripts in detail

Celtx exports scripts as either text or HTML (click on **Scripts** then **Export Script...**), as shown in the following screenshot:

Exporting a script as text from Celtx preserves those leading spaces we need to import the script in Final Draft, Movie Magic, or other software. For many applications, this is sufficient, but—just like our problem with soft returns when importing from Final Draft —Celtx exports jumbled dialog breaks also.

Unlike our import trick of setting up a file printer, Celtx is one of the few pieces of software this technique will not work with. The reason is technical and has to do with Celtx being built (as we discussed earlier on) on top of Firefox's Mozilla engine. This has many advantages but a few disadvantages, like this one. We hope a solution for this annoying bug will be provided in the next release of Celtx.

Of course, I've got a work around for you! It requires a couple of intermediate steps, but works quite nicely. First, click on the **TypeSet/PDF** tab at the bottom of the main Celtx window to create a PDF of your script. As shown in the following screenshot, our script is nicely formatted but does have page numbers, which we do not want or need as the new program, in this case Final Draft, will see them as text that is part of the script:

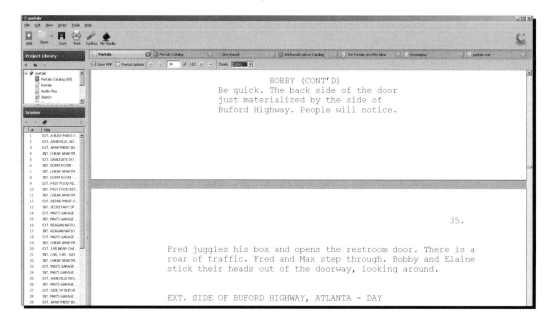

However, as Celtx creates its PDFs out on the web for us, there's no way to kill the numbers. No problem, I'll show you how to get rid of them easily.

Okay, now click once anywhere in the script and press *Ctrl+A*, (or *apple+A* on a Mac), which selects the entire script. It changes color to white text on a blue background, as we see in the following illustration:

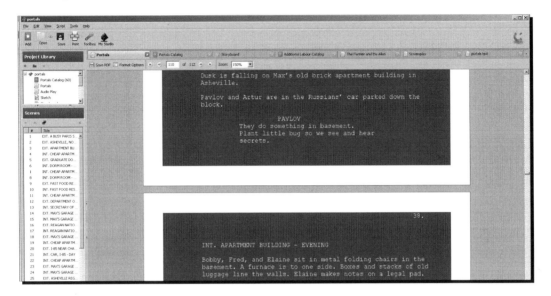

Type *Ctrl+C* (*apple+C* on Mac) to copy the entire script onto the computer's clipboard.

Now, open a new document in Word or Open Office's free clone of Word, click on the blank doc, and type *Ctrl+V* (*apple+V* on Mac) to insert the complete script from the computer's clipboard. Note that it is properly formatted and in the Courier font, which is standard for Screenplays.

Okay, looking good so far, but what about those pesky page numbers? As we see in the following screenshot, the script breaks in weird places and the page numbers from the PDF in Celtx are now in the middle of the pages:

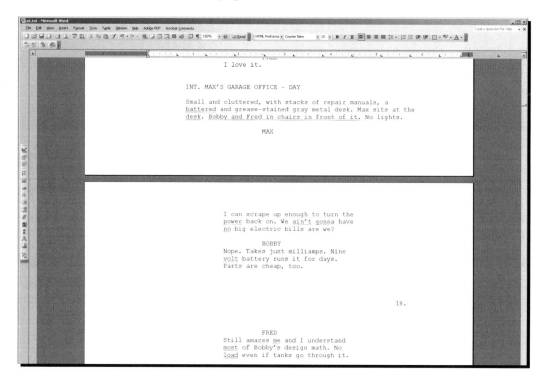

No sweat. It's a whole lot easier to find and edit out errant page numbers than finding and fixing jumbled dialog.

In fact, if you want to do it with a global search and change, we can use Word (or Open Office) for that right now. Call up the **Find and Replace** dialog box in Word, as shown in the following screenshot and use wildcards:

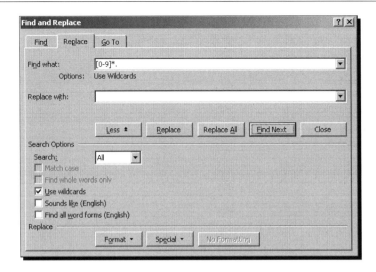

Wildcards are special characters that will find any character based on the criteria we supply. In our case, we want to get rid of these page numbers, which have a pattern of numbers followed by a period. So, in **Find what:** (after clicking on **Use wildcards**), we put the search term **[0-9]*.**—which will find and (if desired) replace any number followed by a period.

Do not, however, actually do an automatic global change. This search term will occasionally find something we want to keep. Use the **Find Next** button and the **Replace** button if it is a page number, or the **Find Next** again if the search item needs to be kept. Of course, the **Replace with:** term is blank, so that we replace the page numbers with nothing—which is what we want. This procedure is very quick and certainly better, again, than looking for jumbled lines.

Okay, with page numbers gone, we're ready to save the file. The only erroneous stuff that should be remaining are some blank lines, but I've found it to be better, if the import is into Final Draft, to wait and fix them there. Final Draft has a scan feature that finds and fixes stuff like that automatically.

Save the file from Word as plain text, and it's now ready for import into Final Draft. Simply open the file as a text file in Final Draft, being sure to click the box to import as a script.

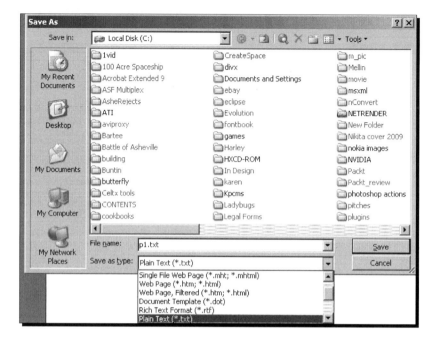

I'm all for saving work and we got these spiffy computers and neat software like Celtx. It's wonderful!

Pop quiz – advanced Celtx

1. Why do we call Celtx projects "containers" and what is the wonderful advantage of this?

2. Why does Celtx have a small "footprint" (take up fewer resources) on our computer and how is this accomplished?

Summary

In this chapter, we've looked at some of Celtx's more advanced features and even gone beyond that with import and export workarounds to save time and effort.

Specifically, we learned first about multiple projects in a single container. Unlike conventional screenwriting software, we saw that we can have many files in the same Celtx project, even unrelated scripts, Word files, photos, video clips, and much more.

Thanks to Celtx's small footprint (economical use of our computers' resources), we can have several copies of it open at once—in other words, several projects open, each of those containing many more projects. This, too, is real power.

We also used two techniques (Celtx's and my own) in this in-depth look at getting already written scripts into Celtx.

Finally, since the entire world does not yet use Celtx, we examined accurate ways of putting our completed scripts out in formats that others can use.

This book, up to now, has been more about how to use Celtx rather than what to use it for. So, hey, let's write a screenplay now using Celtx! We'll do that by using the tools Celtx provides us.

7
Writing Movies with Celtx

This chapter is what I call the money chapter! A money chapter is the chapter or topic which, when I am standing in a bookstore paging through a book or checking its table of contents on Amazon.com, *pushes me into buying the book. Most computer books on a topic of interest will have good stuff in it but there is that one topic that sizzles like a delicious meal just set before you—something that really makes sense and you know you just got to learn how to do.*

In these pages, we will use the features of Celtx for outlining and writing an entertainment industry standard feature movie script, short film, or animation—all properly formatted and ready to market. I enthusiastically encourage you to actually start a script of your own and follow along with all the practical, real-world examples. There is no better way to learn and become comfortable with using Celtx.

If you want to write and sell spec scripts, this chapter will be more than exciting. If you are, let's say, an independent producer (an indie) wanting to create and produce movies yourself, this chapter will be of interest also. If you want to write scripts of any sort, here's a practical guide to using a great piece of software in writing your own equally great script.

To emphasize, this chapter shows not just how to format a script but how to write a screenplay (feature or short), and you are encouraged to actually start writing one—that being the very best way of all to learn both Celtx and writing scripts.

In this chapter, we will learn:

- **Preparing**: I've tried both ways and it's a whole lot easier to write your script from an outline (a "skeleton" or roadmap of your script) or a treatment (character sketches and your story in paragraph form) than just meandering around without direction. All standard stuff is easily accomplished using Celtx's plain text editor. This section shows how to write loglines, synopses, treatments, and outlines—all inside Celtx—to give us a head start and ensure success in writing winning screenplays.

- **The first two words**: We FADE IN and start the first scene. Here we get to see and use the entertainment industry standard elements of scripts. It's not all that complicated—there are only seven.

- **Scenes**: How to set up and use scenes in your screenplays and how Celtx makes it easy to both create, rearrange, and track scenes—all enhancing our creative writing.

- **Action**: "And complications ensued"—turning our plot into action. Tips and examples of using the Action element.

- **Character**: Using the Character element along with introducing and bringing to life (characterization) the people in our script.

- **Parenthetical**: Ralph, (writing furiously) I got to get this script finished (frequent use of parenthetical action in scripts is discouraged these days but here's how it's done).

- **Dialog**: What he said and she said and how to keep it interesting and properly formatted.

- **Shot**: How to specify shots (the way the camera is set up for the scene). Like Transitions, we won't be specifying shots in the scripts we want to sell (let the director worry about this, it's his or her job and they get prickly if someone tries to take it away from them). However, in the media that you're helping to produce, you'll want to put these in for sure.

- **Transition**: CLOSE ON as Ralph holds up the page showing Transitions. Then Ralph hastens to explain that you do not add Transitions to spec scripts you're writing in hopes of selling to Hollywood or Bollywood or wherever. Of course, if you're actually involved in production, you will definitely want to put in the transitions.

- **Text**: Text is a "catch-all" format, not one of the standard script elements, but it is great (as we will soon see) for doing treatments and outlines or, indeed, using Celtx as an ordinary word processor. You could even write short stories or a complete novel easily enough using it.

- **Printing it out**: A more practical look at printing our scripts, both to PDF (more often requested by agents, managers, and producers these days), and on paper (three punched holes, not two), and how to properly bind the paper script.

By the end of this chapter, you will understand screenplay formatting and how Celtx takes all the hard work out of putting together your script, leaving you free to concentrate on action and dialog, and you should already have a script or other project underway.

Preparing to write a Screenplay

I've been using my screenplay Portals as an example throughout this book. Portals—a full 110-page feature movie screenplay is now out in the market and has already gotten several read requests from Hollywood producers.

A read request happens when you send a query e-mail or letter to a producer or agent and they reply to you with something along the lines of "...an interesting concept, I'd like to read it." These requests mean you've got something good enough, at least, to be considered. I have more for you about how to market and get read requests in *Chapter 12, Marketing Your Scripts*.

In this chapter, I'll share my secrets in creating and writing a screenplay using Celtx. Actually, they're not really secrets but rather good practices developed by many scriptwriters over the years. We will, however, see how to use them the Celtx way.

First, we create a project container.

Creating a project container

As we learned in *Chapter 6, Advanced Celtx*, Celtx projects are containers. Our first step is to set up a container where we'll put all the elements relating to our script. These can include (but are not limited to) the following:

- The screenplay itself
- Logline
- Outline
- Master Catalog of characters, props, and over 30 other categories
- Sketches of action, camera angles, position of characters, and so on for various scenes
- A Storyboard depicting action, and so on in all the scenes
- Research information
- Links to websites
- Schedules needed for writing, production, and ease in tracking other calendar-related events
- A collection containing photographs of costumes, possible actors, locations, and so on
- Query letters and other marketing matter

And much more—we can have literally hundreds of items, whatever helps in writing, presenting, and selling our script

Let's get started!

Time for action – setting up the project

First, we need to make a home for our container. Create a directory on your computer.

Open Celtx and on the Splash screen choose the **Film** project. This opens a project container that has, by default, a **Screenplay** in the **Project Library** window which supplies us with the proper elements needed for formatting a feature movie screenplay (scene, action, character, dialog, and so on).

Now, in our new Celtx project, click on **File**, then **Save Project As**, and we get the following screen:

Save in the directory you just created.

Okay, now. In the **Projects Library** window, right click on the default name **Screenplay**, choose **Rename...**, and change it to the actual title of your screenplay. In the following screenshot, I'm changing mine to **PORTALS** (I like to use all caps for screenplay file names):

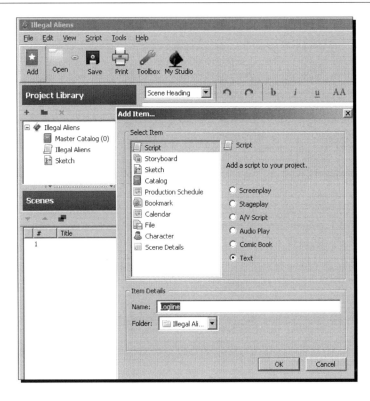

Is this easy or what? Now, we can start the actual creative work, the first being simple but exceptionally important—creating a logline.

Loglines

The first step in writing a Screenplay is both the shortest and the hardest—creating a log line. While this term is really two words, we'll most often see it used today as just one.

A logline is a one-sentence summary of your script and is the way we get the attention of a producer or agent. These folks are deluged by perhaps hundreds of queries—a letter or almost always these days, an email—trying to interest them in a script. You've got about two seconds maybe to get their attention before they move on to the next query. Don't waste it!

As a sample, here's a logline for *The Wizard of Oz*:

After a twister transports a lonely Kansas farm girl to a magical land, she sets out on a dangerous journey to find a wizard with the power to send her home.

Loglines are used for pitching a screenplay to agents or producers. We pitch (throw) a concept at a busy studio executive, producer, agent, manager, or someone who can move our script forward toward actually becoming a movie.

The term logline comes from the old Hollywood days. The studios had script vaults where screenplays were stored. All this was long before the days of computers and electronic files—everything was pounded out with typewriters on paper. Readers would condense what the screenplay was about and write a one line summary on the spine of the script and/or the front cover and, of course, enter it in a log somewhere.

A good logline is critical in grabbing the interest of producers and agents to sell our scripts, but it is even more important in the start up process to make sure we know what we're writing about. If we can't pitch the story in a single sentence, we need to think about it some more before beginning the writing process.

Where to put the logline: We need a place in our project container for the logline, so let's create one. With the mouse cursor on the blue **Add** box to the upper left of the Celtx screen (the one with the white star in it), left click on it as shown in the following screenshot:

In the **Add Item...** dialog box that comes up, click on the **Text** (in Celtx 2.9 and later, select **Novel** here) choice to add a **Text** item to our project, as shown in the following screenshot:

Further down, in **Item Details**, change the name to **Logline**. Click on **OK** at the very bottom. We now have a logline item in the **Project Library** and the large script window of Celtx is open as a text processor.

Celtx's **Text** (now Novel) is essentially a standard word processor. The advantage is that you can edit text inside of Celtx, which makes it quite handy for all sorts of longer documents relating to script projects such as research, character sketches, outlines, and treatments (more about that in just a moment).

Here's another advantage of using this text editor. While we could do loglines, outlines, and so forth in Microsoft Word or another word processing software and actually include those files in our Celtx project container (click on **Add**, click on **File**), those files cannot be edited inside the project. We would have to use the external program.

The problem with using files requiring external programs is—if you pass the project around to a co-author or others involved, or share it through Celtx Studio—not everyone has the same programs you do. Using the Celtx text item keeps everything easier for everyone involved to read and modify, and also keeps it more portable (that is, more widely used document format).

Writing the logline: The **Logline** is open by default from when we created the text item (shown in the following illustration), so we now write our logline. I like to add just a bit more. From top to bottom in the Celtx script window (actually a text window in this mode), we have the title, the genre (the type of story—comedy, thriller, romance, western, mystery, and so on), a pitch (a sort of mini-logline as a hook to get more attention paid to our logline, just something I like to do), and the logline itself.

The following is my pitch and logline for **Portals**:

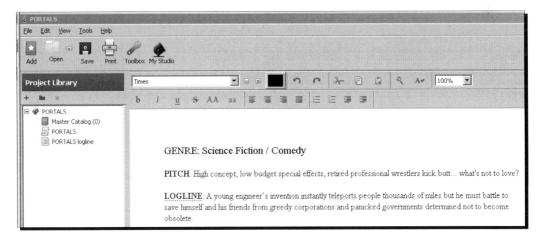

Saying something like "well, that's pretty much it" is inappropriate here. A logline is just one sentence but—done right—it can be harder to write than the complete 110-page screenplay.

A logline is very helpful in starting our script. Condensing the plot into one sentence forces us to think about our story, sparks creativity, and leads us logically into the next step in the process, generating an outline of the script.

If you're not sure of exactly how to structure a logline, a good starting point for this and the following items of synopses, treatments, and outlines would be the **Writer's Development Kit (WDK)**, by Karel Segers from `http://celtx.com/learningTemplates.html`. It's only $2.89 and downloads directly into Celtx.

We will (and should) often go through several versions of our logline before locking it in. I went through about twenty versions of the logline for Portals before coming up with a short, succinct version I felt okay with letting agents and producers see.

Yes, it's a lot of work for just one sentence, but the logline is the most important sentence by far that we'll write in our entire screenplay project. Success depends on getting just the right blend of enlightenment, enticement, and excitement. In other words, something that shows the reader in a second what the story is about, in a way that makes them want to learn more, and excites them about the process. Like I said, the most important sentence we'll write.

Here are some more examples of loglines for scripts of well-known movies:

Rocky: `A struggling boxer finally gets a shot at the heavyweight championship.`

The Fugitive: `After being falsely convicted of the murder of his wife, a once prominent surgeon escapes custody to find the real killer and clear his name.`

Raiders of the Lost Ark: `Just before the outbreak of World War II, an adventuring archaeologist named Indiana Jones races around the globe to single-handedly prevent the Nazis from turning the greatest archaeological relic of all time into a weapon of world conquest.`

Pirates of the Caribbean: `A 17th Century tale of adventure on the Caribbean Sea where the roguish yet charming Captain Jack Sparrow joins forces with a young blacksmith in a gallant attempt to rescue the Governor of England's daughter and reclaim his ship.`

Okay—after a certain amount of work—we have a logline in a format ready for cutting and pasting into an e-mail and sending out to producers and agents. However, don't send it yet. Wait until there's a completed script. After all, what if they like the concept and ask to read the script? It's a no-no not to have it ready.

By the way, when I use the term *producers and agents*, that's a shortcut; many people can possibly move a script along toward actually being made into a movie. We have producers (who make films), agents (who represent actors and writers and others in the entertainment industry), directors (who direct films), managers (who guide the careers of writers, and so on), readers (who are the first line looking at scripts for agents, producers, and so forth), and lots of others connected with getting movies from script to screen. So, there are lots of ways to market your script, and we'll explore those in *Chapter 12* of this book.

Okay, the logline is the first step in getting ready to write our script. The next three are the synopsis, the treatment, and the outline—of these, I consider the logline and outline to be mandatory for any kind of good script to result.

Synopses and treatments are very helpful, but if you have a good outline (and I'll show you how you get that) and know your story, they can be skipped for now. In marketing, you'll often need a synopsis and some producers might ask for a treatment.

If, however, you have a complicated story with lots of action and characters, you'll probably want to do a synopsis and/or treatment. This enables you to better see and devise all the necessary components of the script.

Believe me, all this stuff saves you from floundering around and writing a meandering script that gets immediately rejected. A little work up front yields big rewards later!

Synopses

A synopsis is a summary of your script in two paragraphs to two pages. Make it exciting and entertaining and above all, concise and to the point. The synopsis is useful for several reasons, including the following:

◆ Shows we have a story we understand

◆ Demonstrates there is enough material for a full-length movie (about two hours)

◆ Gives us an exciting preview of the story

Like the logline, we first use a synopsis in planning our script, then as a sales tool.

In Celtx, we again use the **Text** item. Click on **Add** and choose **Text** (just like we did for the **Logline** item in our **Project Library** window). Specify the name as **Synopsis**—labeling it as we do (it saves confusion later when there are many more items in our project container).

The following is an example of a very short synopsis (two paragraphs). It's one I used in an e-mail campaign for a script based on one of my published novels:

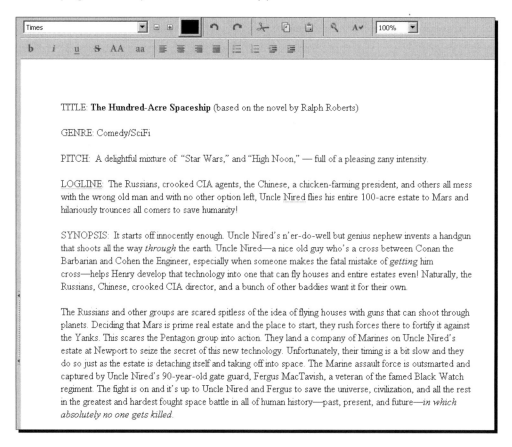

TITLE: **The Hundred-Acre Spaceship** (based on the novel by Ralph Roberts)

GENRE: Comedy/SciFi

PITCH: A delightful mixture of "Star Wars," and "High Noon," — full of a pleasing zany intensity.

LOGLINE: The Russians, crooked CIA agents, the Chinese, a chicken-farming president, and others all mess with the wrong old man and with no other option left, Uncle Nired flies his entire 100-acre estate to Mars and hilariously trounces all comers to save humanity!

SYNOPSIS: It starts off innocently enough. Uncle Nired's n'er-do-well but genius nephew invents a handgun that shoots all the way *through* the earth. Uncle Nired—a nice old guy who's a cross between Conan the Barbarian and Cohen the Engineer, especially when someone makes the fatal mistake of *getting* him cross—helps Henry develop that technology into one that can fly houses and entire estates even! Naturally, the Russians, Chinese, crooked CIA director, and a bunch of other baddies want it for their own.

The Russians and other groups are scared spitless of the idea of flying houses with guns that can shoot through planets. Deciding that Mars is prime real estate and the place to start, they rush forces there to fortify it against the Yanks. This scares the Pentagon group into action. They land a company of Marines on Uncle Nired's estate at Newport to seize the secret of this new technology. Unfortunately, their timing is a bit slow and they do so just as the estate is detaching itself and taking off into space. The Marine assault force is outsmarted and captured by Uncle Nired's 90-year-old gate guard, Fergus MacTavish, a veteran of the famed Black Watch regiment. The fight is on and it's up to Uncle Nired and Fergus to save the universe, civilization, and all the rest in the greatest and hardest fought space battle in all of human history—past, present, and future—*in which absolutely no one gets killed*.

The preceding example, I see now, is more general than a synopsis should be. We should write synopses like they are a mini-outline of the script. In the Writer's Development Kit mentioned earlier, the author suggests a five paragraph format consisting of Act One, Act Two before Mid Point, Mid Point, Act Two after Mid Point, and Act Three.

Again, you can purchase this Learning Series item from the `http://celtx.com` site for details of what to include and how to structure a synopsis.

Basically, a synopsis is a brief summary of your story where a logline is more of a teaser. Again, the Writer's Development Kit is a good starting point. The following screenshot shows what the beginning of the synopsis lesson in the WDK looks like:

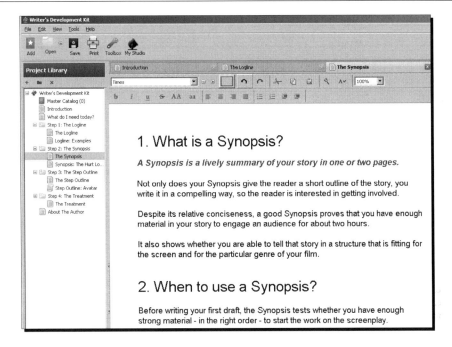

Treatments

A **treatment** is pretty much whatever the person requesting one says it is. Treatments range from one page up to 40, 50, or more. Short treatments resemble synopses and it's hard to say where one leaves off and the other begins.

Long treatments use a narrative format covering all the action in every scene in the movie and often also including bits of dialog.

Start by visualizing the story in your head, jotting notes down. Many script writers use index cards, one scene per card. The cards can be shuffled around until the right order of the scenes to tell the story is found.

Celtx gives us an electronic version of this method of plotting in the **Index Cards** tab at the bottom of the main script window (see *Chapter 2* for details).

The following screenshot shows a portion from my treatment for *Indian Sidekick*, showing the narrative style:

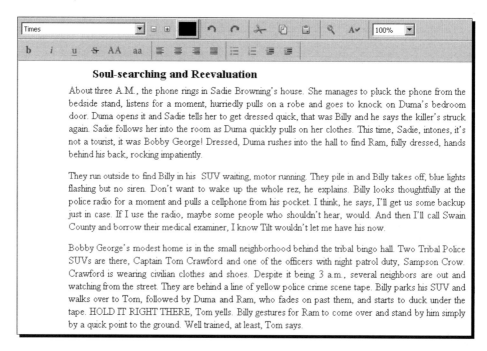

In short, just write in present tense like you were actually telling the story to someone. It's a great technique to work out all the details. In fact, this treatment is one of the longer types at over forty pages and some 18,600 words. The complete Indian Sidekick screenplay is only 22,000 words, so I knew that plot well while writing it.

To set up a treatment in the Celtx project container, again employ the **Text** item. Click on **Add**, choose **Text** (just like we did for the **Logline** item in our **Project Library** window), and change the name to **Treatment** (or, really, whatever is unique and you will remember and know what it is).

Treatments—the same as loglines and synopses—work well before we start the script to help us in getting the story worked out and ready to write, and afterwards as a selling tool.

Something I like to include in treatments are detailed biographies of the main characters. The more we know about the people in our scripts, the better we can tell their stories.

Now, we come to something absolutely necessary before we start writing, an outline!

Outlines

In storytelling, there is a thing called "the Rule of Threes." Three items are easy to remember. Examples in stories include The Three Little Pigs, The Three Musketeers, The Three Wise Men from the Bible, and of course, The Three Stooges. Movies and stage plays also usually have three acts. So using groups of three in writing is:

- Easy to remember

- Something we are preconditioned to from childhood (remember those three little pigs!)

- Stronger than two or four or many points

In creating spec Screenplays, a critically important list of three applies:

- Logline: Without a good logline, agents and producers will not read our screenplay. That's the way the movie industry works. Period.

- Outline: Without a good outline, we will meander around and not produce a nice, tight story that producers will want to film.

- Screenplay: Without a good story in the proper format, our movie will not get made.

To sum it up, a good logline gets read requests for our script and the outline (which is just for our use) makes sure we have a good script to send. Agents and producers will never see our outline, but they'll sure be able to tell if we had one.

A screenplay outline can be as short or long as we like. It can have lots of detail or, if we have the story firmly in our head, shorter. I've found that the more detail, the better. Outlines let us try out story elements in various combinations to see which structure makes the story the most interesting and exciting.

The most common type of outline for screenplays is the step outline (outlines the story step by step), also called a beat sheet (because movies have a rhythm). The WDK features the step outline; the beginning of that section is shown in the following screenshot:

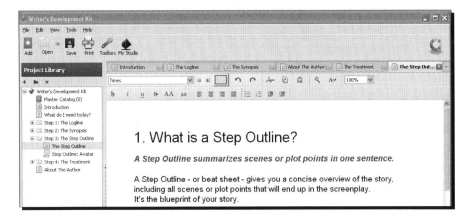

While good to use, I'm going to let you guys in on one of my secrets. If you really want to learn how to write an effective outline (beat sheet), the recognized master was the late Blake Snyder. His books *Save the Cat!* and *Save the Cat! Strikes Back* helped me tremendously and I recommend them highly! Like this book, they can be purchased from `Amazon.com`.

Before I found this book, I did not realize how important having an outline was. I would be writing merrily along and a new plot twist would hit me. That meant I had to go back through and try to rewrite scenes to lay the foundation for my new twist.

It is much easier to do these reworks in the outline than have to scrap your terrific dialog because it no longer fits the revamped story. Think of the outline as a dress rehearsal for your script. Better to find and fix problems this way—where they can easily be fixed—than halfway through your script when hours or days of rewrite might be needed.

Okay, let's do an outline for our Screenplay.

Once more, we add a text object in our Celtx project container, this one for the outline (see the following illustration). Use the title (or at least part of it) and the word "outline" just to keep things from getting confusing later on. Click on **Add** and select **Text**, as shown in the following screenshot. Title your outline as I have mine, so you'll know what it is later.

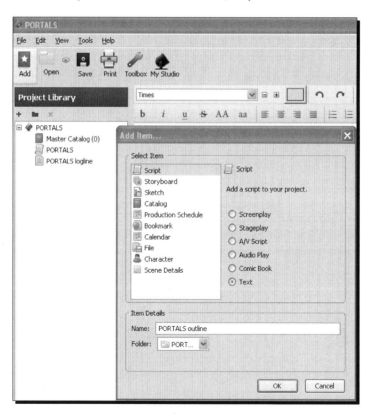

Now, we're ready to start writing the outline. If the outline is not open, just double click on it in the **Project Library** window and we can start writing in the main script window. Again, this is a Text script and like a standard word processor in use. We can use bold, italic, underline, and so on.

As this is just for our own use, no rules of formatting apply, but I like to make it neat and readable. The following screenshot shows the start of the Portals outline.

So, here's the way I do it and this method seems to work well in giving me all I need to write a complete 110-page (or thereabouts) Screenplay. First, the title and byline (just in case I do let someone else look at it for comments).

Next, just for ease of referral, I include the logline (see the following screenshot) despite the fact it's already in a separate file. Keep the logline handy. It should be an inspirational road map to your story or you might realize it needs changing, as your outline comes together and the story takes more solid form.

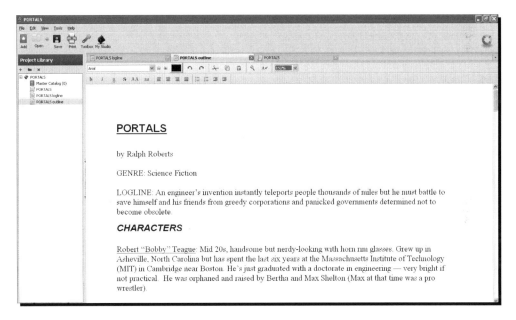

Also, I include thumbnail bios of my main characters (as below for Portals). Knowing as much as possible about the actors in our screenplay up front will make it easier to make the outline and is invaluable while writing the actual script.

Understanding where characters come from, their motivations, their experience in life (which determines reaction to stimulus), is called characterization. These are the things which make characters come to life instead of just being flat, uninteresting cardboard cutouts.

Let me condense the preceding point for you: stories are about people. Storytelling puts certain people in stressful situations and our enjoyment as films goers comes in great part from watching how these characters react.

Put together fascinating people interacting in interesting ways and you have a story. Complicate their life with threats, villains, hurricanes, a huge comet destroying New York City, cattle rustlers, pirates, and so on and you have a movie! ... Hmm. Maybe, even all of those things plus the mother-in-law from Hades and a couple of aliens. The following is what it looks like:

CHARACTERS

Robert "Bobby" Teague: Mid 20s, handsome but nerdy-looking with horn rim glasses. Grew up in Asheville, North Carolina but has spent the last six years at the Massachusetts Institute of Technology (MIT) in Cambridge near Boston. He's just graduated with a doctorate in engineering — very bright if not practical. He was orphaned and raised by Bertha and Max Shelton (Max at that time was a pro wrestler).

Things that need fixing:
1. Bobby's broke ... owes big student loans, wants to pay back Max.
2. After six years in Boston, he feels a little inferior because of his mountain accent and upbringing (some students have been snobbish).
3. He's still carrying a torch for his high school sweetheart, Elaine Freeman.
4. He feels guilty for all those years away at college while Max's life got worse and worse.
5. He wants to make a real contribution to the world but feels his knowledge is all theoretical, that he can't do anything practical.

Frederick "Fred" Mozingo: Grew up on a farm in Iowa. Fred has been Bobby's roommate at MIT — almost as bright as Bobby, more practical.

Max Sheldon: Former professional wrestler and diesel truck mechanic. His garage went broke and his only assets are the dilapidated building that housed it and an equally dilapidated apartment building. He and his deceased wife raised Bobby after his parents died.

Elaine Freeman: Bobby's high school sweetheart, now an FBI agent and the Special Agent-in-Charge of the Asheville office.

Wilson Thickett: Secretary of Commerce. Newly appointed Cabinet officer — formerly CEO of Massive Airways and, in his younger days, a CIA operative.

James Blake: Secret agent. Has worked for the CIA and other clandestine spook agencies but has been "burned" and is no longer employed. He grew up with Thickett and they worked together during Thickett's CIA days. Blake specializes in "wet work" and in getting the job done at all costs.

Sergei Romanoff: Russian Minister of Defense and one of the most powerful men in the Russian government — cunning, very corrupt. Immediately sees the implications in Bobby's invention and determines to get or suppress it. He knows both Blake and Thickett from their early intelligence careers and despite being on opposite sides, worked together .

In my character list for Portals, I felt I knew the characters well enough where I could (and did) add characterization on the fly. Sometimes, however, I'll write several paragraphs about a character detailing his or her complete life up to the beginning of the story. Do as much or little as you need to create a guide for you to write lifelike, exciting characters.

Don't forget that the bad guys need reasons to be doing all that nasty stuff. What happened in their life to make them such big, bad meanies?

Also, don't forget character development. For stories to grip us, the characters (especially your hero or heroine) need to have weaknesses they must overcome to win out in the end.

For example, a guy who thinks he's a coward winds up as a soldier. He finally (after trying and failing a couple of times) overcomes his weakness and fear (by drawing on some already established inner strength), and saves his fellow soldiers in battle.

In my preceding character bios, note the list of "things to be fixed." Those are weaknesses that Bobby Teague, the hero, has. He has to master each of these in order to achieve his goals and save Elaine, Fred, and Max.

The *The Save the Cat!* book mentioned earlier is a great starting point to understand characterization as well as all the other storytelling components in a good movie.

Opening and closing scenes: Now we start the outline itself. Speaking of starting, we need to know where our story begins. In the case of Portals, it begins when Bobby finally gets his instant travel invention to work, making a connection between North Carolina and Paris.

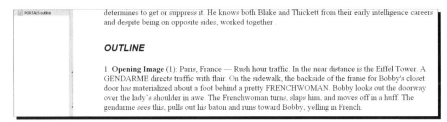

Once we know the beginning, we can figure out the ending. A good movie often echoes the opening image in its closing image. This is a storytelling technique that just feels right to the viewer or reader.

In Portals, after all the setbacks, moments of weakness, the final overcoming of these weaknesses, and the ultimate triumph (happy ending), the final scene mirrors the first scene, by Bobby achieving another milestone with his portals:

> 15. **Final Image** (110): A pressurized airlock hatch appears on a rocky Martian plain near one of the Mars rovers, which swings its cameras around to observe.
>
> Bobby, Elaine, Fred, and Max — dressed in spacesuits — step out and look around. Bobby holds out his gloved hand. They all slap it.

The numbers in parentheses after the scene names in the preceding two figures, refer to page numbers in the screenplay.

In Blake Snyder's Save the Cat! books, certain elements appear on specific pages. For example, the theme of the movie is always stated (usually by a supporting character) on page five. In the following screenshot, Fred states the theme of Portals:

2. **Theme Stated** (5): Fred says, "Bobby, you know this thing is gonna change the world."

3. **Set-up** (1-10): With Bobby's instant teleport connection to Paris, he knows at long last his invention works! He teleports himself to MIT, wakes his roommate Fred, picks up his mail including doctorate notification and dun for back tuition. He returns to Asheville with Fred. Fred meets Max. Elaine is hinted at. Bobby, Fred, and Max discuss Bobby's pending patent. Looking at Bobby's circuit, Fred mentions he's not seen one part of it before. Just some insurance, Bobby tells him. Max tells them about the convention of former professional wrestlers to be held soon in Asheville and how much he looking forward to seeing his old buddies again.

4. **Catalyst** (12): In looking at the rest of his mail, Bobby finds a letter from the Patent and Trademark office. His application is denied! His invention is unprotected. Bobby realizes the only way to protect and control it, is to develop it into a commercial venture before anyone else can.

Enables scene introducing Thickett and Blake — Thickett has learned of the patent application, understands its revolutionary import, wants if for himself, instructs Blake to get the technology and eliminate its inventor. Says he has both Russian support. A lot of money in it for him and Blake!

5. **Debate** (12-25): Bobby thinks he knows his limitations. He has no practical business experience. "How can I promote this instant travel that will change the world with no money and no idea of how to go about it?" He knows they will become targets. How can they protect themselves, much less his technology? He, Fred, and Max discuss and try to come up with solutions.

Blake is putting his operation to steal Bobby's invention into play. Since he has few assets in the States, he and Thickett contact Sergei Romanoff, who supplies Russian military intelligence agents in America to help them.

6. **Break into 2** (25): The decision is made! The three of them — Bobby, Fred, and Max — will form an instant travel company, Galactic Transport. GT's first terminal will be Max's old diesel truck garage where Bobby also worked as a teenager. They get started converting it and planning routes.

7. **B Story** (30): The FBI has people everywhere, including in the Department of Commerce (Thickett may be new but he's already under investigation for corruption because he *is* corrupt). They find out something is going on in Asheville that Thickett is interested in and breaking rules about. The FBI alerts its agent there, SAIC Elaine Freeman. She visits Bobby and Max. It turns out Bobby's not the only one still carrying a torch. Their romance rekindles as Elaine investigates.

The setup of characters and problems is on pages 1-10. The catalyst (that pushes the main character into solving the problem) is always on page 12 (not 11 or 13), and so on.

See Blake's books for all the elements of the beat sheet outlining the method and what goes where and why.

Step outlines or beat sheets usually run two to four pages and are fantastic tools for experimenting with and nailing down the screenplay's story elements. This process requires very little time, really jogs creativity, and saves hours upon hours of time in the actual writing of our screenplay.

Writing a screenplay is like riding a race horse. You thunder out of the gate hanging on for dear life. An outline is the reins, bit, saddle, and stirrups letting you control the gallop, guiding the horse to the finish line.

To summarize the preparations for riding… err, I mean writing a successful spec screenplay, we first craft a succinct logline and then an outline to guide us.

Time for action – creating a title page

Next in the preparing-to-write phase, let's create the title page.

I don't know about you guys, but putting together the title page is a moment of commitment for me—I can see the finished script in my head. It both sets a goal and gives me confidence.

To get to the title page, double click on the name of your Screenplay. In the second illustration below, **PORTALS**, by itself is the screenplay we set up when we first created this project container.

Remember, we find all our scripts, loglines, outlines, and all other files relating to our project in the **Project Library** window.

We bring up the title page form by clicking on the button at the bottom of the main script window, as shown in the following screenshot:

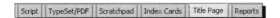

The title page form opens in the main windows and all we have to do now is fill in the blanks.

The **Title:** box is pretty obvious, huh? We type the title of our screenplay here in ALL CAPS.

As explained in *Chapter 2*, there's a bug that causes the title to sometimes not be properly centered. Here's a workaround, if you want your title to look better. On a PC keyboard, hold down the *Alt* key and in the numeric keypad (not the numbers along the top of the letter keys) type 0160. That key combination is *Alt+0160*, which inserts a non-breaking or hard space. Insert however many of these it takes to center the title and byline to your satisfaction.

The next form box should have the word **By**, as shown in the following screenshot:

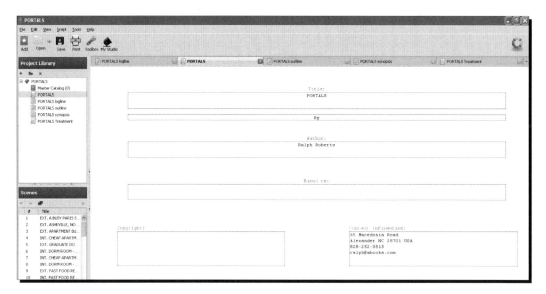

In the **Author:** entry box, put your name and the names of any co-authors.

The **Based On:** box is only filled out if this screenplay is based on a book or short story or some other already written piece that you have the rights to use. Also, this box is used if you are using someone else's characters (again, be sure you have permission). Alternatively, you could put an "With apologies to" if it's parody or satirical material. Whatever you put in this or the other boxes here appears on the title page, of course.

Leave the **Copyright** box blank. Yes, you want to have a copyright or, more usually, register it with the Writers Guild (WGA). But, and this is a *big* but, it is considered amateurish to include that on your title page. Copyrights in the U.S., by the way, occur automatically when you finish a work. What you do by filling out a copyright form (more about that later) is simply register the already (by law) existing copyright. It adds another layer of protection, but you do not need to (nor should) show that on a spec script title page.

Agents and producers assume you have protected your work. If they want to know the particulars, such as the WGA registration number, you'll be asked for that on a release form.

While we're discussing protection, the quickest, least painful way of protecting a finished script is by going online to `http://www.wgaregistry.org/webrss`. Pay $20 online and upload a PDF copy of the script you are registering and get the registration number immediately. Most Hollywood writers use this service. Membership is not required to use this service.

The following screenshot shows the beginning webpage with explanation and instructions:

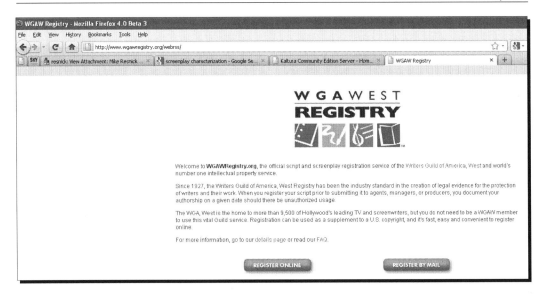

While WGA registration—either from the WGAW (west of the Mississippi) or WGAE (east of the Mississippi) is quite useful to protect your rights in a script, the ultimate protection in the United States is through the Copyright Office of the Library of Congress.

Copyrights are more expensive but have a stronger legal status, at least outside the entertainment industry. Copyrights also last longer than WGAW or WGAE registrations, being the lifetime of the author plus seventy years! That gives the writer and his or her estate the greatest protection.

The Guild registrations (WGAW and WGAE) are only for five years. Your screenplay (or other manuscript) is automatically destroyed at the end of that term. However, the registration may be renewed up to ninety days prior to expiration and during a grace period of ninety days after expiration. While copyrights are stronger, having WGA registration is the standard thing to do within the entertainment industry.

What you might want to think about is what I do. Register all your completed scripts with WGAW or WGAE (depending on the geographic location).

As to copyright, once you finish writing the work, you have an *automatic copyright*. All you're doing (as described following this paragraph) is registering that copyright. Which, of course, increases your legal status in ownership, but it's expensive and so perhaps not needed immediately. That's a decision you'll need to make for yourself.

To register a copyright, go to `http://www.copyright.gov/register/`, as shown in the following screenshot:

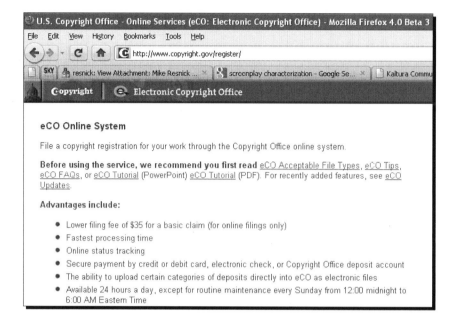

Portals is registered as WGA 1443147, so my use of examples from it in this book is protected. Once a script is registered online, as described earlier, you receive the registration number immediately. A paper certificate is also mailed. The following screenshot is the one for Portals:

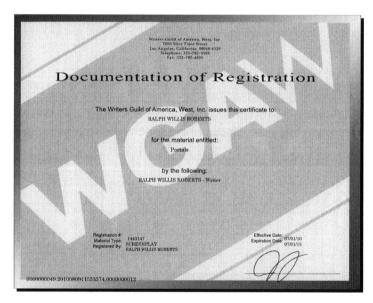

Finally we fill out the **Contact Information:** box with our mailing address, telephone and fax (if any) numbers, and e-mail.

Now, let's check out our title page—on the same line of buttons at the bottom of the main script window of Celtx.

Click on the **TypeSet/PDF** button to format your script. The title page will be created and automatically included each time we format our script.

In *Chapter 2*, we learned how to generate a PDF file, which is done online. I'll also review that for you at the end of this chapter.

One final warning about title pages: Do not use fancy graphics, colors, or anything other than plain old vanilla Courier type done exactly like the example that is following.

Scripts—and more about that just down the page from here—must be done exactly to the traditional technical specifications set down decades ago during those greasy-geared old typewriter days. Ignore these standards at your peril. There's good reason for these rules, which I'll divulge momentarily. Meanwhile, the following is what the PDF of the title page looks like:

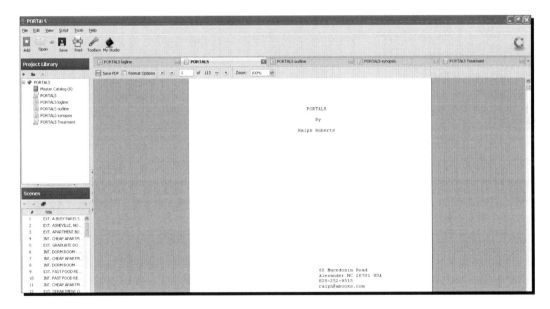

Now, let's start! Left click on **Script** on that bottom row of buttons to return to the script.

Beginning a script—the first two words

The first two words traditionally of a spec screenplay are FADE IN. While falling out of use and a shot on top of that (remember shots are not to be used in spec scripts) most of us still start with this and end with FADE OUT.

However, first (as promised) some more words on format.

Formatting includes the physical layout of words on a script page and which script element to use in describing the action to be filmed. The latter (script elements) we'll be using throughout the remainder of this chapter. The former (physical layout) is thankfully handled for us by our buddy, Celtx.

For example, none of us probably want to be bothered with the fact that character names begin 3.7 inches from the left margin (twenty-two spaces in the 12 point Courier typeface), and it had better be the same every time a character name appears. Industry standard screenplays place a heavy emphasis on the word *standard*.

Imagine the sheer heck those guy and gal scriptwriters went through back during the typewriter days. Every page on every script had to be formatted the same.

Why? It goes against the grain for most of us creative people to do the same thing, the same way, in the exact same place for page after page after page.

The reason is exceptionally important. Money, lots of money!

Movies are expensive to make. A script page, formatted to industry standards, equates to about a minute of film time. Each minute in studio produced movies costs from several thousand dollars to sometimes over a million dollars or more! Producers and the financial officers of studios take screenplay format very seriously. None of us will get away with ignoring it.

The good news is Celtx takes care of most of this onerous formatting automatically. Celtx does the drudge work, so we don't have to. Celtx makes us look good and doesn't even ask for a cut of the big bucks when we sell a script.

If you want to know more about screenplay formatting, I suggest *The Screenwriter's Bible* by David Trottier. It's a huge book full of both physical formatting and, more importantly to us, how to do all sorts of things in a studio approved manner.

For example, I needed a montage of quick shots in Portals showing the rapid development of Galactic Transport. David's book gave me the answer. Have it on your reference shelf. Just make sure your shelf has a couple two by fours under it, this is truly a massive book.

Now, back to our script in progress, or it will be as soon as we select **Text** from the script elements drop-down menu (we'll be using this menu a lot) to the top left of the main script window and type (in ALL CAPS) the words "FADE IN:" (yes, with a colon behind). It looks like the following screenshot:

Don't worry about the title and leading credits—that's the director and producer's job.

The term "fade in" means the screen comes up from total black to showing the action, such as revealing Billy Bob bravely holding his pitchfork as the vicious green aliens charge out of their just-landed spaceship. The movie's off to an exciting start.

Okay, now imagine a finished script of around 110 pages done, the story completed, and we come to the glorious, audience-standing-on-their-seats-applauding ending.

Use **Text** again (these are probably the only two times you'll use it in a script). On the line below the last piece of dialog or action in the script, type "THE END" and put spaces in front of it until it is centered on the page.

On the next line, type "FADE OUT" and space it out to the right margin, as shown in the following screenshot:

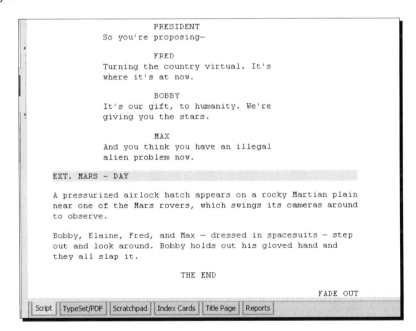

Again, the director and producer will come up with the end credits. This is not your job; your job is done! You've got a script!

The ending should look as shown in the preceding screenshot.

Wow! Now that we know how to plan, start, and end a script, writing it is a mere trifle, eh? So, for the rest of this chapter we'll do just that, using the script elements in that drop-down menu.

Limber up those fingers, here we go!

Scenes

Movies tell stories by a series of **scenes**. A scene is a sequence of action (actors doing stuff or scenery moving by) and dialog (actors talking). We see a scene in which something happens in our story. Another scene of action and/or dialog follows in which something else occurs advancing the story, and so on.

So let's write our first scene. Since we have an outline, we already know what's in it.

To make writing easy, I like to have my outline handy in Celtx also. If your outline is not open, just double-click on it in the **Project Library** and it will open in the main script window, as shown in the following screenshot:

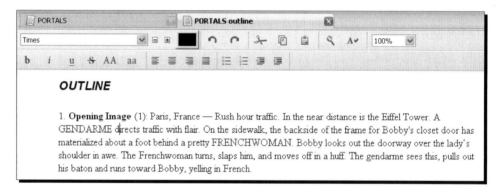

Now that we have tabs for the screenplay (currently hidden), and for the outline (now showing), it's easy to switch back and forth between script and outline by just left-clicking on the tabs.

We start the scene with a scene heading (also sometimes called a slugline). Celtx will format this for you (scene headings are always in ALL CAPS). Just select **Scene Heading** from the drop-down menu. A grayish bar shows the text is in the scene heading format as shown in the following screenshot:

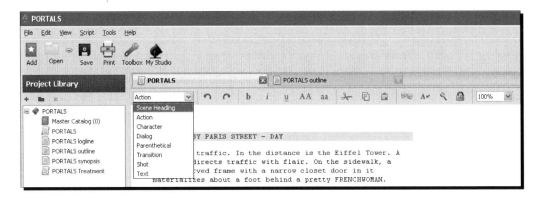

A scene heading is just a structured line saying whether this action is happening outside or inside (type EXT. for outside or INT. for inside), the location (A BUSY PARIS STREET), a hyphen (-) for separation, and the time (DAY). As ever in scripts, it is important that all your scene headings are done exactly this way.

The following are some more examples of scene headings, all from Portals:

INT. CHEAP APARTMENT – DAY

INT. APARTMENT BUILDING BASEMENT - EARLY MORNING

EXT. GALACTIC TRANSPORT OFFICES – DAY

INT. THE INTERNATIONAL SPACE STATION - EARTH ORBIT

In the last example above, the concept of day and night does not quite fit space, hence the use of "EARTH ORBIT."

Also, try not to get too cutesy. Me, I sometimes can't resist:

INT. OLD MINE TUNNEL - KINDA DARK

The following screenshot shows what the first scene in Portals looks like:

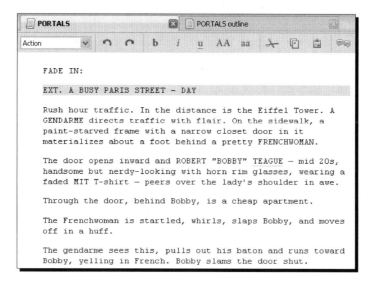

Scene headings are basically three parts, with a more rarely used possible fourth element. EXT. is an abbreviation for exterior and INT. for interior. Those two terms show the location of the camera. If the camera was inside, shooting out of a window, the scene heading would be INT. despite the action happening on the outside. It's the camera's viewpoint that counts.

Next, of course, is the location, then the time of the day.

The rarely used fourth part is if some kind of out-of-the-ordinary occurrence or location requires additional identification, such as these following examples:

EXT. VJ DAY IN TIMES SQUARE – DAY – 1945

INT. INSIDE A VOCANO – NIGHT – MARVIN'S FEVERISH DREAM

David Trottier in *The Screenwriter's Bible* suggests the following format as also being valid:

EXT. VJ DAY IN TIMES SQUARE – DAY (1945)

INT. INSIDE A VOCANO – NIGHT (MARVIN'S FEVERISH DREAM)

Also, you can have secondary scene headings, such as the primary scene:

INT. BILLY BOB'S MOUNTAIN SHACK – DAY

The action starts in the kitchen. Then the characters move to the living room and we put in a secondary scene heading:

LIVING ROOM

Some action occurs. Then:

BEDROOM

The characters engage in some more action, which possibly results in an R rating for the movie, and so on.

Please keep in mind that movies are visual. We want to keep things buzzing along. Avoid long scenes like the plague (and clichés, too, eh?).

Again, script pages are about one minute of screen time. Scenes of one and a half pages on average make a movie nice and snappy and not boring.

If you need a bunch of very short scenes to rapidly advance action, consider the montage like I mentioned earlier. The following is what one (of the two in Portals) looks like:

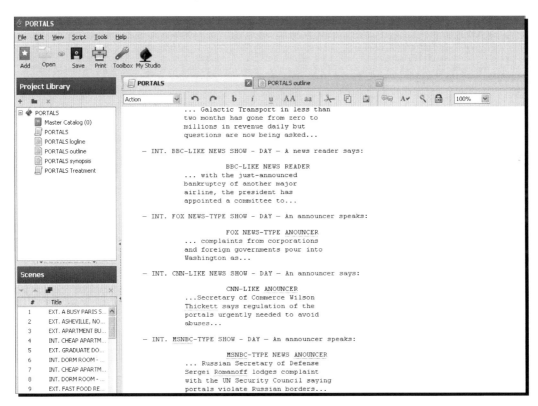

As you can see, montages follow slightly different (but still rigid) rules of format. You can also understand by now why, even with the help of Celtx doing all that automatic formatting, a good formatting reference is also mighty handy at times.

Flashbacks and dreams: Good writing practice is to use these sparingly, but let's say you quickly wanted to show why a character is so afraid to ride in cars. The following is the accepted method:

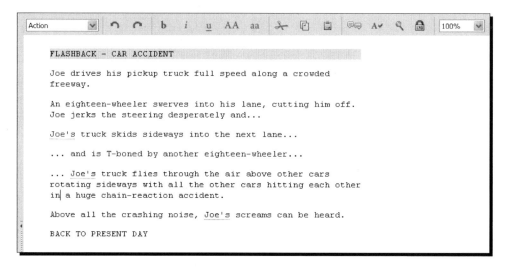

We can also indicate time, such as:

EXT. I-40 NEAR KNOXVILLE – NIGHT (FLASHBACK)

If several scenes are called for, use:

EXT. WOODS – EARLY MORNING – FLASHBACK SEQUENCE

Dreams use a similar format:

DREAM – JOE RELIVES HIS ACCIDENT

Establishing Shot: An establishing shot is a quick shot to show where the action is taking place, so that the viewer follows the story and is not confused about its current location. Do these as just a regular brief scene in Portals, as shown in the following screenshot:

```
EXT. THE WHITE HOUSE, WASHINGTON D.C. - DAY

An American flag waves in front of the home of the
president.


INT. OVAL OFFICE - DAY

The PRESIDENT OF THE UNITED STATES — a tall black man —
sits behind his desk in the Oval Office.

In front of him, cups of coffee balanced on their knees, sit
Bobby, Elaine, Fred, and Max.
                        PRESIDENT
            Director Kirby assures me that all
            of you are true heroes.
```

There are other lesser used ways of formatting scene headings/sluglines—for those instances, keep a reference like *The Screenwriter's Bible* handy.

Time for action – formatting scene heading

Be sure that your scene headings are all in the **Scene Heading** element, as shown in the following screenshot:

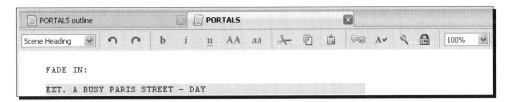

There is a bar indicating this in my example.

1. To determine which element a line is in (inside a Celtx script), left click anywhere in that line to get an editing cursor (vertical flashing bar) and look in the box to the upper left where the drop-down menu for elements is.

2. If it's in the correct format (Scene Heading), we'll see those words. If not, click on the down arrow on the right side of the elements window and click on **Scene Heading**. This puts the entire line in the correct format.

To properly track our scenes, Celtx has to know where the scene headings are. This emphasis on proper element formatting applies to everything including the other formats we'll be looking at in the rest of this chapter—**Action**, **Character**, **Dialog**, **Parenthetical**, **Transition**, **Shot**, and **Text**.

Okay, we know how to title our scenes. So, what goes in them? Basically, it's action and dialog. Let's write some.

Action

When we type a scene heading in a Celtx script and hit the *Enter* key, Celtx automatically puts us into the `Action` element, as show in the following screenshot:

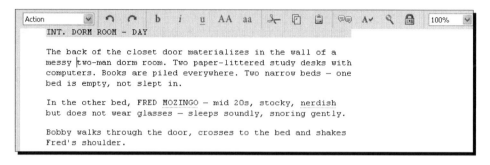

The **Action** script element is for narrative descriptions in which we show such things as (preceding example) setting, new character introduction, and action.

If you're new to writing scripts and unsure of what goes where in this unique form of visual storytelling, there are only three things that go in action. These are:

1. Action
2. Settings and characters
3. Sound

We write narrative description in present tense, such as:

```
Ralph says "write in present tense."
```

In other words, write **Action** as if it is happening at this very moment.

 Now here's an important tip! Keep action sparse and lean—never exceed four lines in length in either **Action** or **Dialog**. Two or three is even better. White space in scripts is good!

Be dramatic, don't just describe action—*show it*. The following screenshot shows an example from Portals of both keeping action in short paragraphs and making it move:

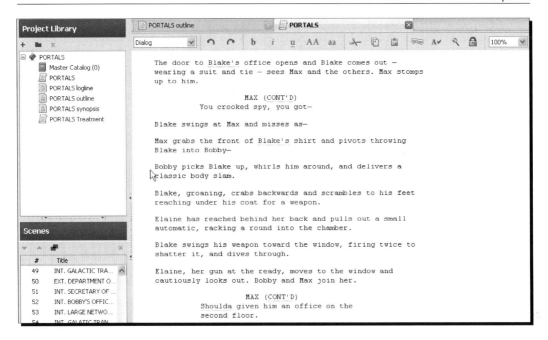

Being sparse means leave out any incidental action or description that does not advance the story. For example, two characters sit at a restaurant table talking. We would not show one character lifting a glass and sipping his drink unless it was part of the story. (Like someone is poisoning him). Otherwise, *don't mention* it.

However, don't be sparse to the point of leaving out things needed to set up part of the plot. Let's say one of the characters needs to find out directions to somewhere. We could make that possible like this:

In one corner of the room, a computer sits on a table, its screen lit up.

Just one line, sparse enough, but it does show a computer, powered up, is available for checking something like Google Maps or MapQuest to get directions.

We can use action to do characterization also:

Billy Bob clomps into the room with his cap still on and demands immediate attention.

Sue smiles and pats Betty's dog. The dog wags its tail and licks her hand.

From the preceding examples, the viewer knows Billy Bob to be impatient and not polite and that Sue is a nice lady loved by dogs.

Also avoid redundancy. An example of this would be:

```
INT. BOZO'S BAR - NIGHT
```

```
Billy Bob clomps into Bozo's Bar.
```

That's repetitive, so instead write:

```
INT. BOZO'S BAR - NIGHT
```

```
Billy Bob clomps in.
```

As we learned about **Scene Heading**, click anywhere in an action paragraph to make sure that the word **Action** appears in the script element drop-down box. Keeping our scripts properly formatted is easy, so long as we tag them with the right element.

That's it for **Action**. Check books such as *Save the Cat!* and *The Screenwriter's Bible* for greater depth in formatting and using action in scripts.

Now, let's look at the people in our screenplay.

Character

A **character** is a person (actor) in our script. In introducing a character, we need to keep the description as nonspecific as possible (so that casting can pick the right actor to play the part), but include anything that is important to the story. The three areas we need to cover in the first appearance of a character are:

- His or her name (ALL CAPS the first time used) and age (keep all this simple)
- How they are dressed (if important to the story)
- Any distinguishing attitudes or anything else that might determine how they react to people
- Keep all that under four lines

An example is:

```
HERMIE WEINER — late 50s, short, bald, wearing a thread bare suit — slams
open the door to the drugstore and stomps  in. His expression and attitude
are that of a tough little guy used to getting his own way.
```

The **Character** element is how we indicate their name and cause Celtx to properly format it, as shown in the following screenshot:

```
                          FRED
            Bobby, you know this thing is gonna
            change the world.

                          BOBBY
            Not just the world, Fred.
            Instantaneous travel to Mars, to
            worlds around other stars.

            Lots more research to do. But we
            can go anywhere on Earth we have
            GPS coordinates for. We-

    A loud knocking sounds. Bobby and Fred look at the closet,
    then realize it's coming from the apartment's front door.

                          BOBBY (CONT'D)
            Shut the closet!

    Bobby goes to the front door and opens it.

    MAX SHELDON — 60s, big, powerful, a former professional
    wrestler, colorful clothes — stands there glaring.
```

The **(CONT'D)** next to Bobby's name in the preceding screenshot is standard script formatting automatically put in by Celtx whenever a character speaks, some action occurs, and he speaks again (that is, before any other character speaks).

In the preceding screenshot, we also see how a character that has not previously appeared in the script is introduced or mentioned in a scene. In the Action description, the name of the character, *this first time only* in descriptive narrative, is in ALL CAPS, which tells the director or anyone else reading our script that someone they haven't met before has entered the story.

During this first appearance, again, give a short physical description of the character and how he or she is dressed, and any other distinguishing items that fit into the story.

In the case of Max, we later learn that he's intimidating on first appearance but as his characterization continues, he turns out to be a loving second father to Bobby and a good friend to have. Of course, cross him or try to hurt the ones he loves and he can still twirl bad guys above his head and body slam them like he used to do in the ring years before.

Always provide the name of characters when they first appear in the story. Don't refer to a YOUNG WOMAN and a few pages later give her name as MARCY DOAKS. In the case of unnamed characters, be sure that they are identified uniquely, such as POLICEMAN #1 and POLICEMAN #2.

There are all sorts of indirect ways to characterize people. In Portals, when Max first arrives, Bobby slips through the portal in the closet to turn off the alarm clock in their dorm room. Max does not know about the portals yet, so he's baffled. This gave me a chance to add to Bobby's character (that is, he's a shy guy who does not realize how attractive he really is to the ladies):

```
He dashes to the closet, sidles through the door so that Max
can't see inside, and pulls it shut.

Max looks at Fred. Fred shrugs. The alarm clock cuts off.

                    FRED
          Maybe he's wants to come out of the
          closet.

Max snorts.

                    MAX
          Not Bobby. All the girls love him.

                    FRED
          Bobby?

                    MAX
          He just ain't figured it out yet.
```

We can also visually tag people to characterize them. A great example is in the old B Western movies when the good guys wore white hats and the baddies black. You might not want to be quite that obvious. Stereotypes happen for a reason.

Other items of clothing or accessories that characterize might be sunglasses (cool dude) or a bowtie (fussy, precise), or carrying a cane (elegant), and so forth.

Whenever one of our characters speaks in the script, we use the **Character** script element, so that his or her name will be in ALL CAPS and centered at a proper distance from the left margin (all of which Celtx does for us automatically).

Characters should always be referred to in the same way throughout the script.

Usually just the character name appears on a line by itself, as we see in the preceding screenshot. However, there are elements that can modify the character such as (O.S.) and (V.O.). O.S. means *Off Screen*. This shows someone speaking who's in the room but the camera does not see that person. A woman behind a dressing screen for example. V.O. is *Voice Over*. A narrator speaking would be V.O. or if we wanted to let the viewer hear both sides of a telephone conversation, the guy on the phone would be V.O. Keep in mind that O.S. and V.O. are not the same.

Now, our characters need to speak.

Dialog

Movies have been "talkies" since the late 1920s. That means characters speak. The following screenshot shows an example of Bobby, Fred, and Max "bouncing" off each other in Portals:

```
                                                          17.



                    FRED
          So... Several recruiters offer us
          hundred-thousand-dollar-a-year jobs
          in fancy labs with hot and cold
          running secretaries but we're—

                    MAX
          Eating off the dollar menu for
          breakfast.

                    BOBBY
          Yep.

                    FRED
          Six years of constant hard work
          with no time for fun and now we're—

                    BOBBY
          Pretty much going to do more of the
          same.

                    FRED
          Starting up a new business-

                    MAX
          In my old garage.

                    FRED
          -with no capital.

                    BOBBY
          We had capital but you wanted an
          extra sausage biscuit.

                    FRED
          I love it.
```

The same general rule of keeping to four lines or less applies to dialog just like in action. This is one of those little things that, if violated, causes our script to scream "amateur" when we really want it to be confidently and persuasively purring "buy me, I'm a winner".

The following screenshot shows an example of breaking up a long dialog and handling a phone conversation, with a little characterization thrown in. Blake is one of the bad guys in Portals, an ex-CIA killer, and general nogoodnik.

```
EXT. REAGAN NATIONAL AIRPORT, WASHINGTON D.C. - DAY

A jet is on final approach to Ronald Reagan National
Airport.


INT. REAGAN NATIONAL AIRPORT TERMINAL - DAY

James Blake is in a departure lounge, over by himself in a
corner by the window, talking on his cellphone. Other people
sit in the rows of seats waiting on their flights.
                    BLAKE
          Pavlov? ... Blake. James Blake. ...

          Yeah, yeah. Good to talk to you
          again, too. ... Right, Sergei's
          already told you to help. ...

          Pay's good, don't worry. You're in
          Charlotte, right? ... Good, that's
          two hours drive from Asheville.

A young boy comes close to Blake and looks out at the
planes. Blake glares at him and he moves away.
```

In Celtx, there is a special way to break dialog and still keep the **Dialog** element format—hit *shift+Enter* twice. This puts the necessary "soft" returns in to keep it in **Dialog**.

Celtx assists us to write faster, as we've already learned earlier in this book. One of these ways is when we type a character's name and hit return, the format element automatically changes from **Character** to **Dialog**.

Celtx also keeps dialog together by preventing a character name being at the bottom of a page and the dialog beginning on the next (which is the standard rule in formatting screenplays).

If we have a call for people talking over each other, we can use the dual dialog format as in the following example from *Chapter 2*:

```
EXT. SMALL PRIVATE PROPELLER AIRCRAFT - DAY

A small plane wings its way through a cloudless blue sky.


INT. SMALL PRIVATE AIRCRAFT - DAY

BOB - 30s, chubby, wearing a Hawaiian shirt - and ROY - 40s,
moustache, thin - are the pilots.
          BOB                      ROY
We're low on fuel. Did you-   Me? I thought you-


          BOB                      ROY
I had to go file the flight   I assumed you had paid for
plan. I gave you the credit   the fuel when-
card and-


          BOB                      ROY
You did bring the             I laid them on your desk
parachutes? Where-            so-
```

Now, here's another way we can modify dialog, by using the **Parenthetical** element.

Parenthetical

The **Parenthetical** script element allows us to give direction to the actor where absolutely necessary. Use this sparingly (directors like to, well, direct) but know that it is available. Here's an example from Portals that (looking at it now) is perhaps not needed. Of course, he would be gasping if he just ran in from this sort of situation.

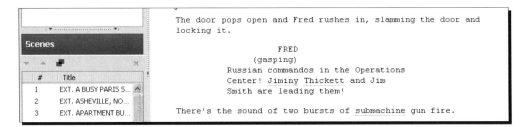

Here are two more ways we can use the **Parenthetical** element:

```
                    JOEY
        My turn to pay for the beers? ...
              (slaps his back pocket)
        ... Oops. I seem to have left my
        wallet at home.

                    SAM
                  (frowning)
        You seem to do that a lot, Joey.
```

Once more, in the modern spec script, do not use the **Parenthetical** element very much. Our next element, **Shot**, should not be used at all in a spec script—never ever.

Shot

A **shot** is a camera direction. In the following example, **POV** (highlighted) means Point of View and it tells the director to use the camera to show the scene from Billy Bob's eyes. **BACK TO SCENE** returns it to the full scene where we again see Billy Bob:

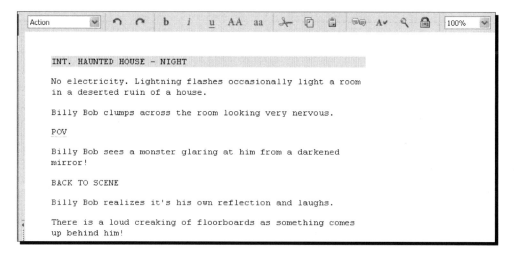

Other camera shots include **INSERT**, which is a quick close-up of a detail. For example, a man walks under a hanging sign. The **INSERT** shot shows the chain holding up the sign pulling loose from the wall. We return to the full scene as the sign starts to fall.

CLOSEUP tells the director to do a headshot where just the heads of one or two characters are in the frame.

A **LONG SHOT** is when the camera is a good distance away.

We can also indicate **SERIES OF SHOTS**, which are quick mini scenes such as:

SERIES OF SHOTS

Monsters jump into the back of Billy Bob's fleeing pickup truck

Billy Bob sees them in the rear view mirror and screams

A monster's huge fist breaks through the rear window

Billy Bob opens the door and tumbles down a bank

The pickup truck blasts on down the highway with a monster at the wheel and all the rest howling in laughter.

Billy Bob stands up, yanks his cap off, throws it to the ground, and jumps up and down on it.

BACK TO SCENE

And so on through many more. The following screenshot shows a page captured from the Internet's Wikipedia showing links to articles about various types of camera shots:

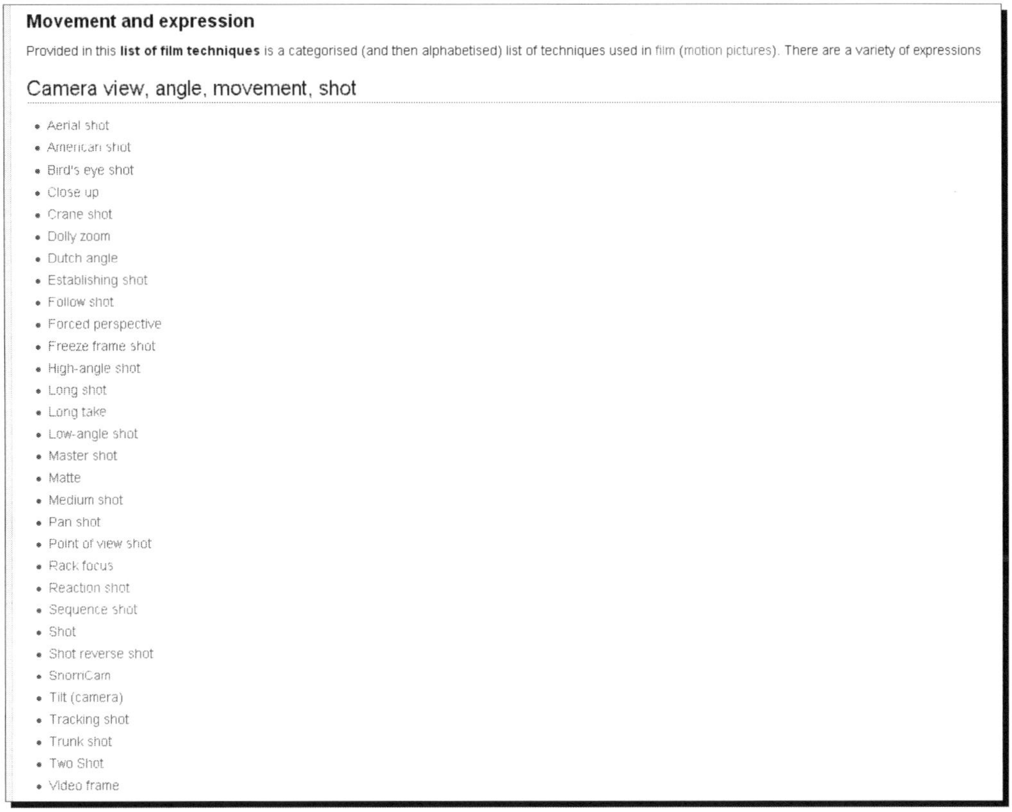

Movement and expression

Provided in this **list of film techniques** is a categorised (and then alphabetised) list of techniques used in film (motion pictures). There are a variety of expressions

Camera view, angle, movement, shot

- Aerial shot
- American shot
- Bird's eye shot
- Close up
- Crane shot
- Dolly zoom
- Dutch angle
- Establishing shot
- Follow shot
- Forced perspective
- Freeze frame shot
- High-angle shot
- Long shot
- Long take
- Low-angle shot
- Master shot
- Matte
- Medium shot
- Pan shot
- Point of view shot
- Rack focus
- Reaction shot
- Sequence shot
- Shot
- Shot reverse shot
- SnorriCam
- Tilt (camera)
- Tracking shot
- Trunk shot
- Two Shot
- Video frame

Celtx gives indie producers and directors a wonderful tool for building shooting scripts (those scripts with camera directions included), and of course, all those scheduling and tracking features we've already met in previous chapters.

This provides us with a good transition to mention the **Transition** element.

Transition

A definition of transition is "to move between". It is basically an instruction to the film (or video) editor on how to cut (move) from one scene to the next. The default is **CUT TO:**, which means simply that the first frame of the next scene starts immediately after the last frame of the previous scene, which can be a bit abrupt.

So we have **DISSOLVE TO:** where one scene fades gently into the next—much more artistic.

MATCH CUT:, in which the focus point in one scene sort of morphs into the focus point of the next scene.

Celtx properly formats a **Transition** for us when we choose it on the drop-down script elements menu and type out the type of transition desired. As shown in the following screenshot, the format for a transition is in ALL CAPS against the right margin followed by a colon.

This example uses two types of transitions and a camera shot direction.

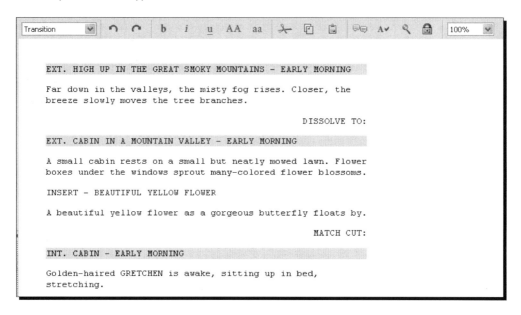

Is that artistic or what?

There are hundreds of possible transitions. I use Adobe Premiere Pro and it has scores. So, the possibilities available to us in specifying transitions are quite wide. Add in all those different camera shots, on top of narrative description and pithy dialog and just imagine all the great movies we can write and produce.

Text

As we learned earlier in this chapter the **Text** selection on the script element drop-down menu is rarely used. Other than typing **FADE IN:** at the beginning of a script and adding **THE END** and **FADE OUT**, I do not find it useful. Text puts in unformatted words and we almost always want lines in our script tagged with one of the standard script elements—**Scene Heading**, **Action**, **Character**, **Dialog**, **Parenthetical**, **Shot**, or **Transition** (but not those last two in a spec script).

Printing it out

The standard file format for screenplays is Adobe's Portable Document Format or PDF. Celtx, as we learned in *Chapter 2*, generates a PDF file from our scripts that we can save on our computers. However, it does not do the actual creation locally.

This means—when it is time to format—an Internet connection must be available. Celtx sends the script to a server out there somewhere (we don't care where), turns it into a PDF, and returns it to us (without saving anything out there, by the way). By doing this, Celtx gives us more formatting power than our own computer can and keeps our local software lean but powerful and, above all, free.

To turn your script into a PDF, left click on the **TypeSet/PDF** button at the bottom of the main script window, as shown in the following screenshot:

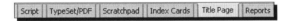

Celtx takes a moment to work its magic (a progress bar runs at the top of the main script window while formatting is occurring)—the script is transferred to the formatting server which sends back a PDF file. Once the PDF appears in the main script window, we can review and save it. We can also print out a hard copy if we like, by clicking on the **Print** button on the main toolbar, as shown in the following screenshot:

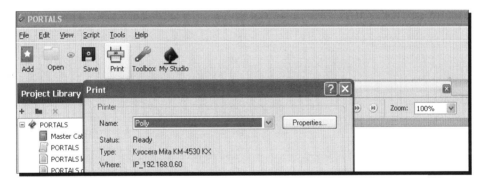

Once we've saved the PDF to our computer hard disk, we can also open it in Adobe Reader (the free program from `http://www.adobe.com`) and print it from there or in any other program that reads PDF files. Alternatively, we can, as most agents and producers seem to prefer these days, e-mail them the PDF of our script for review.

Should they ask for a paper copy, you'll need to print and bind it in the approved manner. The easiest way is to get paper already punched with three holes (the big box office supply stores have this). Also get brads and brad washers from The Writers Store (`http://www.writersstore.com/`), and a cheap rubber hammer to flatten the brads after binding. Put brads in only the top and bottom holes (yes, this is a rule).

For a complete guide to binding scripts, watch my eight-minute video on this topic in the Script Writing section of my site at `http://forums.1vid.com/index.php/topic,1370.0.html`.

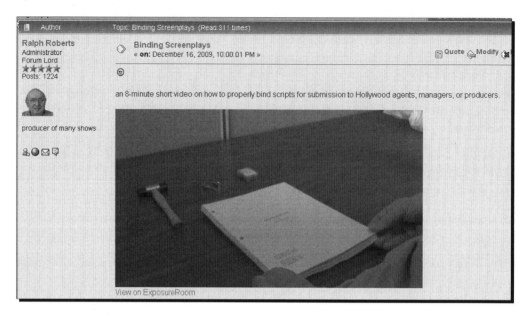

Have a go hero – write a screenplay!

Okay, hero. Now's your chance to make your own heroes into heroes, using the techniques and tools discussed in this and earlier chapters to finally write a screenplay. To visualize, create, and record a story formatted to industry standards. Can you do it? Yes. You can! For you are a true hero and, like any good hero, have a trusty sidekick to keep you moving forward. Celtx.

The steps I've given you in this chapter are the same ones you'll get if you pay big money to attend expensive screenwriting courses. They are simple, powerful, and work hand-in-glove with Celtx. To give you an overview, you plan and write a screenplay in the following way:

1. Write a logline (if you can't tell the story in two or three lines, you're not ready to write it yet).

2. Outline the story. I again recommend checking out Blake Snyder's "Save the Cat" books for some great techniques on writing outlines (he calls them "Beat Sheets"). You can use the note cards in Celtx to match the way Snyder suggests you hone your outline.

3. Write a synopsis (optional). A synopsis lets you develop your story in even greater detail but using methods such as "Save the Cat" or the step outline we looked at earlier, you may have such a good grasp of your story that the synopsis can be skipped.

4. Sit on a chair and write the script. Once you have a good outline and an excellent tool like Celtx. Writing the screenplay itself is by far the easiest and most satisfying part of this whole process.

You go, HERO!

Summary

In this chapter, we learned how to write loglines, synopses, treatments, and outlines—all inside Celtx—to give us a head start and ensure success in writing winning screenplays.

We typed FADE IN and started the first scene. Here we got to see and use the entertainment industry standard script elements and found it not all that complicated—there are only seven after all.

We used all the good stuff Celtx provides for setting up and using scenes, and saw how Celtx makes it easy to create, rearrange, and track scenes—all enhancing our creative writing.

We found out how to turn our plot into action and use the Character element along with introducing and bringing to life (characterization) the people in our script.

We examined parenthetical action.

What he said and she said is dialog and we looked at how to keep it interesting and properly formatted.

We also delved into how to specify shots (the way the camera is set up for the scene). Like transitions, we won't be specifying shots in the scripts we want to sell (let the director worry about this, it's his or her job and they get prickly if someone tries to take it away from them). However, in the media you're helping to produce, you'll want to put these in for sure.

Transition: CLOSE ON as Ralph holds up the page showing transitions … Then Ralph hastens to explain that you *do not* add transitions to spec scripts you're writing in hopes of selling to Hollywood or Bollywood or wherever. Of course, if you're actually involved in production, you will definitely want to put in the transitions.

Text, we found out, is a "catch-all" format, not one of the standard script elements, but it is great (as we will soon see) for doing treatments and outlines or, indeed, using Celtx as an ordinary word processor. You could even write short stories or a complete novel easily enough using it.

We took a more practical look at printing our scripts, both to PDF (more often requested by agents, managers, and producers these days) and on paper (three punched holes, not two), and how to properly bind the paper script.

So, now we have more than just the basics of screenplay formatting and know how Celtx takes all the hard work out of putting together our script, leaving us free to concentrate on action and dialog. Let's keep on keeping on and turn out those great screenplays!

If you're into audio visual productions, documentaries, and so forth like me ...
Well, that's next!

8
Documentaries and Other Audio-Visual Projects

*Writing documentaries and other nonfiction scripts is a bit different than movies. Celtx's integral audio-visual editor is perfect for docs (documentaries), commercials, public service spots, video tutorials, slide shows, light shows, or just about any other combination of visual and other content that is not just sound alone (use **Audio Play** for productions having only sound and no picture, such as radio plays or podcasts).*

In this chapter, we will cover the following topics:

- **What an audio-visual production is**: A look at the many types of productions falling under the term "audio-visual" and how Celtx makes them easier to create and use.

- **Starting an audio-visual project**: Building a Celtx project container for our AV project.

- **Creating an AV project in Celtx**: **Scene Heading**, **Shot**, **Character**, **Dialog**, and **Parenthetical**—how to use with examples.

This chapter, using what we have learned previously, enables us to write solid, professional audio-visual projects.

What is an audio-visual production?

The term audio-visual production basically covers anything in the known universe that combines varying components of movement, sound, and light.

Movies are nothing more than big expensive (really expensive) audio-visual shows. Television programs; the fireworks, performed music, and laser lights of a major rock concert; a business presentation; Uncle Spud showing slides of his vacation in Idaho—all are audio-visual productions.

A complex audio-visual production, such as the big rock concert, combines many types of contents and is called a multimedia show, which combine sounds and music, projections of video and photos (often several at once), lights, spoken words, text on screens, and more.

Audio visual shows, those of an educational nature as well as for entertainment value, might be produced with equipment such as the following:

- Dioramas
- Magic lanterns
- Planetarium
- Film projectors
- Slide projectors
- Opaque projectors
- Overhead projectors
- Tape recorders
- Television
- Video
- Camcorders
- Video projectors
- Interactive whiteboards
- Digital video clips

Also productions such as TV commercials, instructional videos, those moving displays you see in airports, even the new digital billboards along our highways—all are audio-visual productions (even the ones without sound).

My favorite type of production, documentaries (I've done literally hundreds of them), are audio-visual shows.

A documentary is a nonfiction movie and includes newsreels, travel, politics, docudramas, nature films and animal films, music videos, and much more.

In short, as we can see from the preceding discussion, you can throw just about everything into a production including your kitchen sink. Turn the faucet on and off while blasting inspiring music and hitting it with colored spotlights, and plumbers will flock to buy tickets to the show!

Now, while just about every conceivable project falls into the audio-visual category, Celtx (as shown in the next screenshot) offers us specific categories that narrow the field down a little.

The following screenshot from Celtx's splash page shows those categories. **Film** handles movies and television shows, **Theatre** (love that Canadian spelling, eh?) is for stage plays, **Audio Play** is designed for radio programs and podcasts, **Storyboard** is for visual planning, and **Comic Book** is for writing anything from comic strips to epic graphic novels.

Text (not shown in the following screenshot) is the other project type that comes with Celtx and is great (as we found out in *Chapter 7, Writing Movies with Celtx*) for doing loglines, synopses, treatments, outlines, and anything else calling for a text editor rather than a script formatter.

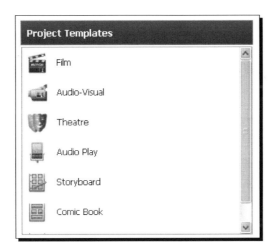

Just about everything else can be written in an **Audio-Visual** project container! Let's think about that for a moment. This means that **Audio-Visual** is by far and away the most powerful project provided by Celtx.

In the script element drop-down box, there are only five script elements—**Scene Heading**, **Shot**, **Character**, **Dialog**, and **Parenthetical**—whereas **Film** has eight! Yet, thanks to Celtx magic, these five elements, as I will show you in this chapter, are a lot more flexible than in **Film** and the other projects. It's pretty amazing.

So, time to start an audio-visual project of our own.

Starting an AV project in Celtx

What better example to use than a short documentary on... wait for it... Celtx. This film I actually plan on producing and using to both promote Celtx (which certainly deserves letting people know about it) and also showing that this book is great for learning all this marvelous power of Celtx, so run out and buy one or more. They make fantastic holiday gifts, and so on.

The title: "Celtx Loves Indies."

Indies is slang for independent producers. An independent producer is a company or quite often an individual who makes films outside Hollywood or Bollywood or any other studio system. Big studios have scores or even hundreds of people to do all those tasks needed in producing a film. Indies often have very few people, sometimes just one or two doing all the crewing and production work. Low budget (not spending too much money on making films) is our watchword. Celtx is perfect for indies—it is, as I point out in the documentary—like having a studio in a box!

So, my example project for this chapter is how I set up "Celtx Loves Indies" in Celtx.

Time for action – beginning our new AV project

We start our project, as we did our spec script in the last chapter, by making a directory on our computer. Having a separate directory for our projects makes it a lot easier to organize and to find stuff when we need it.

Therefore, I first create the new empty directory on my hard drive named `Celtx Loves Indies`, as shown in the following screenshot:

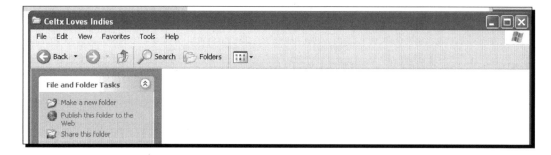

Now, fire up Celtx. In a moment, we'll left click on **Audio-Visual** to open a project container that has an **Audio-Visual** script in it. However, first, since I have not mentioned it to date, look at the items outside the **Project Templates** and **Recent Project** boxes in the lower part of the splash page, as shown in the following screenshot:

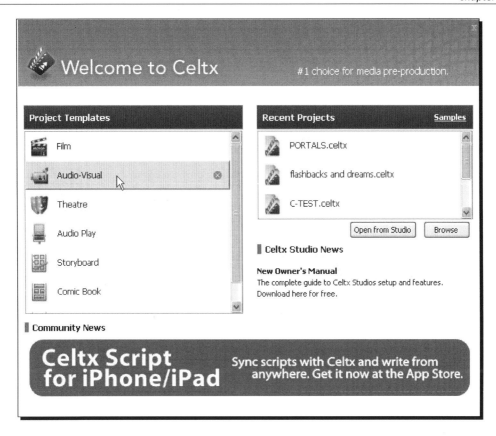

As Celtx is connected to the Internet (or should be, see *Chapter 1*, *Obtaining and Installing Celtx*, as to why and for instructions on how to set this up on your computer), we get some information each time Celtx starts up from the servers at: `http://celtx.com`.

This information from online includes links to news, help features, ads for Celtx add-ons, and announcements.

The big news here is that Celtx has added an app (application) to synchronize projects with iPhones and iPads. That's not in my outline of this book, but I'll make a place to cover it later on. However, check these messages out each time you open Celtx.

Next, we open an **Audio-Visual** project in Celtx.

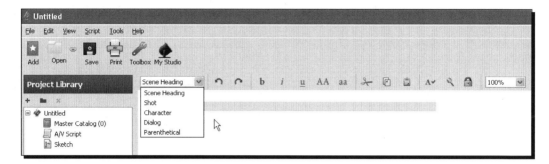

This gives us a chance to check out those five script elements we met earlier by left clicking on the downward arrow next to **Scene Heading**. In the next section, we'll examine each and use them.

Time for action – setting up the container

Continuing with our initial setup of the container for this project, rename the A/V Script in the **Project Library**. I renamed mine, naturally, Celtx Loves Indies. Also, remember we can have hundreds of files, directories, subdirectories, and so on in the **Project Library**—our research and more. This is why a Celtx project is really a container as emphasized in previous chapters.

Just right click on **A/V Script**, choose **Rename...** and type in the new title, as shown in the following screenshot:

Left click on **File** at the top left of the Celtx screen, then on **Save Project As...** (or use the *Ctrl+Shift+S* key shortcut) to save the project into your new directory, all properly titled and ready for action, as shown in the following screenshot:

Title page

I like to add a title page to all my scripts. To have a title page included in the print out of an **Audio-Visual** project, left click on the **TypeSet/PDF** button at the bottom of the main script window, as shown in the following screenshot:

When the Typeset/PDF screen opens in the main script window of Celtx, left click on the **Format Options** button at the top. The **Format Options** dialog box opens, as shown in the following screenshot:

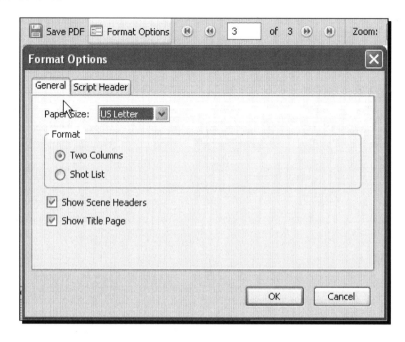

Under the **General** tab of the **Format Options** dialog box (in the preceding screenshot), we need to make sure several options are checked off.

Paper Size is the print output page size of the PDF file (not necessarily that of your printer).

For example, you might live in Europe and print on A4 paper using the **Print** button at the top of the Celtx screen. However, the script is being submitted to a producer in America, who would be printing on the U.S. Letter. Using the **Paper Size** option, we can generate PDFs having different paper sizes than might be our local standard.

Next, down in the box, click in the circle to the left of **Two Columns**.

Industry standard audio-visual scripts use a two-column format. The left column contains camera shots and the other directions. The right column has characters and dialog (who speaks and what they say). This is shown in the following screenshot:

	1
VIDEO	**AUDIO**
TITLES: Titles roll as an exciting montage consisting of quick-cut bits of scenes from indie movies play.	
INTRODUCTION: MEDIUM: shot of me with green screen behind. Use video wall effect with outtakes from several of my documentaries playing.	RALPH Hi, I'm Ralph Roberts — author of the CELTX BEGINNER'S GUIDE and producer of hundreds of documentary films. As an independent producer or *indie*, I know our two most favorite words in all the universe are *low budget*.

As we're right at it, let me mention the **Shot List** choice. Once our audio-visual script is finished, we can check here to generate and print a list of shots. This would be useful for the camera operator in setting up scenes, and looks like the following:

SHOT	TYPE OF SHOT	DESCRIPTION
1.1		Titles roll as an exciting montage consisting of quick-cut bits of scenes from indie movies play.
2.1	MEDIUM	shot of me with green screen behind. Use video wall effect with outtakes from several of my documentaries playing.
2.2	MEDIUM	graphic with the words LOW BUDGET in all caps on green screen.
2.3		Make me smaller, show excerpt from Rapid Ralph Runs the Roads #40 on green screen (Willow Creek).
2.4	MEDIUM	Stock photo of big Hollywood studio on green screen.
2.5		Make me smaller. Splash page of Celtx on green screen.

For now, we want the two-columns format selected. To finish out this tab, check **Show Scene Headers** (we want to see the titles of the scenes in our sample script) and **Title Page** because as stated earlier, we want to include a title page.

We won't use the **Script Header** tab in this project, but if you ever want to, it replaces the title page with a data page listing the fields that can be filled out in this tab, as shown in the following screenshot:

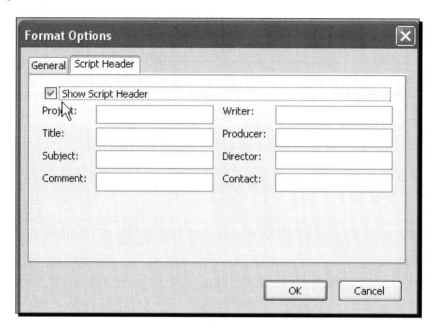

You would find a script header more useful for internal use in a large company where several people work on the project and the data is more important than appearances. This dialog box does not allow you to select both if you wanted a title page and the script heading data. However, that's easy to get around; just duplicate the finished script by right clicking on its name in the **Projects Library** and selecting **Duplicate**. You'll have two scripts of the same name. In one, you can have a title page and in the other the PDF prints out with the script header data. You might want to change the name slightly, so it's obvious which has what.

Time for action – adding a title page

Okay, now that we've told Celtx we want a title page included, let's set one up. Left click on the **Title Page** button at the bottom of the main script window, as shown in the following screenshot:

The title page form, as we've seen most recently in *Chapter 7*, appears in the main script window of the Celtx screen, as shown in the following screenshot:

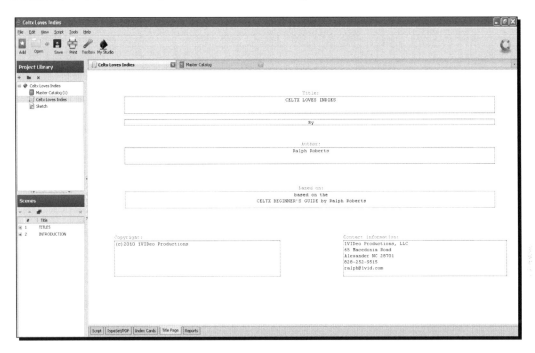

Fill it out by typing in the boxes. I've entered my title, my name as author, the work it's based on (this book), and my contact information.

Also add a copyright! Use a c in parentheses (c) to indicate the copyright symbol. While you could type the *Alt-0169* key combination for an actual "c in a circle" copyright symbol, the PDF conversion program out there on the Internet does not convert it correctly, so use the above workaround. It's just as legal.

What I said in *Chapter 7* about not putting a copyright only applies to spec scripts. Everything else, including audio-visual scripts, should have a copyright notice.

Now, the way copyrights work is simple, especially under U.S. law (Title 17, U.S. Code is the law covering copyrights). When you finish a work, it is automatically copyrighted. Filling out forms (see *Chapter 7* for how to do that online) and sending in money only registers the copyright, which already exists. It's another layer of legal protection. However, if you do want it, just do it online (currently costs $25).

Do not go to an attorney to get a copyright done. As a publisher, I come across authors who have. They paid $250 or so for the attorney (or more likely one of his or her paralegals) to do what they could have done themselves for a whole lot less.

Unless your job is for big bucks or with someone you have reason not to trust (and in that case, why are you working with them?), the copyright notice is all you really need. With the title page entries all filled out, we're ready to see what it looks like after the PDF is generated—both to check for errors and as encouragement for us to write the rest of the script. Hey, you got one page done already, eh?

Click on the **TypeSet/PDF** button again (bottom of the main script window), as shown in the following screenshot:

Celtx sends our title page out on the Internet (as described in the last chapter and elsewhere in this book), formats it, and returns it to our computer, displaying it in the main script window, as shown in the following screenshot:

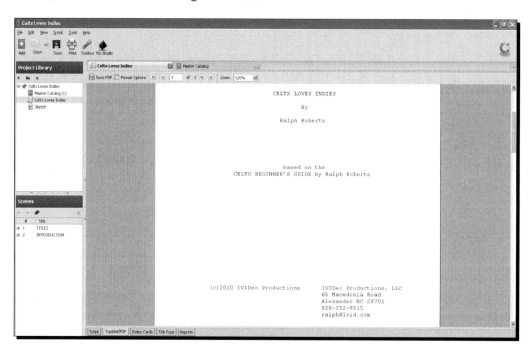

We could save the title page as a PDF file to our hard disk by clicking on the **Save PDF** button at the top of the main script window, but it's not worth it until we have some of the script written.

The data we filled out and changes in configuration made already are saved every time the Celtx project gets saved, so nothing is lost.

Celtx power

Now, just as a reminder of Celtx's power. Look at the **Project Library** box and double-click on **Master Catalog** (the main database of Celtx). I've already started my script, so it has one entry so far, myself as a character, narrating, as shown in the following screenshot:

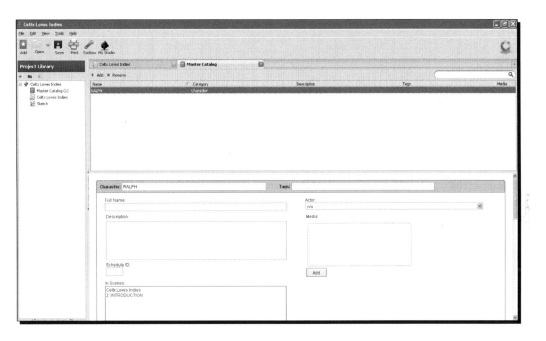

This entry was made automatically by Celtx as the script was being written. As we saw in *Chapter 2, All those Wonderful Writing Features*, we can fill out the data fields in the various categories that Celtx tracks for us. Currently (in Version 2.7 of Celtx) there are 35 categories tracked. We find those on the right side of the main script window when a script is open for editing.

Again, as detailed in *Chapter 2*, we are not limited to only 35—we can create and add literally hundreds of categories, whatever needs tracking. The power of Celtx compared to the high dollar programs, that basically only write scripts, is immense. Not bad for free!

It's time now to actually write our audio-visual script. Go to the script by clicking on the **Script** button at the bottom of the main script window (see the following screenshot) or double click on the script's name in the **Project Library**.

Writing an AV project in Celtx

An audio-visual script is written using the five script elements in the **Audio-Visual** project script, which are **Scene Heading**, **Shot**, **Character**, **Dialog**, and **Parenthetical**.

A script in progress—my *Celtx Loves Indies*—is shown in the following screenshot:

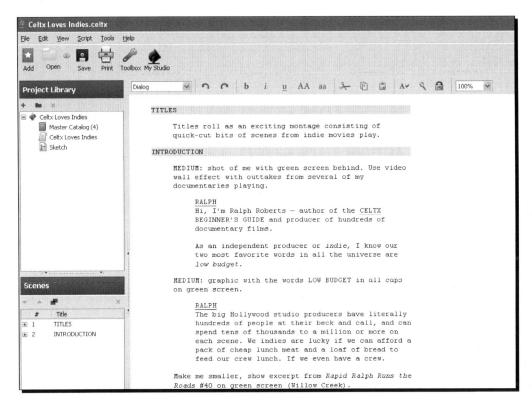

A few pages ago, we discussed how wide a variety of audio-visual productions Celtx's audio-visual project script edit covers, and all done with those five script elements found in the drop-down menu at the top of Celtx's main script window. You can see it in the preceding screenshot; it is showing **Dialog** at the moment.

Once finished and sent out on the Internet for an almost instant conversion to PDF, a completed page looks like the following:

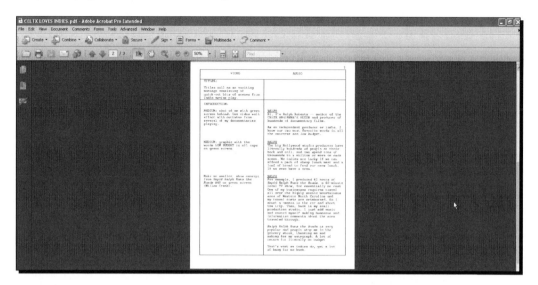

All nice and neat, and to get it that way, we must be careful to tag each item we write with the correct script element. I emphasized that in the previous chapter, I'm doing it again now, and I'll do it two or three more times before this book ends. It is critical.

Do that and it's amazing, the power we have in crafting all those zillions of types of audio-visual shows, presentations, and more.

So, let's go through and look at what each of the script elements does for us.

Scene heading

Scene headings work precisely like they did for us while writing the spec script in *Chapter 7*, only they look a bit different. The word INTRODUCTION: in the following screenshot is the name of this scene:

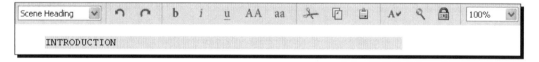

We type the scene heading in any mix of upper and lower case and, so long as we have **Scene Heading** selected in the script elements drop-down menu, Celtx puts it in ALL CAPS and adds a colon when it formats into a PDF. The preceding screenshot shows how it looks in our script. Here it is when formatted into a PDF:

```
INTRODUCTION:

MEDIUM: shot of me with          RALPH
green screen behind. Use         Hi, I'm Ralph Roberts -- author of the
video wall effect with           CELTX BEGINNER'S GUIDE and producer of
outtakes from several of         hundreds of documentary films.
my documentaries playing.
```

Scene headings automatically appear in the **Scenes** box to the left of the Celtx window under the **Project Library**. As in any type of Celtx script, we can use these scene headings in the box to move scenes around in the script, delete scenes, or as a navigation aid in moving to a selected scene in the script. Also, clicking on the small box with a plus sign (+) in it (if more than one shot is in the scene) gives us a list of shots, as shown in the following screenshot:

Shots

The **Shots** script element refers to camera shots. These can be industry standard shot names, or more informal instructions for the camera operator or video editor, or a combination like the following:

```
MEDIUM: graphic with the         RALPH
words LOW BUDGET in all caps      The big Hollywood studio producers have
on green screen.                  literally hundreds of people at their
```

Selecting the **Shot** script element and typing the shot causes Celtx to format it in the left column when the PDF is created.

Character

The **Character** script element denotes someone who speaks. In the preceding example, that would be me. When we type a character name with the **Character** element selected, Celtx capitalizes and underlines it, and places it in the right column.

Oh yes, Celtx makes our typing faster by prompting us. Type a scene heading, hit the *Enter* key, and we are automatically in shot mode. Type the shot and hit *Enter*, we are in character, then in dialog, and back in character, and so forth. We covered key shortcuts earlier; they can really speed up your productivity.

Dialog

The **Dialog** element is for the spoken word. Celtx formats it, when PDFs are created, in the right column. Remember, in your script, just click on any groups of words and the script elements box shows you which element it is in. To change the type of script element, simply select that element in the drop-down menu. Dialog looks like the following screenshot in the finished PDF (right column):

```
Make me smaller. Splash page     RALPH
of Celtx on green screen.        Well, here's the dream of every
                                 indie producer in the world. All the
                                 resources of a Hollywood studio in
                                 a box! It's called Celtx -- spelled
                                 C-e-l-t-x but pronounced with a K.
```

Parenthetical

This is a kind of "catch all" for anything that does not easily fit in the other four script elements of Celtx's **Audio-Visual** project. Anything we type in Parenthetical is formatted in the right column with parentheses around it.

One example of using a parenthetical would be reminding myself to promote this book in the preceding script:

(hold up book)

Pop quiz – What Are Audio/Visual projects?

1. Which of the below is not an audio/visual project?

   a. Documentary about India

   b. Slide show of your Uncle Monty's vacation to Bermuda

   c. TV commercial for Honest Bob's Used Cars

   d. Podcast in which you tell us how successful Celtx has made you

2. Should you add copyright information on the title page of an A/V project?

    a. Yes

    b. No

Summary

In this chapter, we took a look at the many types of productions falling under the term "audio-visual" and how Celtx makes them easier to create and use. We learned how to build a Celtx project container for our AV project and to use the AV script elements of **Scene Heading**, **Shot**, **Character**, **Dialog**, and **Parenthetical**.

This chapter along with what we have learned previously enables us to write solid, professional audio-visual projects.

Now, exit stage right and we'll get ready to write a play using Celtx's **Theatre** project.

9
Raising the Curtain on Plays

Plays are pretty much like movies except for the car chase scenes (just kidding). There are differences but Celtx assists us in mastering those differences and writing for the stage.

In this chapter, we will cover:

- ◆ Act I, Scene I—writing a play: We will learn about dramatic stage plays and outline a play using Celtx's **Theatre** editor's **Text** element
- ◆ Starting a theatre project: We will learn how to set up a project container for our play
- ◆ Play elements: Act, Scene, Stage Direction, Character, Dialog, Parenthetical, and Transition
- ◆ Printing our plays
- ◆ Keeping track of the cast

Using what we've learned previously and the new material that will be presented in this chapter, we will be able to write exciting, professionally-formatted stage plays.

Act 1, Scene 1—writing a play

Plays are a form of storytelling which have come down to us from prehistoric times. I like to think of them as prehysteric times, because being chased around by wooly mammoths and sabertooth tigers was no laugh.

Cavemen and cavewomen had a rough life. Telling and acting out stories in the cave at night was a nice break from hunting, gathering, and outrunning big animals. In fact, a good case can be made for this type of playacting being that old cliché "the second oldest profession."

The oldest profession, of course, is computer book writing. Think I'm kidding? Look at all those cave paintings showing how to program bison and mammoth hunts and the like. Do you believe those writers got paid the big skins and shiny stones like those storyteller actors? Nah.

According to Wikipedia, the first recorded theatrical event in history was a performance of the sacred plays of the myth of Osiris and Isis (ancient Egyptian gods) in 2500 BC in Egypt. That would be over 4,500 years ago.

The history of Eastern theatre dates back to 1000 BC with the Sanskrit plays of ancient Indian theater, and the Chinese who were putting on plays too during this era.

Within a few centuries, the Greeks had developed plays into highly formalized popular entertainment with special places to view these dramatic presentations—theaters. The word theatre means "place for seeing" from the ancient Greek language. The Greeks also invented dramatic criticism, acting as a career, and theater architecture.

By the way, I am alternating between the Americanized spelling of theater with the Canadian/British theatre. The latter looks kind of weird to me but that's the way it's spelled in Celtx because, of course, a Canadian company oversees the development of Celtx. However, sometimes, I just got to use the er ending.

Down through the ages, plays have continued to be popular. William Shakespeare being one of many playwrights (those who write plays, like us) who has given this art form a boost along the way.

Plays remain a favored entertainment today with venues ranging from the lights of Broadway "the Great White Way" down to schools and community theater productions all over the world.

Thankfully, we have means of writing plays today far easier than those guys back in prehistoric times. Like one of those storytellers approaching a wall painter.

"Hey, man, want to publish my play?"

"Sorry, dude, got to get this computer book painted and playwriting software hasn't been invented yet. See me in about 8,000 years when you can download Celtx off the Internet. Watch out for that sabertooth tiger behind you!"

This now brings us back to the present. Let's write a play but, what exactly is a play?

What are plays?

The scripts for plays (dramatic stage presentations) are like any other script we write in Celtx—a blueprint (directions) for the final production.

Being something performed in a limited area (a stage), plays rely a lot more on dialog (the spoken word) than screenplays where the action might roam across continents or entire solar systems (or at least appear to, thanks to the movie magic of special effects). Dialog is all important in writing a play.

A good example of a play is included with Celtx, The Importance of Being Earnest by Oscar Wilde, first performed in 1895. It's a comedy about Victorian society often performed even today.

I got to digress just for a moment to relate this anecdote. Wilde was quite a character in his day and attracted some ill feeling and had numerous enemies. One of these was a Scottish nobleman, the Marquess of Queensberry, John Douglas. He is famous for sponsoring the Marquess of Queensberry rules, which are named after him and the foundation of the modern sport of boxing.

Anyway, the Marquess was upset with Wilde because his son and Wilde were an item (told you Wilde was a character). So, the old Marquess showed up at the theater the evening The Importance of Being Earnest premiered, loaded down with vegetables he planned on throwing at the playwright. If he had not been stopped at the door, the play might have gotten a different sort of review indeed.

Anyway, to get to this sample play, open Celtx and to the right of **Recent Projects**, click on **Samples** as shown in the following screenshot:

The **Recent Projects** box now changes to a **Sample Projects** list. Several examples of the types of projects Celtx can help us write are listed. Scroll down and click on the **Importance of Being Earnest (Theatre)** choice, as shown in the following screenshot:

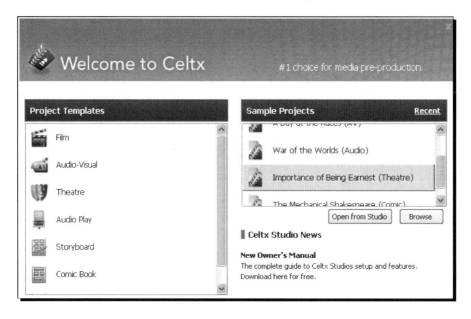

As follows, you can see that this play is a very good example of a **Theatre** project container with several items in the **Project Library** (check out Oscar's biography) in addition to the stage play itself. This is why I call it a *container*.

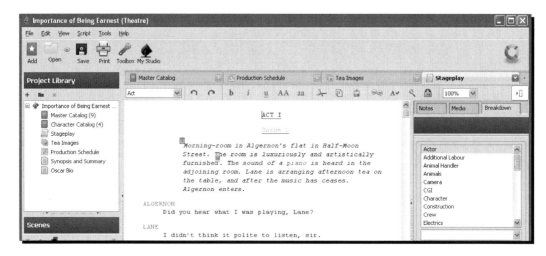

Parts of a stage play script

What is a stage play? Well, we know it's a blueprint—a plan for the staging of the play.

Plays normally occur in three to five acts. Each act might have several scenes. The one-act play is also popular. As the stage play writers (also called a playwright), we are responsible for three major elements, which are as follows:

◆ Characters: Several people (played by actors) who show and tell the play's story—the latter more so than in screenplays again because, of the limited area on a stage.

◆ Setting: Where and when the play takes place so that the set designer will have an idea of the props, backgrounds, and so on to build for the play.

◆ Stage directions: What the characters do and how they react. In writing stage directions (which the audience never sees) we give hints to the director as to how he or she will need to have characters speak, react, move, and so forth. Directions we'll provide include the following:

❑ Entrances (when characters come onto the stage)

❑ Exits (when they leave such as the famous "Exit, stage right")

❑ Events (like a murder happens)

❑ Actions (what characters do physically)

❑ Pauses in dialog not covered by action; perhaps characters are shocked by the murder and look to each other for support

We do not design the costumes (although we can write in items of clothing that impact the story), backgrounds, show how the sets should be constructed, schedule rehearsals and performances, and so on. Unless, of course, it's a small production and that is also our job and we just happen to have Celtx which makes it all so wonderfully easy.

Now it's time to create our theatre project container.

Time for action – starting a theatre project

Creating a project container for a play is accomplished the same general way as it was accomplished for screenplays and audio-visual scripts.

We first create a new directory on our hard disk. In my case, I'm planning a stage production entitled An Evening with Professor Celtx, as shown in the following screenshot:

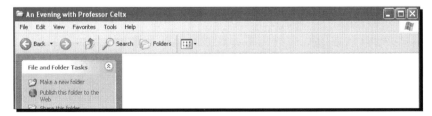

Now we start Celtx and choose the **Theatre** project on the Splash page, which gives us a new **Theatre** project container. Note, the following screenshot comes with ACT I and Scene 1 headings already in place:

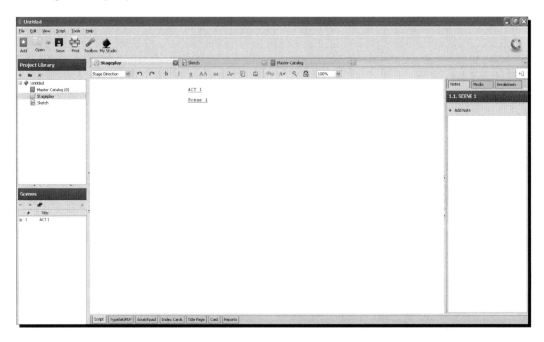

Finish up by:

1. Right clicking on the generic **Stageplay** script and changing its name to something closer to the name of your script (in my case **An Evening with Professor Celtx**). You could also, at this time, delete the generic **Sketch** just to avoid confusion. Should you want one later, it's easy enough to create it with the blue **Add** button.

2. Click on **File** to the upper left of the Celtx window and choose **Save Project As...** or use the *Ctrl+Shift+S* shortcut key combination, as shown in the following screenshot, and save it in the directory you made on your hard disk as the name of the play:

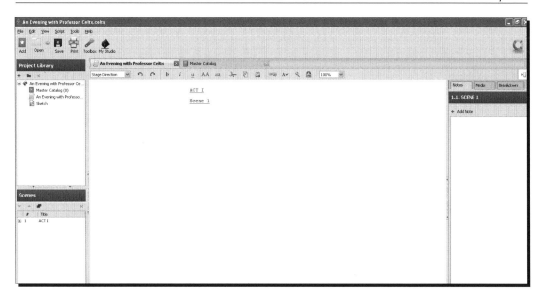

Do this for every project and you will be thankful many times later when trying to find stuff. Believe me; I learned this type of discipline the hard way.

Time for action – creating the title page

Like the spec screenplay we set up in *Chapter 7, Writing Movies with Celtx*, and unlike the audio-visual project in *Chapter 8, Documentaries and Other Audio-Visual Projects*, where we had to specify we wanted a title page, the **Theatre** project provides a title page by default.

We simply fill out the title page form and a properly formatted title page will be added in front of our script every time a PDF is created.

To get to the form, to fill it out, click on the **Title Page** button at the bottom of the main Celtx script window, as shown in the following screenshot:

Now, we enter our title, the name of the author (or authors), a copyright notice, and contact information. As I mentioned in the last chapter, the spec screenplay title page is the only title page you do not put a copyright notice on. That's something unique to Hollywood during the submission process. Actually, even without the copyright notice—at least under U.S. law—your work is protected but, like backups, it's a good habit to get in.

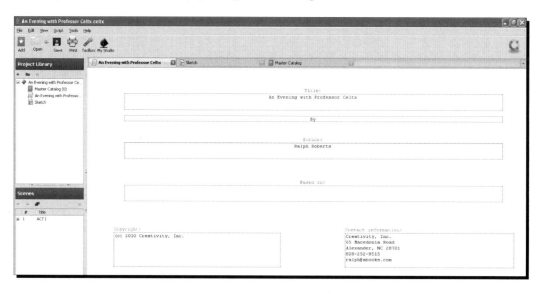

Now, click on the **Typeset/PDF** button and our title page whizzes out on the Internet, is typeset, and returned to us, as shown in the following screenshot:

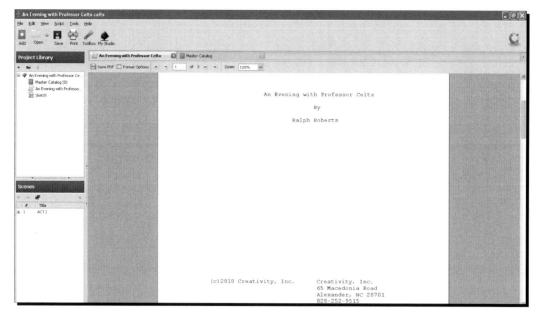

That's it for the title page, but... well... What do we write?

Outlining a play

As we discussed in *Chapter 7*, having an outline makes writing a script easier, more productive, and saves us tons of time.

Celtx's **Text** is a handy text processor and perfect to whip up our outline in. Add one to your **Theatre** project container by clicking on the blue **Add** button, selecting **Text** under **Add a script to your project**, and filling out **Name:** with a title for the outline, as shown in the following screenshot:

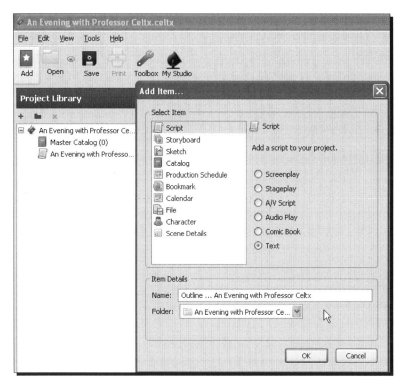

By the way, when we have long file names, I like to put identifiers like "Outline" at the beginning of the title in the **Project Library**, as the entire title won't be visible without widening that column. The latter, of course, eats up valuable screen real estate better devoted to our script.

Now, let's get to outlining. A play needs a plot and how to do that was solved long ago. One of the first to quantify how plays should be structured was the famous Greek philosopher, Aristotle (384 – 322 BC).

Aristotle's influential writings include those about physics, metaphysics, poetry, music, logic, rhetoric, politics, government, ethics, biology, zoology, and theater. He also taught Alexander the Great, who later conquered the known world.

Back then, over 2,000 years ago, in the Golden Age of Greek civilization, there wasn't much on TV, so they spent a lot of time attending plays. Aristotle analyzed the successful dramas of the day and came up with (and I'm being serious now) a simple but still true observation that a play is a whole and that "a whole is that which has a beginning, a middle, and an end."

Twenty centuries later, Gustav Freytag (1816 –1895)—a German dramatist and novelist looked at the ancient Greek plays, those of William Shakespeare (still classics and widely performed today), and others. He came up with a famous analysis of a play structure, Freytag's Pyramid, as shown in the following screenshot:

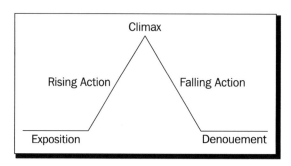

So, we have the basic points for our play's outline. Following is the definition of each:

- **Exposition**: During this initial part of the play, we put scenes needed for the audience to properly understand the story, such as the protagonist (good guy or gal), the antagonist (the baddie), the basic conflict (why they are at odds with each other), and the setting (where the story occurs).

   At the end of the exposition (end of Act I), we write the *inciting moment* that enables the story and sets it in motion.

   The inciting moment in a play is like the catalyst in a screenplay (which we met in *Chapter 7*). Something happens or some condition comes into being that sets the good guys and bad guys against each other and creates conflict.

- **Rising Action**: During the rising action, (first part of Act 2) the protagonist tries to reach his or her goal—a detective tries to solve a murder, a Romeo strives to win his Juliet, Professor Celtx attempts to sell the ghosts of William "Bad Billy" Shakespeare, and Oscar Wilde on the benefits of using Celtx for writing dramatic stage plays.

Secondary conflicts enter from adversaries of lesser importance, such as the ghost of John Wilkes Booth in An Evening with Professor Celtx. Booth, a stage actor, was known for interrupting plays, such as the night he greatly inconvenienced President Abraham Lincoln during a performance of Our American Cousin at Ford's Theater.

Act 2, in our plot, ends with everything going against the protagonist—dark times indeed.

♦ **Climax**: Act 3 begins with the climax where the protagonist, against all odds, turns things around and is on the way to winning or (in a tragedy) losing. Bad Billy Shakespeare kills off Romeo and Juliet in the end, something Professor Celtx (humorously) exhorts him to correct by rewriting his old plays for modern times and tells him what program (Celtx, natch) to do it with. The climax is just that, the most exciting point in the play.

♦ **Falling Action**: From the point of climax at the beginning of Act 3, the action "falls" or slows down as the conflict is resolved by the protagonist winning or losing. The antagonist does not have to be human, it can be nature or a state of mind (the hero fights falling into insanity).

♦ **Dénouement, resolution, or catastrophe**: In the last scene of Act 3, we have some sort of resolution. The murderer is arrested, the boy kisses the girl as they stroll off stage to get married, Professor Celtx beams as Bad Billy Shakespeare (now in love with the power of Celtx), sits rewriting Romeo and Juliet using a laptop running Celtx's **Theatre** project, the hurricane blows the roof off the theater. Oh, wait, that last bit is weather, not plotting, still it's a good complication to keep in mind.

That's our start to how plotting is done. Read more about Freytag's Pyramid and the many elaborations on it since the 19th century, but this structure will really help in outlining a play.

The Outline in Celtx

At the beginning of every outline, I suggest that you include some thumbnail bios of your characters, as I demonstrated in *Chapter 7*, when we looked at outlining screenplays.

The more you know about the people in the play up front, the easier you'll find writing the play, and the characters will respond in believable ways for you (see the following screenshot).

After the characters are defined, include a paragraph or so about the setting of the play. Give the set and costume designers enough hints, so that they know what sort of furniture and background to supply and what sort of clothes the actors will need but don't do their design work for them.

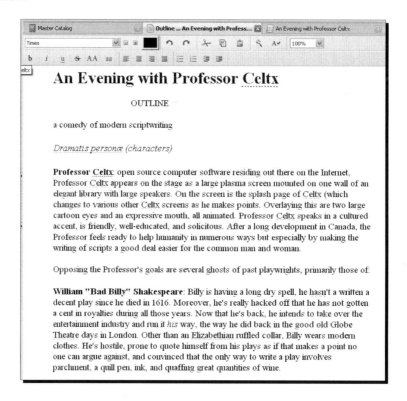

Now that we understand plotting a play and outlining it, and have our characters and setting, it's show time! The time has come for us to begin writing the play using Celtx.

Play elements

Go to the stage play script we created earlier. You'll find it in the **Project Library** window. Just double-click on the name and the script opens in the main script window of the Celtx screen, as shown in the following screenshot:

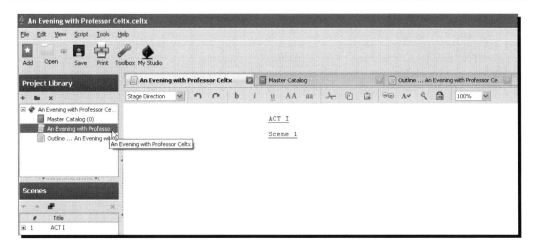

Like all scripts in Celtx, we have the proper script elements to format our stage play. These are **Act**, **Scene**, **Stage Direction**, **Character**, **Dialog**, **Parenthetical**, and **Transition**. As in other types of Celtx projects, they are found in the drop-down menu at the top of the main script window, as shown in the following screenshot:

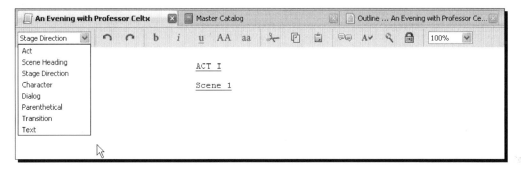

Unlike my example of formatting a screenplay in *Chapter 7*, where I used the **Text** element for the **FADE IN:** and **FADE OUT:** (beginning and end), we will not find a use for **Text** inside a play script. Ignore it, if you will, and following is how the other seven come into (pun as ever, intended) play.

Again (as I have in the two previous chapters), let me emphasize that every line in the script must be in one of these elements. We tag all components of the script in this manner, so that Celtx knows how to format it. Celtx, of course, is always proactive in assisting you to choose the right element. For example, type a character's name in the **Character** element and hit the *Enter* key and the next line will already be in **Dialog** for you.

To tag a line with a script element, click on the script at the place you want to tag, which creates an I-beam cursor at the place of insertion, and then choose the element from the drop-down menu. I'll show you examples of doing this, as we will now discuss each of these seven active play formatting elements (**Text** not being used).

Act

The **Act** element shows the main divisions of a play. A new **Theatre** project script (or if you use the blue **Add** button to insert one in any type of project) already has Act I in place. Note that inserting the I-beam cursor (the line in front of the A in Act I) causes the drop-down menu box (left top) to show the name of the script element, as shown in the following screenshot (it's that simple):

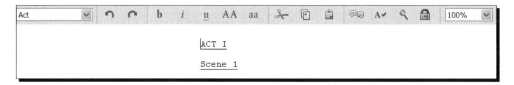

Most plays have three acts. If the play you're writing is a one-act play, just delete the Act I line and start with Scene I.

To create a new act, such as Act II or Act 2 (either Roman or Arabic numbering is okay, just use the same format throughout), click to get the I-beam where you want the act title to be, choose **Act** from the drop-down script elements menu, then type it in. Celtx automatically puts it in ALL CAPS and underlines.

Scene heading

A new scene heading is created the same way as Act except, naturally, we choose the **Scene Heading** script element, as shown in the following screenshot:

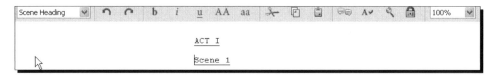

Each time we add a new scene, Celtx automatically includes it in the **Scenes** box (on the Celtx screen's lower left under the **Project Library**). As we've already learned, the **Scenes** box lets you navigate the script by clicking on a scene. To go to that scene in the script window, delete unwanted scenes, or move entire scenes around by just dragging the scene name in the **Scenes** box. Powerful and convenient, that's our friend, Professor Celtx.

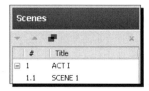

Stage direction

The **Stage Direction** script element allows us to give directions. The following screenshot shows the sample script included with Celtx that we met earlier in this chapter, The Importance of Being Earnest. The set of stage directions under Scene 1 includes such features as embedded notes (covered in *Chapter 2*) and other goodies.

Some play script formats, by the way, have all the stage directions inside parentheses. You can do that if you like, it's optional.

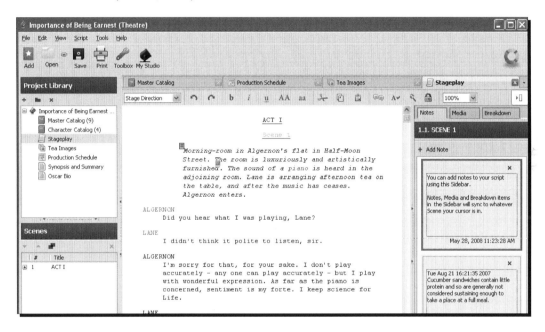

Let me emphasize again, as stated earlier, stage directions are only to give hints to the director, set designers, and so forth. The audience does not see them, only the results that come from the various interpretations by professionals of your hints. Don't try to do it all. Unless, of course, you will also be designing the set, sewing the costumes, directing, and maybe even acting a part or two. If you are, Celtx can handle the planning for all that as well.

Character

The **Character** script element is simply for adding the name of the character who is speaking and formats, in ALL CAPS, even if we type it in lower case. This is shown in the following screenshot:

```
ALGERNON
       Why is it that at a bachelor's establishment the
       servants invariably drink the champagne? I ask merely
       for information.

LANE
       I attribute it to the superior quality of the wine,
       sir. I have often observed that in married households
       the champagne is rarely of a first-rate brand.

ALGERNON
       Good heavens! Is marriage so demoralizing as that?
```

Dialog

The **Dialog** script element shows what a character says, as shown in the preceding screenshot.

Parenthetical

The **Parenthetical** script element allows us to add a direction at the beginning or in the middle of dialog, like in Oscar's speech shown in the following screenshot. As we learned in writing screenplays, it should be used sparingly.

```
                           Scene 1

         In the library. The screen showing Professor Celtx
         is currently still, the eyes unmoving.

         Bad Billy Shakespeare and Oscar Wilde enter,
         looking around, faces puzzled and awed at modern
         conveniences.

BAD BILLY
       But soft! What light yonder breaks? What wonder torches
       so cool and with no flicker.

OSCAR
       It's called electricity, Bill. Had it in my day but
       they seemed to have refined it.
                (he looks up at the screen)
       Taste in art has not held true, though. That is no
       picture of Dorian Gray.

         Professor Celtx rolls his eyes on the screen.
```

Transition

The **Transition** script element is used to show changes between scenes or acts. Two of the more common ones are BLACKOUT (lights dim or even go out briefly) and CURTAIN (the curtain closes and reopens). As shown in the following screenshot, when using this element, Celtx puts the direction in ALL CAPS and right justifies it (puts it against the right margin):

```
    PROFESSOR CELTX
         About about time you two arrived. Playwrights? More
         like play-wrongs, I think.

             Bad Billy and Oscar both jump and look around for
             the source of the voice.

                                                        CURTAIN
```

Printing our play

Once our play is written, we want to send it out for formatting into a PDF file. We do this in all Celtx scripts by left clicking on the **Typeset/PDF** button at the bottom of the main script window, as shown in the following screenshot:

Our play is sent out on the Internet, formatted, and returned to us in a matter of seconds. Once more, this is very secure and the Celtx formatting servers do not keep a copy of your work. It's just a way of extending the power of Celtx for us.

At the top of the main script window is the **Format Options** button (see the following screenshot). We can choose the size of the paper (for the PDF, not your printer), the **International** or **American** formatting versions, show scene numbers (**Both, Left, Right, None**), and **Show Title Page & Cast** (which I'll explain in the next section, it's neato!).

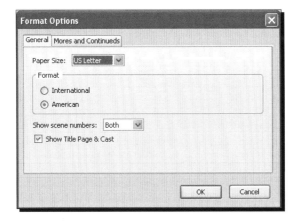

When formatted into a PDF, the American version play looks like the one shown in the following screenshot:

```
                           ACT I

                           Scene 1

                           In the library. The screen showing
                           Professor Celtx is currently still,
                           the eyes unmoving.

                           Bad Billy Shakespeare and Oscar
                           Wilde enter, looking around, faces
                           puzzled and awed at modern
                           conveniences.

                                BAD BILLY
                  But soft! What light yonder breaks? What wonder torches so
                  cool and with no flicker.

                                OSCAR WILDE
                  It's called electricity, Bill. Had it in my day but they
                  seemed to have refined it.
                                (he looks up at the screen)
                  Taste in art has not held true, though. That is no picture
                  of Dorian Gray.

                           Professor Celtx rolls his eyes on
                           the screen.
```

The international looks like the following:

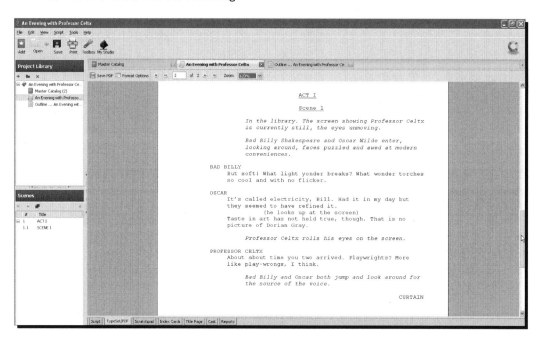

Tracking the cast

As shown in the preceding illustration, there is an extra button at the bottom of Celtx's main script window in a **Theatre** script, second from the right, **Cast**. The following screenshot shows what we get when we left click on it:

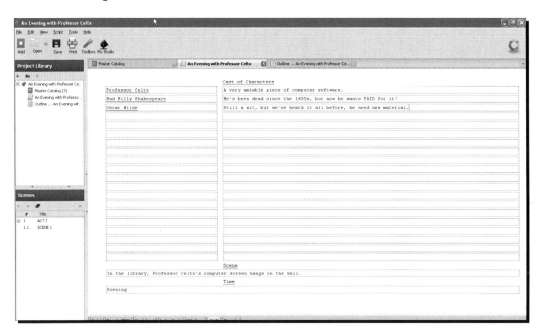

It's a cast list that you fill out and—if the **Show Title Page & Cast** option has been clicked in **Format Options** (as shown in the preceding section), a cast list is added just before the script and after the title page, which looks as follows:

```
                    Cast of Characters

Professor Celtx:              A very amiable piece of
                              computer software.

Bad Billy Shakespeare:        He's been dead since the
                              1600s, but now he wants PAID
                              for it!

Oscar Wilde:                  Still a wit, but we've heard
                              it all before, he needs new
                              material.
```

This feature should not be confused with the **Master Catalog** in the **Project Library** window, where Celtx automatically tracks all characters with a speaking part (and lets us manually add the bit players with nonspeaking roles).

1. How many acts make up a play?

    a. One

    b. Three

    c. Five

    d. Any of the above

2. What are the three main things you describe in writing a play?

    a. Characters, Audience Seating, Setting

    b. Characters, Setting, Stage Directions

    c. Characters, Setting, Number of Stagehands

Summary

In this chapter, we learned what dramatic stage plays are and how to outline them using Celtx's **Text** element. We started a Theatre Project and did the set up of the project container for our play. We also explored Celtx's script elements for a stage play—**Act**, **Scene**, **Stage Direction**, **Character**, **Dialog**, **Parenthetical**, and **Transition**. We then printed out our play and saw what the **Cast** button does.

Using what we've learned previously and the new material presented in this chapter, enables us to write exciting, professionally-formatted stage plays.

Next, listen up please, because we'll be talking about audio plays.

10
Audio Plays, Podcasts, and Other Great Sounds

Celtx's **Audio Play** *editor makes writing radio or other audio plays a breeze. It's perfect also for radio commercials or spots, and absolutely more than perfect for* **podcasts***. Podcasts are easy to write, require minimal knowledge to produce, and are a snap to put on the Internet. We will learn about writing all these audio forms and more in this chapter.*

In this chapter, we will cover the following:

◆ **Listen to this**: How to write scripts that sound fantastic with Celtx's **Audio Play** editor.

◆ **Audio play elements**: Scene Heading, Production Note, Character, Dialog, Parenthetical, Sound, Voice, Music—how to use, when to use.

This chapter, using what we've learned previously and the new material in this chapter, shows us how to turn out audio scripts that sound as good as they look.

Listen to this

Mostly, during the course of this book, we've been discussing visually oriented scripting. Yes, we write dialog but—in screenplays, AV (audio visual) presentations, and stage plays—we see our dialog performed as well as hear it.

The audio play script is different, it's meant only to be heard.

Sound, of course, is very important. In a video or film, the old cliché says that "sound is seventy percent of your video." An exaggeration? No, not when you consider its impact. In producing a video, we can often (and I have) get away with poor lighting and less-than-stellar content if we have good sound, including appropriate use of some stirring background music.

Why sound productions?

A *sound production* is one without a visual component. It is meant to be heard.

This chapter is all about sound. So, as a script writer/producer why is Celtx's audio play script of benefit?

Let's look at it this way. Here's my ranking of imaginative storytelling:

- Written (books, magazines, and so on): Tops the list because it's all happening in our head. The author shows us the story inside our brains! As a writer, if you want intelligent galaxies, no problem (and two of my published science fiction stories have featured these incredibly immense creatures). Any range of emotions, any exotic locality, and any character is only a few words away.
  - Pro: The only limit is the writer's imagination.
  - Con: We live in increasingly visually oriented societies, not nearly enough people read for entertainment anymore.

- Sound (radio plays, storytellers, "stand-up" and "sit-down" comedians, podcasts, and so on): By far the oldest method of telling stories, dating from those cave people in fire-lit caverns thousands of years ago lying their fur-clad butts off (fiction is making stuff up for the amusement of an audience). Pro: Today, technically the easiest to produce and distribute. You do not need printing presses, bookstores, video cameras, video editing software, or any of the other expensive stuff that written and visual media require. Just a microphone and a recorder. It's truly easy and free to put audio on the Internet for instant worldwide distribution. Con: You have to be able to talk... or at least to gesture well.

- Visual (movies, stage plays, audio visual productions, and so on): By now, perhaps the most popular. People like them (me, too) because all that hard imagining is done for you. We see everything in the story, it's visualized for us. Pro: potential for greater impact on more people. Con: really expensive and requires lots of people (collaborative effort) to do right.

The winner is sound! An audio play, a podcast, or any other aural (sound) production is least expensive to produce and a lot less difficult and time consuming than, say, writing a novel or shooting a movie costing millions of dollars.

Radio plays

Radio plays remain at the top of the heap of sound productions.

For a time—from the 1920s, when commercial radio broadcasting first started, until the 1950s, when television finally surpassed radio for fictional entertainment (excluding talk shows, of course)—radio was what the great majority of the public turned on in the evening.

Those of us in America have heard of and even listened to (recordings of those old shows are plentiful) some of these shows. The names are legend: Jack Benny, the Lone Ranger, Fibber McGee and Molly, the Green Hornet, the Shadow, and so on. I listen to a lot of those on satellite radio in my car—there's a channel that rebroadcasts these old shows 24/7.

Radio plays, new ones, are becoming popular again just because they are so easy to write and produce—especially with Celtx.

An example of a classic (and very famous radio script) is included with our Celtx installation. Let's open that as we look at the elements of writing scripts for sound productions.

This script is H.G. Wells' *War of the Worlds*. The radio adaptation was written by Orson Welles (no relation to H.G.) and first broadcast on October 30, 1938. It was so realistic that people tuning in late thought the program was an actual news show and that we really were being invaded by the Martians!

To open the script, left click on **Samples** on the Celtx Splash screen (shown when the program first opens). It's on the right, as shown in the following screenshot, on the same line as **Recent Projects**:

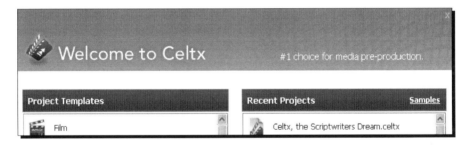

After we click on **Samples**, the **Recent Projects** window changes to the **Sample Projects** window. Go down the list to **War of the Worlds (Audio)** and again left click and the script sample will open in the script window of the main Celtx screen.

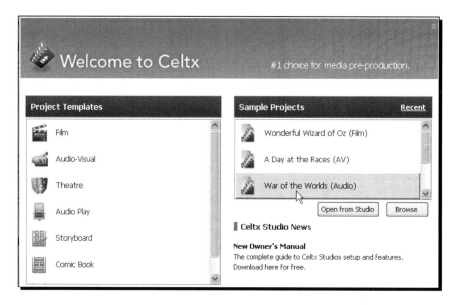

Once open, the *War of the Worlds* radio program script looks like the following:

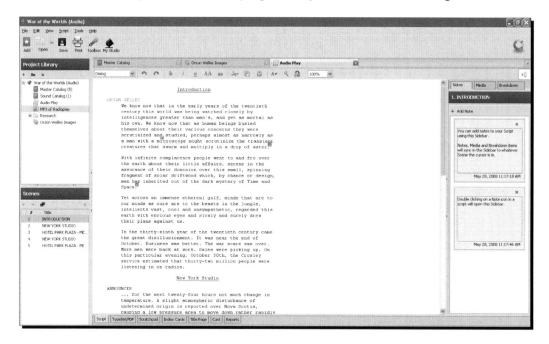

By the way, inside the **Project Library** in the *War of the Worlds* Celtx project container, there is an MP3 (audio) file of that 1938 broadcast. Most computers are already set up to where just double-clicking on the title will play the sound file. Items in the container that are not Celtx components (that is, the built-in script formats) will use whatever system components are available. That means media files like audio, video, or pictures will play or display if you have your system set up to do so (consult help files for your particular operating system).

Orson Welles was an extremely talented man. This radio show had tremendous impact and is replayed every year by perhaps hundreds of radio stations on Halloween.

Welles went on to produce many radio shows and quite a few movies. He is best known for two works, the radio adaptation of *War of the Worlds* and the film *Citizen Kane*—the latter of the two won him an Oscar and is thought of by many (myself included) to be the best movie ever made.

The same case can be put forward that *War of the Worlds* is, if not the best, certainly the radio program that's had the most impact over the past hundred years!

So, it's an excellent example to use in writing audio plays.

Welles used exactly the same script elements that Celtx gives us in its **Audio Play** script, and a description of them follows.

Time for action – setting up our audio play project

Okay, time now to prepare our own **Audio Play** project. We do it like we did in earlier chapters for **Film**, **Audio-Visual**, and **Theatre** project containers.

Again, the only difference between Celtx script projects (leaving out **Storyboard**, which is different) is the type of initial script appearing as default.

We could, for example, open a **Film** project, delete the **Screenplay** in **Project Library**, and use that big blue **Add** button to put in an **Audio Play** script and have exactly the same thing.

It's just convenient to choose the type of project matching the initial script.

So to set up our Audio Play project, start Celtx and click on the Audio Play choice as shown in the following screenshot:

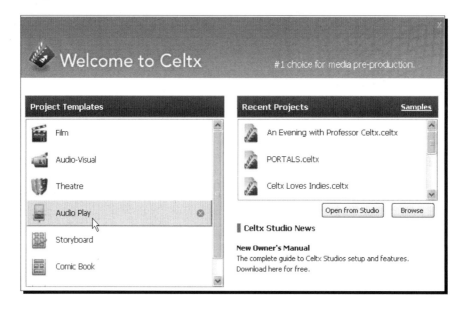

We get an untitled, empty project as follows with an **Audio Play** script linked to the **Project Library** and open in the main script window, ready for us to start writing.

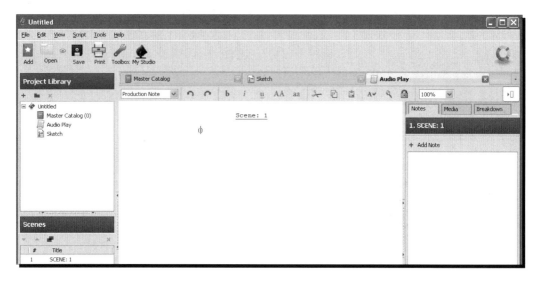

Before churning out the script, however, we'll want to save our project in a place easy to find again. I suggest making a separate directory for it, as shown in the following screenshot, for my audio podcast in progress, *Celtx, the Scriptwriters Dream*.

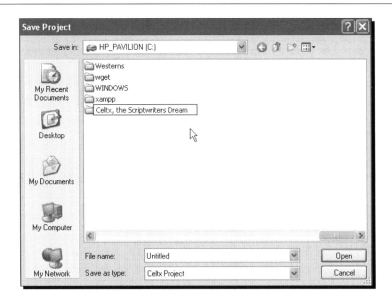

Go back to Celtx and use the **Save Project As…** (or the *Ctrl+Shift+S* key shortcut) to save our project under its title in the new directory.

We also right click on **Audio Play** in the **Project Library**, select **Rename…**, and change the title to that of our forthcoming audio play.

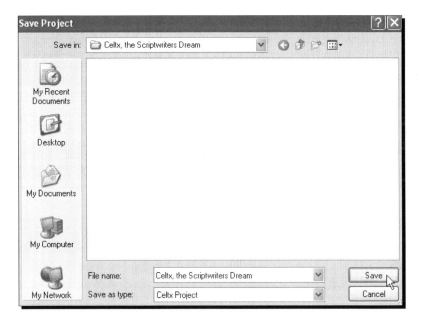

Now we're ready to learn the audio play script elements and start writing.

Audio play elements

A Celtx audio play script contains eight possible script elements: Scene Heading, Production Note, Character, Dialog, Parenthetical, Sound, Voice, and Music.

The drop-down menu at the top of the main **Audio Play** script window works just like those in the three previous scripts we've looked at—**Film**, **Audio-Visual**, and **Theatre** (in each of the three previous chapters respectively).

Scene heading: Umm, calling them scenes in a radio play might seem sort of counterintuitive (means "not logical, Spock"). By now, we've seen how scenes are used in movies, plays, and even audio-visual productions to describe and show action. Well, we do exactly that in writing a radio play scene, except all the action takes place inside the listener's head.

Radio plays as an art form are closer to short stories in scope and power of imagination than movies are.

 I'm a long-time writer and a few (okay, a lot of) years ago, I wrote in an article that "...writing lets you intimately touch strangers without getting slapped" since you are directly in their minds, running around and kick-starting their imaginations.

Later, I found this to be not completely true as you can get slapped—at least figuratively—by reviewers and readers pointing out a dumb mistake that got by you and your editors. Not me, of course, but other writers, eh?

Okay, so since we're working inside imaginations, the word scene fits quite nicely.

Scene names in radio scripts are usually minimal, often just numbered as in `Scene 1`, `Scene 2`, `Scene 3`, and so on. In the sample portion of the "War of the Worlds" radio play, simple sections or locations—like `Introduction` and `New York Studio`—are used.

To enter a scene name in Celtx's **Audio Play** script editor, use the drop-down menu of script elements as shown in the following screenshot, exactly as in every other type of Celtx script with the exception of **Comic Book** (coming up next chapter) which has pages.

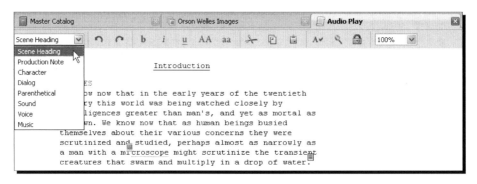

Unlike the other scripts we've worked with to this point (**Film**, **Audio-Visual**, and **Theatre**), scene names are not in ALL CAPS but upper and lower case, centered, and underlined.

Scene names do appear in the **Scenes** box under the **Project Library**, just as in all previous scripts. We can click on these scene titles in the **Scenes** box to navigate (to go), rearrange the order of scenes, or delete entire scenes as already shown several times in this book.

Welles labeled the next three scenes by location—New York Studio, Hotel Park Plaza - Meridian Room, and back to New York Studio.

The following screenshot shows the Introduction portion of the "War of the Worlds" script mentioned earlier:

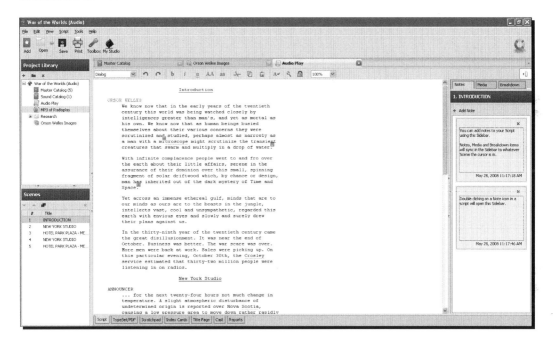

In this famous radio play, Orson Welles starts with an introduction as the first scene. Here he foreshadows that some evil is coming our way from Mars.

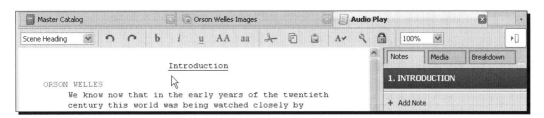

We get a weather report (shown in the following screenshot), just like normal radio, and move into a ballroom big band program (popular on 1930s radio) just like a regular broadcast schedule was being followed.

```
                        New York Studio

ANNOUNCER
        ... for the next twenty-four hours not much change in
        temperature. A slight atmospheric disturbance of
        undetermined origin is reported over Nova Scotia,
        causing a low pressure area to move down rather rapidly
        over the northeastern states, bringing a forecast of
        rain, accompanied by winds of light gale force. Maximum
        temperature 66; minimum 48.
```

Then, the scheduled program is interrupted by a special bulletin.

```
                        New York Studio

ANNOUNCER TWO
        Ladies and gentlemen, we interrupt our program of dance
        music to bring you a special bulletin from the
        Intercontinental Radio News.
```

So Welles is doing what we, as radio play writers want to do, messing with your mind and creating events in your imagination. If you tuned in late and missed the introduction, then you might think this an actual news broadcast (as thousands of people did in 1938), and panic.

Production note: A production note is just that, something we include to indicate equipment needed for the engineer or any other information. The **Production Note** script element formats in ALL CAPS and inside parentheses (). In the following example—my script-in-progress mentioned earlier, the podcast Celtx, the Scriptwriter's Dream—I show the equipment I'll be using. If you need sound effects, special music, or anything else, they are included in this listing as well.

Sound effects, by the way, are called *Foley art* and someone who specializes in sound effects is a Foley artist. The term comes from Jack Foley who—in 1927 as sound was becoming common for motion pictures—invented the concept. Foley art livens visual productions and, of course, is absolutely critical in radio plays. The crunch of footsteps, the clop of horses, gunshots—all these add to the rich tapestry of imagination radio plays invoke.

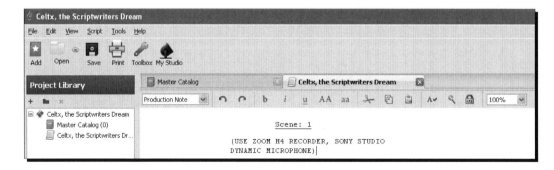

In the radio scripts I've seen—both classic and modern—production notes are perhaps the least used, but Celtx gives us that option.

Character: The **Character** script element looks much like the same element in our previous look at screenplays, audio-visual productions, and stage plays. It formats in ALL CAPS and, in an **Audio Play**, is placed against the left margin for you by Celtx:

The preceding example from *War of the Worlds* might cause those who already write a lot of audio scripts to question why no number appears to the left of the character name. Many modern audio scripts use numbering and I'll show you how to get that format later in this chapter. Celtx, as ever, has us covered.

Dialog: The preceding screenshot also shows how dialog is formatted in Celtx's **Audio Play**. While this example is more than four lines, again that rule applies only to screenplays for Hollywood (as detailed in *Chapter 7*). Your dialog can be any length you like. Especially in writing podcasts, it tends to be long. I do suggest starting new paragraphs occasionally for greater readability for whoever is voicing the dialog.

Parenthetical: The **Parenthetical** script element in **Audio Play** is used inside dialog to give the talent direction, as shown in the following screenshot. It formats in ALL CAPS inside parentheses ().

```
RANGER BOB
        You're joking, right Cap?
        (LAUGHS)
        Me go after those outlaws alone?
        (PAUSE)
        You're not joking, huh?
        (GROANS)
```

Sound: Sound effects are a very important tool in radio plays. Gunshots, footsteps, wind whistling, and more, all add to the atmosphere and action of the story. The following screenshot is an example of using the **Sound** script element. I've turned on numbering just to show what that style of formatting looks like:

```
4  SOUND: A HORSE CANTERING

5  RANGER BOB
        Sure is lonely out here in the desert.

6  SOUND: GUNSHOTS, THE HORSE GALLOPS

7  RANGER BOB
        Make for those big rocks, boy!
```

Voice: The **Voice** script element is not to be confused with **Dialog**. **Sound** (which we saw just above), **Voice**, and **Music** are all effects aiding in storytelling.

All three of these elements format the same way.

The use for **Voice** includes human speech, yelps, the other end of a phone conversation, or whatever that may require special processing. Examples would be a PA announcer announcing a bus now boarding (hollow, echoing sound), Indian war cries in the distance as they chase Ranger Bob with the intent of giving him a really close haircut, and so on.

These sounds, would most likely be recorded ahead of time and dropped in the proper spot during the reading of the script as would be most sound effects. In a script, the **Voice** script element looks like the following:

```
RANGER BOB
      Okay, boy, we're behind these rocks and I think we've
      lost the outlaws.

VOICE: WAR CRIES OF A SIZABLE INDIAN BAND, COMING CLOSER

RANGER BOB
      Ut oh. Time to call it a day!

SOUND: HORSE GALLOPING, GUNSHOTS

VOICE: INDIAN WAR CRIES CLOSER

RANGER BOB
      It don't get no worse than this.

SOUND: A LION'S ROAR, CLOSE AND LOUD

RANGER BOB
      A lion in a Western? Who's writing this crazy show?
```

Let me take this opportunity to emphasize again that we don't just type SOUND: or VOICE:. Use the drop-down menu, so that Celtx knows what the element is and formats it correctly. This is *really*, *really* important to do.

Music: Like the preceding two script elements, **Music** formats as shown in the following screenshot, in the *War of the Worlds* sample that comes with Celtx:

```
                        Hotel Park Plaza - Meridian Room

MUSIC: SPANISH THEME SONG ["NO MORE," A TANGO]... FADES

ANNOUNCER THREE
      Good evening, ladies and gentlemen. From the Meridian
      Room in the Park Plaza Hotel in New York City, we bring
      you the music of Ramón Raquello and his orchestra. With
      a touch of the Spanish, Ramón Raquello leads off with
      "La Cumparsita."

MUSIC: "LA CUMPARSITA" STARTS PLAYING, THEN QUICKLY FADES
OUT
```

That concludes how the eight script elements in **Audio Play** work. Using only these few formatting instructions, we can create and populate entire galaxies for science fiction shows, write exceptionally erudite (smart sounding) blogs, snappy radio commercials, or anything else that is performed as audio only. As has been said before, "it's the theater of the mind."

Now, as promised, here's how to get numbering in an **Audio Play**.

Time for action – numbering elements and creating a PDF

Orson Welles, late in his life, turned (like many aging stars) to doing television commercials. Most famously, the ones for a wine company in which he intoned, "We will sell no wine before its time." Were Welles still around today, he would probably be churning out new radio scripts and pontificating, "We will send out no script before it's made into a PDF." (He could make that sound good!)

Maybe not, but we still have to get our scripts, audio, and otherwise into a PDF to e-mail or print out.

As in the other script editors, click on the **TypeSet/PDF** button at the bottom of the main script window, as shown in the following screenshot:

Clicking on this button causes Celtx to send our script out on the Internet, format it, and return it as we have already seen several times (but it's still a powerful magic). However, we can make changes to the format, and Celtx automatically recreates the PDF.

One of those changes is numbering elements. At the top of the PDF window, click on **Format Options** and the **Format Options** dialog box appears, as shown in the following screenshot:

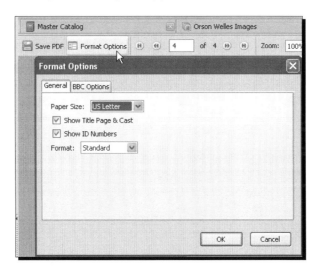

In this box, under the **General** tab, we can change the paper size, show title page and cast (I always turn these on as shown in the previous chapter on the **Theatre** script editor), show ID numbers (this is the one we want).

Check **Show ID Numbers** and we get the numbered format as shown in the following PDF I created of the sample from War of the Worlds:

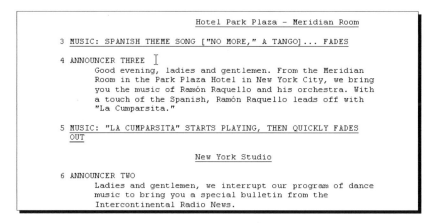

```
                          Hotel Park Plaza - Meridian Room

  3 MUSIC: SPANISH THEME SONG ["NO MORE," A TANGO]... FADES

  4 ANNOUNCER THREE
          Good evening, ladies and gentlemen. From the Meridian
          Room in the Park Plaza Hotel in New York City, we bring
          you the music of Ramón Raquello and his orchestra. With
          a touch of the Spanish, Ramón Raquello leads off with
          "La Cumparsita."

  5 MUSIC: "LA CUMPARSITA" STARTS PLAYING, THEN QUICKLY FADES
    OUT

                          New York Studio

  6 ANNOUNCER TWO
          Ladies and gentlemen, we interrupt our program of dance
          music to bring you a special bulletin from the
          Intercontinental Radio News.
```

BBC formatting

The **BBC** or **British Broadcasting Corporation** has long been arguably the best radio network in the world. The BBC is still a great market for audio scripts. They do, however, have certain requirements in formatting.

Time for action – using BBC formatting

In the **Format Options** dialog box, the final selection, **Format:** is a drop-down menu featuring two BBC formats, **BBC Cue** and **BBC Scene**, as shown in the following screenshot:

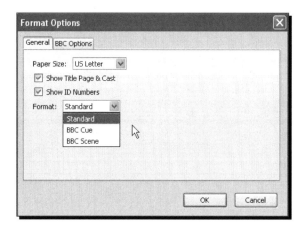

The BBC Cue looks like the following:

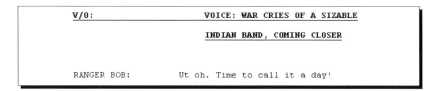

The BBC Scene is shown in the following screenshot:

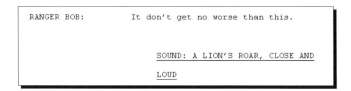

Finally, we have the **BBC** tab of the **Format Options** dialog box. Click on it and we get the following screen:

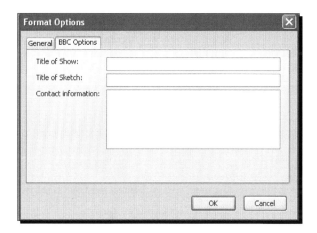

Fill out the preceding fields and that information is included in your audio script.

Have a go hero

The easiest audio production to write and produce is a podcast, as it can be simply anything you want to say. Podcasts are easy to edit (check out the free audio program on Windows and Linux, Audacity—it will do all that you need in editing and preparing podcasts for broadcast on the Internet).

So, hero, spread your wings, and write a podcast. Record the audio by reading your script (you can use Audacity and a USB microphone for that), maybe fancy it up a bit with a snippet of music introduction, and it's ready to be uploaded on the Internet. Google for podcast free hosting and you'll find somewhere to publish it. Let me hear you, hero!

Pop quiz

1. What is the easiest, cheapest type of production?

    a. A stage play with no sets and naked actors.

    b. Black and white film.

    c. Audio plays.

    d. A slide show of Uncle Mort's vacation.

2. The radio broadcast of Orson Welles' "War of the Worlds" on October 30, 1938 caused widespread panic because:

    a. People were a lot stupider back then.

    b. Those "spinning the dial" and tuning in late thought it was a real news show.

    c. Everyone knew the Martians were aggressive and likely to invade at any time.

    d. A meteor shower that night made people think UFOs were landing.

3. Celtx formats audio play scripts and other types of scripts:

    a. By using Adobe Acrobat which must be installed on your computer.

    b. Through a third party open source PDF creation software on the local network.

    c. With a powerful but large module that is installed on your computer as part of Celtx.

    d. By sending the script out on the Internet to a server where it is quickly formatted and returned to Celtx, saving on the use of your computer's resources (memory and disk space), and making Celtx a lot smaller and less complex than it would otherwise need to be.

Summary

In this chapter, we learned how to write scripts that sound fantastic with Celtx's **Audio Play** editor. We also became familiar with the script elements for audio scripts: **Scene Heading**, **Production Note**, **Character**, **Dialog**, **Parenthetical**, **Sound**, **Voice**, and **Music**.

This chapter, using what we've learned previously and the new material in this chapter, showed us how to turn out audio scripts that sound as good as they look.

Now, it's comic book time!

11

WAP! POW! BANG! Writing Comic Books with a Punch

Comic books, graphic novels, comic strips, and so on are modes of widely popular method of storytelling.

We, comic fans, know that writing for comic books is very close to writing for the movies. In fact, for a writer, marketing scripts for the comics is easier and has less competition than trying to sell a script.

In this chapter, the following topics will be covered:

- **Banging out a Comic Book script**: How to write scripts with Celtx's **Comic Book** editor.

- **Comic Book elements**: Page, Panel, Caption, Character, Balloon Type, Balloon—how to use, when to use.

- **Navigating, deleting, and reordering pages**: How to move around, delete, or reorder pages.

Using what you've learned previously and the new material in this chapter will show you how to write comic book scripts with a BANG!

Graphic storytelling

Okay, I've written just about everything in the world in my career except comic books—although now that I see how easy it is using Celtx, you can bet I will be. However, I've churned out extensive words about comic books over the years, writing for such publications as *Comic Buyers Guide*. What's more—and here's the real brag—something not many folks can say, I've actually been a comic book character!

It happened back in 1982. I had a young friend who was trying to break into comics as an artist. Butch was very good and I, along with everyone else, encouraged him. Well, he made it and (as Jackson Guice) is still making it big time. He was kind enough to include the comics shop owner—my late friend, D.W. "Doc" Howard—and myself as Dire Wraiths in *Rom Annual* #1 (1982).

My comic character had a short career but, although banished to another dimension, could come back some day. That's me in the middle below. I smoked a pipe then but quit in 1988 and have not smoked since—cuts into writing time too much.

What are comics?

A comic (to define the form) is a series of static pictures laid out to tell a story with more art than words, although dialog and captions play an important part.

The name "comic" referring to graphic storytelling comes from the fact that most early works in this media were humorous. Comics today cover a wide range from horror, super heroes, mystery, supernatural, science fiction, fantasy, and so on to, yes, some really hilarious stories.

Earlier examples of the comic storytelling form are noted by academics, but graphic storytelling as we know (and love) it today really started in the nineteenth century. A good example of its birth is the early cartoons in magazines, such as the British humor publication, Punch.

Meant primarily to amuse, unlike the earlier political cartoons which were mostly satire, by the 1860s they were moving beyond single panel cartoons into *comic strips* (a series of related panels in a row that told a story).

In the 1890s, Richard F. Outcault developed *The Yellow Kid*, the first recurring character in a comic strip. The *Yellow Kid* was very popular and helped build comic readership in papers.

By the 1920s, publishers were printing "books" (cheap pulp concoctions) that featured longer strips filling entire pages to tell stories and the comic book was born. The 1930s and 40s are referred to as the "Golden Age" of comics and introduced characters still widely popular today—super heroes such as Superman, Batman, Wonder Woman, Captain America, and funnier characters, such as Archie, Donald Duck (with nephews Huey, Dewey, and Louie), and Donald's money bin filling Uncle Scrooge.

Today, the rich legacy of comics has developed into a highly-popular, worldwide industry of increasingly sophisticated graphic novels and the like.

For the comic book writer (that's us, thanks to Celtx's Comic Book editor), there is a strong market for good comic book scripts. The following websites are two good starting points on the web for learning about writing and selling comic book scripts:

```
http://www.superheronation.com/
```

```
http://www.hoboes.com/Comics/Creators/
```

Time for action – opening the sample comic book script

Celtx comes with a sample comic book script. Let's open it up and take a look. To get to the sample material, start Celtx, and click on Samples, as shown in the following screenshot. See, I've included my finger pressing the **Samples** button to show you how it's done, or you might have better luck left clicking on it with your mouse cursor:

Wait, is that an advertisement above? Yes, just to remind ourselves here, Celtx is connected to the Internet, so the company which develops Celtx adds messages there, usually about availability of add-ons or special offers. This is how they support themselves while keeping Celtx itself free for our use—a small enough favor which I, for one, do not mind granting.

After we left click on the **Samples** button, the **Sample Projects** menu appears, as shown in the following screenshot. Scroll down and left click on the last selection, **The Mechanical Shakespeare (Comic)**.

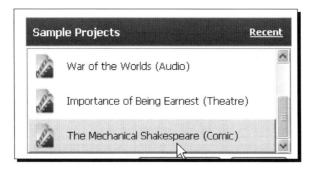

This brings up a **Comic Book** project container with the script open in the main script window. Looking in the **Project Library** window (shown in the following screenshot), we see some other items there as well, such as **Research Images**, **Page 1(final)**, and **Page 2 (final)**. Again, a Celtx project container can hold and organize literally thousands of items for us.

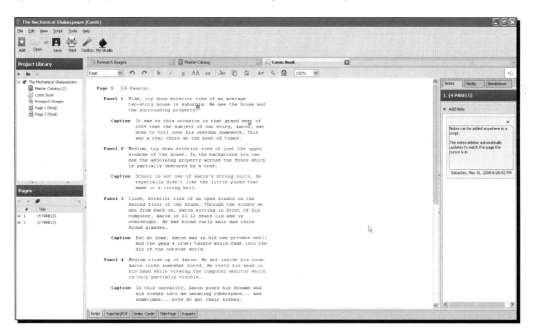

Now most types of scripts in the edit format like above, that we've seen so far, look reasonably close to the final printed version—except, of course, the audio-visual project, which has lines around it and a vertical divider put in place when the **Typeset/PDF** is used and it's sent out on the Internet and returned as a PDF. Comic scripts also get lines after they are converted into PDF, as shown in the following screenshot (this being the sample comic script we just opened):

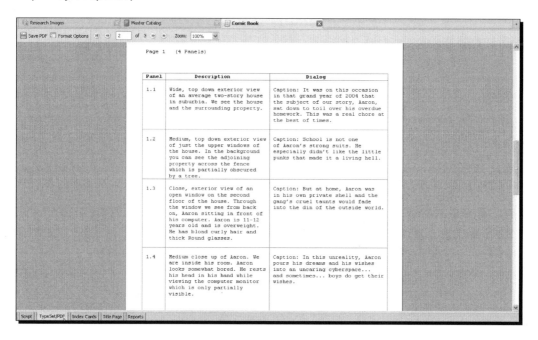

All of the above, by the way, is one page in the comic book—four panels, each panel being one of those cartoons strung together in sequence to tell a story.

Now, let's create our own comic book script.

Time for action – creating a Celtx comic book container

Okay, time to create our own Celtx comic book project container. We first make a directory on our computer to hold it.

In my case, I'm thinking about writing a comic book featuring that mighty superhero, Celtxman! By day a mild-mannered computer book writer, by night a lightning fast scripter able to leap tall metaphors in a single bound, fighter of grammar and spelling mangling gremlins, champion of scriptwriters everywhere! Celtxman, our hero. Anyway, I've created a Celtxman directory, as shown in the following screenshot:

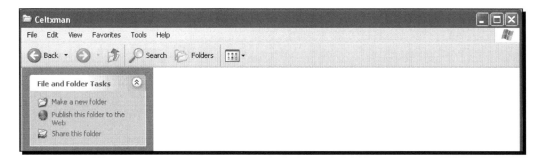

Now, we open Celtx again (and a reminder, you do not have to close the instance of Celtx we already have open with the sample comic book project, more than one at a time runs nicely).

On the Splash screen (shown in the following screenshot), left click on **Comic Book** to open that type of project:

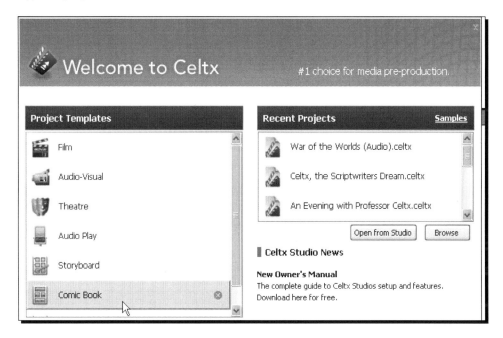

We get a new empty project ready for use with a new **Comic Book** script included and open for business, as shown in the following screenshot:

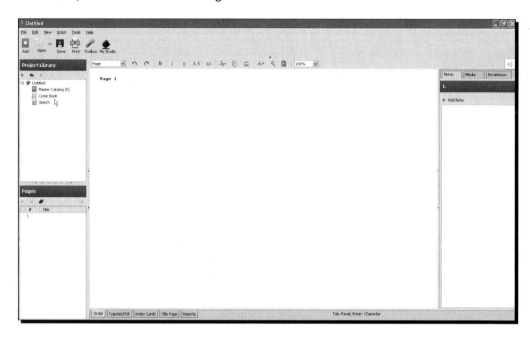

Next, let's rename the generic script. Right click on **Comic Book** in the **Project Library**, and in the **Rename Item** dialog box that pops up type in the name of your script as I have mine in the following screenshot:

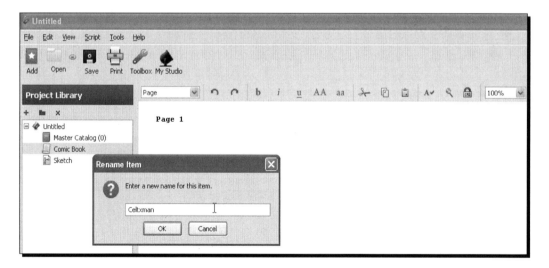

Remove the **Sketch** object for now by left clicking to select it, then left clicking on the small **x** beneath the words **Project Library** to delete it. Now left click on **File** and then on **Save Project As…**, enter the title of your script in the **File name:** box, making sure you're in the directory we just created. Left click on the **Save** button, as shown in the following screenshot:

It may seem a trifle obsessive to go through this setup procedure, as I have in the last four chapters for each type of script. It is not. I serve as computer guru to a number of other writers, some longtime, seasoned pros (like the old grizzly bear here). The single biggest failing a lot of them have is poor organization of files on their hard disk. They spend an inordinate amount of time calling me to help them find a lost project they wrote only yesterday.

Get in the habit of starting a Celtx project like we've been doing, naming it something logical, and putting it in a place you can easily find tomorrow, next week, four years from now.

You'll thank me, and I won't have to charge you for calling me and interrupting my writing.

Time for action – building the title page

As I've suggested in other projects, take the time now to build a title page. It will make you feel good to have it and seems, to me, to give a little kickstart to the creative process of actually committing script to paper.

Open the title page form by left clicking on the **Title Page** button at the bottom of the main script window, as shown in the following screenshot:

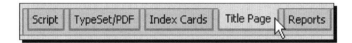

Fill out the form with title, author(s) name(s), copyright notice, and contact information. Remember what I told you earlier: Use a letter c in parentheses or (c) to indicate copyright (as shown in the following screenshot). Do not use the *Alt+0169* key combination, which gives a regular copyright symbol ©, as that symbol, due to a glitch in Celtx's online formatting, is returned as a garbage character. Until that's fixed, use the preceding workaround.

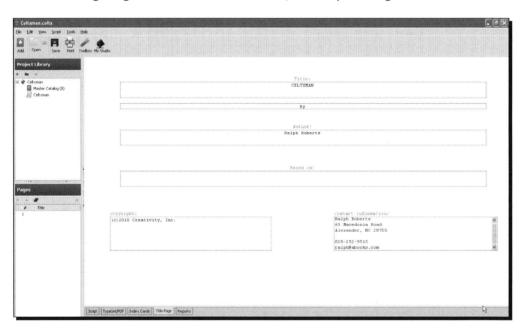

Typeset your title page to make sure it looks okay (convert it to PDF) by left clicking on the **Typeset/PDF** button at the bottom of the main script window, as shown in the following screenshot:

Okay, looking at the following screenshot, I see no typos on mine:

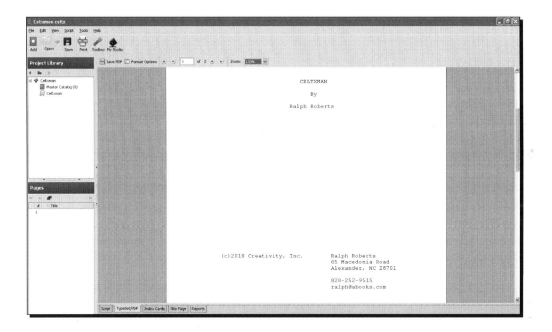

While we're on the PDF screen, left click on the **Format Options** button at the top of the main window, as shown in the following screenshot. Unlike the other script editors where we've found several options, here we have paper size (that's the paper size of the PDF, not your local printer although both can be the same), and a check box to turn the title page on and off (print one or not). I suggest including a title page.

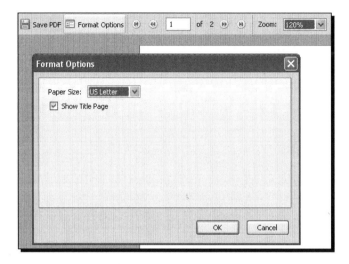

Okay, now let's explore Celtx's script elements for writing comic books.

Comic book elements

The comic book editor in Celtx only has six script elements—Page, Panel, Caption, Character, Balloon Type, Balloon.

We access each of these elements as in all the other Celtx scripts by using the drop-down menu at the top of the main script window, as shown in the following screenshot:

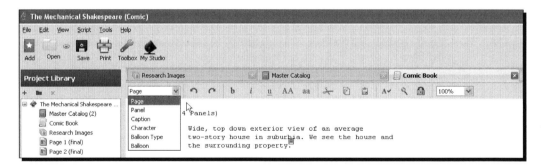

We also make sure that every line in the script is in a format, preferably the correct format for that element, so that Celtx can help us by properly formatting our finished scripts to industry standards.

Page

Okay, here we go, but where are we going? The following screenshot shows an empty comic book script under the editing bar at the top of the main script window. We're on the first page.

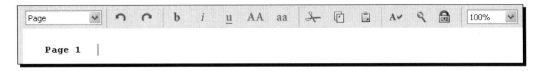

Well, there are two schools of thought on page descriptions. The sample script we've been looking at simply tells us how many panels exist on the page:

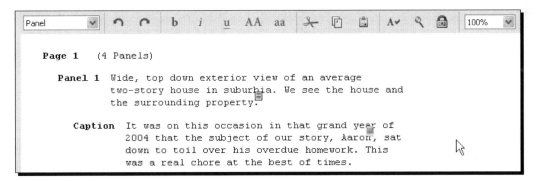

That method is kind of minimalist (like having no detail, dude).

A short description works a lot better, I believe. Remember, we're providing guidelines for the artist here. Don't make him guess too much, eh?

Providing directions works better:

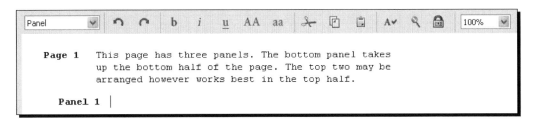

So, we write the description of Page 1 as shown in the preceding screenshot and Celtx helps us out by popping in Panel 1 with our I-beam cursor now positioned, ready for writing Panel 1.

Panel

We describe what's to be seen in the first panel, writing in the present tense just like doing screenplays, except here we can use "we". That is, use constructs like "we see." After all, this description is just for the artist.

Conciseness counts, as it does in writing screenplays. My panel description in the following screenshot could probably stand a bit of work, but let's get some more of the story in before rewriting.

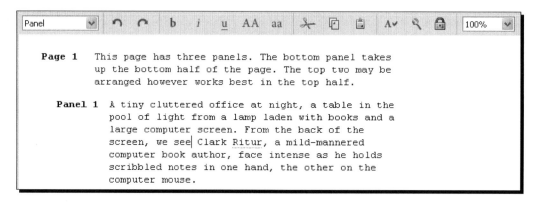

Yes! We've almost written our first panel, but it needs something else, something to help the reader better identify what's going on.

Caption

A caption, of course, helps the reader better identify what's going on and is a major part of this unique form of visual (in this case graphic) storytelling. So, we add a caption to the panel in progress, as shown in the following screenshot:

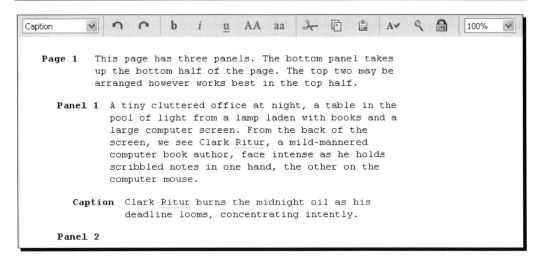

That helps!

What have we got so far? Let's convert it into PDF (use the **TypeSet/PDF** button).

The following screenshot shows the page description and the first panel the way it will look in the finished script:

Panel	Description	Dialog
	Page 1 This page has three panels. The bottom panel takes up the bottom half of the page. The top two may be arranged however works best in the top half.	
1.1	A tiny cluttered office at night, a table in the pool of light from a lamp laden with books and a large computer screen. From the back of the screen, we see Clark Ritur, a mild-mannered computer book author, face intense as he holds scribbled notes in one hand, the other on the computer mouse.	Caption: Clark Ritur burns the midnight oil as his deadline looms, concentrating intently.

Now we can move on to the second panel.

To start a new **Panel** from **Caption**, hit the *Enter* key twice or use the drop-down menu.

Character

The **Character** script element in the Celtx **Comic Book** editor works like in most scripts, that is, Celtx formats it centered and in ALL CAPS.

We add Clark as a **Character**, so he can speak and also so Celtx can put him in the **Master Catalog** as a character and track him.

All this is accomplished automatically the first time we type his or any other character's name in the **Character** format, as shown in the following screenshot:

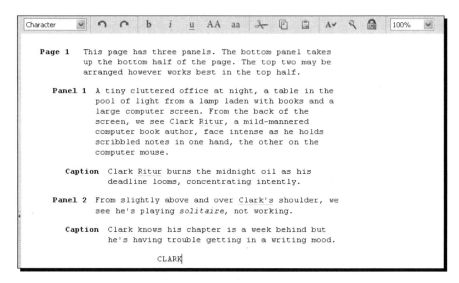

Balloon type

Use this element the same way you would a **Parenthetical** element in a **Film**, **Theatre**, or **Audio Play** project.

So, by using **Balloon Type** to put in (thinking) as shown in the following screenshot, I tell the artist to draw a balloon with circles below it in the classic "inside the character's head" speech balloon.

```
Panel 2  From slightly above and over Clark's shoulder, we
         see he's playing solitaire, not working.

Caption  Clark knows his chapter is a week behind but
         he's having trouble getting in a writing mood.

                         CLARK
                      (thinking)
                 Say, I wonder if Packt would let me do my next
                 book on Solitaire? It's darned complicated!
```

Balloon

Finally, in the sixth script elements in the comic book, is the **Balloon**. Now it's time for Clark to speak, and the **Balloon** script element is used for that. This element is really the same as the **Dialog** element in other scripts and looks the same while writing our comic book script:

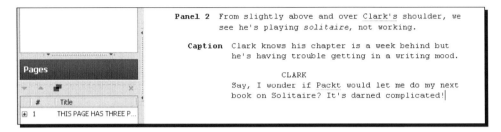

Navigating, deleting, and reordering pages

In a **Comic Book** project, we do not have the usual **Scenes** box under the **Project Library** but rather a **Pages** box. However, it works the same way, automatically tracking page names and letting us navigate quickly to them by just double clicking on the page description. We can also delete pages.

Left clicking on the little box with the plus sign in it next to a page number expands it to show the panels, which you can act on in the same way.

Now, a final thought on writing comic books scripts. Many comic writers find the comic format hard to use and use the screenwriting format instead. That's also a part of the power of Celtx—you can do what you need to do, not what the software says you must.

Pop quiz

1. How do scripts for comics differ from all the previous Celtx projects that we've learned?

    a. They are printed out differently

    b. You are describing artwork instead of action

    c. You must use two-dimensional characters

    d. Comic character dialog is not like actors speaking

2. The word 'panels' in comics refers to:

    a. The artists and writers who answer our questions at comic conventions

    b. A type of decorative wall covering that we can tape our scripts and drawings to

    c. The one or more drawings per comic page

    d. None of the above

Summary

In this chapter, we learned how to write scripts with Celtx's comic book editor. In doing so, we became familiar with the comic book script elements of Page, Panel, Caption, Character, Balloon Type, and Balloon, and when to use each of these. We also examined the techniques of navigating, deleting, and reordering pages.

This chapter, using what you've learned previously and the new material in this chapter, shows you how to write comic book scripts with a BANG!

This completes learning about Celtx, but I am adding a chapter next on how to market your scripts using, naturally, Celtx!

12
Marketing Your Scripts

Okay, your script is finished and polished, and looks and reads great. So, how do you sell it? This chapter gives you some of my hard-won secrets in marketing—how to inexpensively get the attention of agents, managers, producers, and others who will not only read your script but actually pay you money if they like it.

Here we are looking primarily at marketing spec (written on speculation) screenplays. If you turn out a great screenplay and a Hollywood producer buys it, you could get several hundred thousand dollars up front and perhaps a million or more if the script actually gets filmed. Kind of worth learning the rules for, eh?

In this chapter, we will cover the following topics:

- ◆ **Appearances are everything**: How your script looks is critical in every way!
- ◆ **Loglines and queries**: Get their attention but do it right.
- ◆ **Ways to get noticed**: Some methods of putting your work before a lot of people.
- ◆ **Places to get leads**: First you have to find 'em, then you can pitch 'em.
- ◆ **Be persistently persistent**: The only philosophy of marketing that actually works.
- ◆ **Marketing using Celtx**: How we can keep track of everything using Celtx.
- ◆ **Getting support from your fellow writers**: Online bulletin boards, film festivals, and so on.

This chapter gets you started with marketing and selling scripts, and if it doesn't make you more than the price of this book, you really shouldn't have accepted that first lowball offer, eh?

Appearances are everything!

The title of this section—as I've stressed numerous times in these pages—says it all. *Appearances are everything*! I kid you not on this.

No matter how great your writing may be, no matter how earthshaking the idea behind it, no matter how clever the action and dialog are, if it doesn't look right, they won't read it. ("They" being people like producers and agents who can cut those big checks to you.)

Celtx, our buddy, gives us a head start in turning out scripts that *look right* (that is, are correctly formatted for Hollywood and other markets). It's a big start, too.

Here's a dreadful secret: By far the majority of scripts churned out by would-be scriptwriters across the world have no chance of even being read by producers because they are improperly formatted.

As a judge in scriptwriting contests, I've seen many hundreds of these scripts that had wonderful concepts, riveting plots, fascinating characterization, but which also had a one-way ticket direct from envelope to an agent or producer's trashcan because of glaring format errors. All those hours upon hours of hard work murdered most foully by little bitty glitches so easy to cure.

Yes, Celtx helps you avoid these script-killer mistakes, but you still have to know and understand formatting.

The Screenwriter's Bible

For all those little formatting details, I recommend *The Screenwriter's Bible* by David Trottier. A massive 8.5 x 11 inch book with 386 pages, it is a "must have" reference. Search for it on Amazon.com. Right now, it's selling for just over $16.

What is a screenplay?

Basically, in the movie industry (feature films), there are just two types of scripts. We've discussed these already but let's review:

◆ The type this chapter is about, a speculative (called a "spec"). This is a script written on *speculation* (no upfront payment) or even invitation to write it. Usually, the plot and characters come directly from the imagination of the writer, although scripts are often also based on books (be sure you have the rights to do so!) or real people and events (rights apply here also).

◆ A commissioned screenplay (sometimes called a "shooting script") is one where the writer is hired to write the screenplay, usually from already developed material. In this type of script, you can include material, such as camera directions, that is frowned on in a spec script (okay, more than frowned on, they are the kiss of death for your script).

Spec scripts are important to us for two reasons. First, lightning can strike and big bucks could be thrown our way. Many aspiring screenwriters, however, use spec scripts to attract the attention of agents and producers (by showing how well they write). They hope, in this manner, to not necessarily sell the spec script but to get commissioned script work, which can pay incredibly well also.

It all comes down to format. You may be the rankest of amateurs in writing scripts, but if you market a properly formatted script with a good story, *you have a chance*. If it looks professional, agents and producers may very well—even if they've never heard of you—read your submission. I've been a professional writer for over thirty years. I learned early on that it's often more important to appear professional than to necessarily be professional.

Of course, you still have to back up that appearance with a really hot story, but it will get you through the door.

What Celtx does for us?

Back in the old typewriter days, formatting scripts was a major pain. Writers had to figure out how many spaces over from the left margin to put the character's name, how many spaces over to start the dialog, and other details that had to be done the same way, every single time.

Celtx takes care of that kind of monkey work for us!

All you have to remember is to use the script elements drop-down menu at the top of the main script window to properly tag the format desired, our choices being: scene headings, character names, dialog, action, and so forth. This lets Celtx know how to format the script. The following screenshot shows how the script elements menu looks in action:

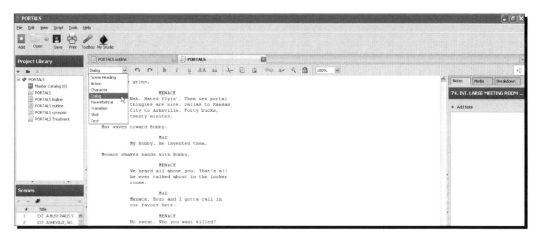

When the script is written, with all elements tagged, send it out on the Internet to be formatted by clicking on the **TypeSet/PDF** button at the bottom of the main script window, as shown in the following screenshot:

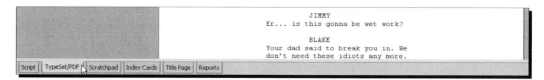

Celtx returns a perfectly formatted script, which meets movie industry standards and is ready for marketing, such as my script Portals, a snippet of which is shown in the following screenshot:

```
                                                           6.


                         BOBBY
                   Ah... be right back!

         He dashes to the closet, sidles through the door so that Max
         can't see inside, and pulls it shut.

         Max looks at Fred. Fred shrugs. The alarm clock cuts off.

                         FRED
                   Maybe he just wants to come out of
                   the closet.

         Max snorts.

                         MAX
                   Not Bobby. All the girls love him.

                         FRED
                   Bobby?

                         MAX
                   He just ain't figured it out yet.
```

However, sometimes we might have to give Celtx a little help.

Where Celtx needs help

There will be times where we need to format something not obviously covered in the drop-down script elements menu. We covered several of these in *Chapter 7, Writing Movies with Celtx*.

By the way, there is one more thing that needs to be beaten on here—the on-screen version of the script will typically differ (slightly) from the PDF (typeset) version of the script. Pagination, line breaks, and continueds often affect the typeset version of the script in ways the on-screen editor has no method of emulating.

Celtx, however, comes close to doing a perfect job of formatting for us, but there are times when it needs help. Here's an example. In Portals, I wanted to add a montage (brief, quick scenes showing a lot of history in a very short time) to show the rapid expansion of Galactic Transport. Thanks to *The Screenwriter's Bible*, finding how a montage was properly formatted was easy. Knowing what it looked like, I could then type it into Celtx, as shown in the following screenshot:

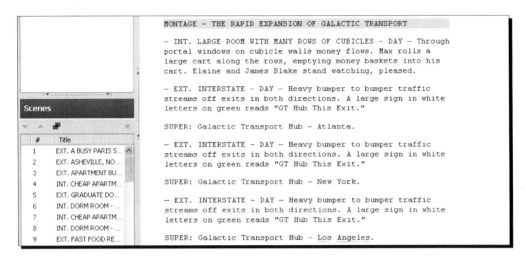

When sent out and turned into a PDF, it looks like the following:

```
MONTAGE - THE RAPID EXPANSION OF GALACTIC TRANSPORT

- INT. LARGE ROOM WITH MANY ROWS OF CUBICLES - DAY —
Through portal windows on cubicle walls money flows. Max
rolls a large cart along the rows, emptying money baskets
into his cart. Elaine and James Blake stand watching,
pleased.

- EXT. INTERSTATE - DAY — Heavy bumper to bumper traffic
streams off exits in both directions. A large sign in white
letters on green reads "GT Hub This Exit."

SUPER: Galactic Transport Hub - Atlanta.

- EXT. INTERSTATE - DAY — Heavy bumper to bumper traffic
streams off exits in both directions. A large sign in white
letters on green reads "GT Hub This Exit."

SUPER: Galactic Transport Hub - New York.

- EXT. INTERSTATE - DAY — Heavy bumper to bumper traffic
streams off exits in both directions. A large sign in white
letters on green reads "GT Hub This Exit."

SUPER: Galactic Transport Hub - Los Angeles.

- EXT. AUTOBAHN - DAY — Heavy bumper to bumper traffic
streams off exits in both directions. A large European-style
sign reads "GT Hub Dieser Ausgang."

SUPER: Galactic Transport Hub - Frankfurt, Germany.
```

So, we now have the correct formatting for a montage in the script.

To accomplish this was simple. I put MONTAGE – THE RAPID EXPANSION OF GALACTIC TRANSPORT in as **Scene Heading** (montages, despite showing a lot of different things, are considered to be one scene). Everything else is tagged as **Action**.

SUPER: means superimposition, which is simply placing a title on the screen.

This is why having a format reference guide handy is worth many, many times its cost. Celtx gets us almost there. A little extra effort on our part finishes the job. Why send out a 110-page screenplay that gets rejected because of a format error on only one page?

No reason to do that when Celtx has us so close!

Sending out a good-looking script!

Celtx creates PDF files for us, all nicely formatted and which can then be saved to our hard disks, as described several times earlier in this book.

More and more these days, agents and producers prefer PDFs be e-mailed to them. If you helped Celtx out on the few small things, as we just discussed earlier, that PDF will look very professional and so will you!

However, you'll still occasionally be asked for a paper or "hard" copy. We went over how to print and bind a script the "Hollywood" way in *Chapter 7*.

To recap (as shown in the following screenshot) print the script on one side of the paper only. You can either punch three holes (has to be three) or buy pre-punched sheets. You also need cardstock to make the front and back covers.

I make front covers by printing the title page on it. That's all they want, so *do not* put fancy graphics. Just the title, the by-line, (if it is based on another work add that), and your contact information.

Do not put the copyright or any registration information such as a WGA number. Just the above and nothing else, and you will look professional (because you will be professional).

Bind it with two brads (shown at the top of script in picture), putting them in the top and bottom holes, leaving the middle hole empty. On the backside of the script, place two washers (in the little box to the right). They are flat and have a slit instead of a round hole to fit down over the brads.

Use a small rubber hammer to flatten the brads against the washers, which tightly binds the script and looks, as already said (but it bears repeating), very professional.

You can get all these supplies and other neat scriptwriting stuff online at the Writers Store, http://www.writersstore.com

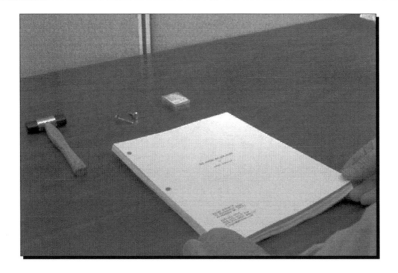

Don't get too funky with the color of the cardstock either. Use a muted, conservative color. I like a sort of beige myself. Burn their eyes out with International Orange or some other fluorescent color and they might not be able to read your script.

If all this sounds rather obsessive compulsive, it is. However, this is the way the business works. You want your writing to stand out, not the physical script—a garish or nonstandard script tends to be discarded because the readers rightly assume the writer does not know what he or she is doing.

Loglines and queries

Loglines and queries are how you market your screenplay.

Marketing a script means sending it out to people who might buy it or give you work because they like your style of writing. It means constantly researching and finding agents, managers, and producers who might be interested in your script.

A lot of other writers—me and a few hundred thousand more—are competing with you for those few high money sales. So, make that extra effort to get your work noticed and read.

As I've stressed in previous chapters, Celtx makes it easy for us to keep things relating to a script all in one place, the file that I call the "Celtx script container."

As shown in the following screenshot, in the **Project Library**, I have the script, its logline, outline, the synopsis, the treatment, and the query handy in one place:

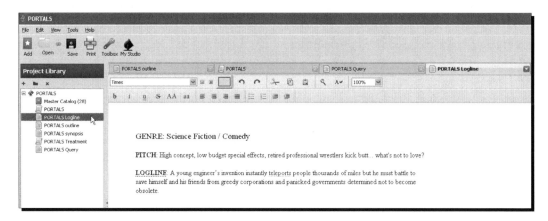

In my actual marketing file (this is just an example for the book) I keep correspondence relating to marketing (people sent to, responses, read requests, and so on). You can have literally thousands of documents in this one container if need be.

By the way, Portals is receiving good response and looks like I have gotten an agent because of the script.

However, you don't get to send your script out right away. Agents, producers, and others in the business do not want to see unsolicited scripts. Ever! Due to legal concerns, too little time in the day to deal with a waterfall of scripts coming in through mail, e-mail, and other good reasons (to them), you'd better not send the entire script until requested.

Instead, we send a logline (usually a one sentence description of the story; see the preceding illustration) and a query letter (or e-mail, most often e-mail these days).

The query letter should consist of the title, the genre (comedy, horror, thriller, romance, or whatever the main emphasis of the story is), the logline, a one or two paragraph synopsis of the story, and a paragraph about your qualifications, if any.

Should you not have any qualifications, it's no problem; just leave that paragraph out. However, most of us have something good we can say about ourselves, which shows we've had some good experience that might just show up in our script.

Yes, the logline and query—despite their shortness—can be (if done right, and they should be) a lot harder than writing the 110-page or whatever screenplay.

A spiffy logline

In *Chapter 7*, we saw how to construct loglines. This section is more about why we need great loglines.

Agents and producers receive sometimes hundreds of queries a day! If anyone at all looks at these queries it's a brief glance at the logline. If that logline does not grab them in the few seconds they spare you, they're on to the next logline, and you never hear from them. So, the logline we send better be good.

The logline is by far the most important sentence you'll ever write in a spec screenplay project. This is it! This is the brief instant of time we get to pitch our script. We *do not* want to blow it.

Don't worry about whether it is fair or not; the entertainment industry is what it is.

Loglines should be short, but not too short. I like to include what I call a pitch (some folks call them taglines) of seven or eight words. This is not a logline, it's more like something you'd see on a movie poster to entice you into the theatre or to buy or rent that film. I think it makes my logline stronger to have an enticer like that, but make up your own mind.

Okay, here's the difference. This is a pitch:

```
Aliens invade Earth and no one notices.
```

That's a nice teaser but it doesn't convey the story. The logline for this concept would be more like:

```
Aliens invade Earth and no one notices, which really irritates them, until
one small girl does and must convince her friends to help save humanity.
```

Now we have a story.

Danny Manus, in an article entitled "Good Loglines" at `http://virtualpitchfest.com` suggests that loglines should be twenty-five words or less ("...preferably less..."), be just one sentence, and have no more than two commas.

Blake Snyder in his book *Save the Cat* (again, highly recommended if you want to write screenplays that sell) shows us that a logline should contain the following elements:

Irony: It must be in some way ironic and emotionally involving — a dramatic situation that is like an itch you have to scratch.

- A compelling mental picture: It must bloom in your mind when you hear it. A whole movie must be implied, often including a time frame.
- Audience and cost: It must demarcate the tone, the target audience, and the sense of cost, so buyers will know if it can make a profit.

◆ A killer title: The one-two punch of a good logline must include a great title, one that "says what it is" and does so in a clever way.

Read *Save the Cat* for an explanation, but as you can see, writing a good logline takes real effort.

Using Danny's suggestion, I've pared the logline for Portals down to 25 words as follows:

An engineer's invention instantly teleports people thousands of miles but he must save himself and his friends from panicked governments determined not to become obsolete.

Now, I need to rewrite it and work in some of Blake's suggestions, although what I have so far is getting me read requests from agents and producers. However, always keep polishing your logline until your baby sells!

Here are three more loglines, these from well-known movies:

◆ **Titanic**: A young man and woman from different social classes fall in love aboard an ill-fated voyage at sea.

◆ **The Godfather**: An epic tale of a 1940s New York Mafia family and their struggle to protect their empire, as the leadership switches from the father to his youngest son.

◆ **Shakespeare in Love**: A comedic portrayal of a young and broke Shakespeare who falls in love with a woman, inspiring him to write "Romeo and Juliet."

Spend time on your logline. The logline is your foot in the door to get your script considered.

As we discussed in *Chapter 7*, doing a logline before you start writing the script is helpful. It spurs creativity, helps us get started on the outline, and is a measure of just how viable our story concept is.

Loglines can be used also to bounce your idea off other writers to make sure you're on the right track.

Getting help on your logline: One great place to get help on your logline (and query and screenplay itself) and to give help in return is DoneDealPro.com. This happens to be my favorite site for getting tips on producers, agents, and managers, and for running trial balloons up and seeing if anyone shoots them down.

The site offers a subscriber section (which is low cost and I think worth the money, and there's more about that later), but the forums are free!

To post loglines-in-progress and to comment on other folks' loglines, queries, and scripts, you have to be a registered member of the forums (which is, again, free). This protects your intellectual property by restricting viewing only to people who have registered and agreed not to abuse this service.

The following screenshot shows a part of the forum, just to give you an idea of its scope. There's a lot more on this site:

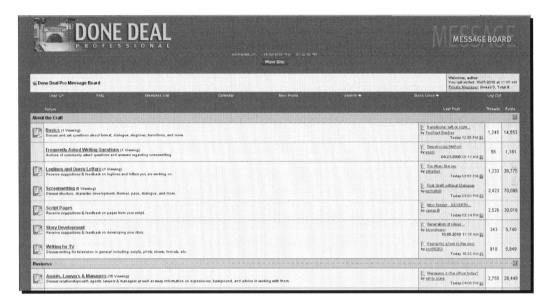

In the **Loglines and Query Letters** forum, you can post your work and get helpful comments on how to make it better.

As also mentioned in *Chapter 7*, if you're not sure of exactly how to structure a logline, a good starting point for this as well as writing synopses, treatments, and outlines is the *Writer's Development Kit* (by Karel Segers) from `http://celtx.com/learningTemplates.html`. It's only $2.89 and downloads directly into Celtx.

Okay, so we have a logline now that causes the reader to say "hmmm" and read on into the query e-mail or letter (most likely e-mail, but more about that later in this chapter). What should go into that query?

An interesting and informative query

We also covered query letters in *Chapter 7*. A quick reminder, query letters should be relatively short, tell the reader what the project is, its length, title, lay a snappy logline on them, a brief synopsis of the story, your qualifications, and your contact information.

The following is an example of the query I'm using for *The Berkeley Berserkers* (which is getting read requests also). This one is sent mostly through e-mail (and I'll show how to find addresses for that soon).

Recently completed 110-page feature screenplay:

TITLE: The Berkeley Berserkers

GENRE: Comedy

PITCH: 1,000-year-old defrosted Vikings play professional football THEIR way!

LOGLINE: Four 1,000-year-old defrosted Vikings have trouble following the rules of modern life much less professional football, yet the fate of the worst team in the league and an entire university's survival rests on their mighty but contrary shoulders.

SYNOPSIS: Dr. Millie Eriksdatter discovers four frozen Viking warriors in the Greenland icecap. Revived after 1,000 years, her university in Berkeley is at a loss what do with the Berserkers and then the government withdraws all funding, leaving the university in desperate shape. Millie's boyfriend — coach of the worst team in professional football — which is also flat broke, seems to provide the answer since his team will fold unless it gets a good running back who is unstoppable, two offensive linemen who can block trains and ENJOY it, and a placekicker who can kick a ball over the moon, threading the goal posts on its way back to Earth. Thorkell the Tall, Ari, Gorm, and Snorri — recently defrosted Vikings with amazing athletic ability fit the bill.

But... things are not that easy. Ex-Congressperson Gruber — scientific advisor to the president (and the one who cut off funding) intends to take the Vikings by any means (she needs them in order to move the research grants to her old university). The Vikings – being more used to raiding, looting, and killing the opposition than obeying rules — have trouble adapting. It all comes down to one final chance for everyone, one football game to win against impossible odds or else.

I would be delighted to send you the complete script either on paper or via PDF.

In my career to date, I have sold over 100 books to national publishers, thousands of articles and short stories, three previous screenplays to Hollywood producers and six options.

Thank you,

--Ralph Roberts

I add my mailing address, telephone numbers, and e-mail. The latter they already have, of course, but what if they print out the query and pass it around? I want them to have that e-mail address.

Also, I add my **IMDb (Internet Movie Database)** link. IMDb is the main reference source used in the movie industry. If you have any credits there, be sure to let them know. We'll have more to say shortly about how you can use IMDb in selling your scripts.

My IMDb page, for those interested, is at `http://www.imdb.me/ralphroberts`. Feel free to check me out.

The preceding query letter is just a suggestion, but it does contain the basics. Agents, managers, and producers (the three main classes of people we want to target our scripts to) are busy folk—so, even shorter than my example is good.

Remember that the end goal is to get them to request a read of your script (the Holy Grail, a *read request*). Realize, however, that the people who can do you good get perhaps thousands of queries submitted to them every single week of the year. Your goal is to, someway without looking stupid, make yours pop out from all the others!

Sound like impossible odds? Nope. Here's the good news. Seventy or eighty percent of those query submissions are so obviously unprofessional, they get rejected out of hand. Those queries are from kids or people who don't do their homework and send a long, rambling missive of a totally nonviable concept (something that won't make money or has already been done to death).

So, all you have to worry about is a few hundred pros or people smart enough to look like pros (like you and me). Thus, thanks to Celtx and all the other stuff you learn by immersing yourself in researching selling screenplays, you become a much bigger target for that wonderful strike of lightning when a Hollywood producer starts throwing money at you while gushing about your great script.

Experiment with several versions of queries, both long and short. The ones that are working are the ones that bring in read requests. The following is an example of a short one that has worked for me:

```
TITLE: The Farmer and the Alien

GENRE: Comedy, science fiction

Think Clint Eastwood in "Every Which Way But Loose."

Clyde is a robot.

An alien cons a Carolina mountain farmer into growing a fearsome crop he
must protect from corrupt government officials and invading alien fleets
IF the Earth itself is to be saved — but the alien done picked on the
WRONG farmer.

"Left turn, Clyde."

I would be delighted to send you the complete script.

In my career to date, I have sold over 100 books to national publishers,
thousands of articles and short stories, three previous screenplays to
Hollywood producers and six options.

Thank you,

--Ralph
```

A short and simple query that is funny if they're old enough to remember *Every Which Way But Loose*. (Some were.)

In the last paragraph, I have a few credits to mention. As we discussed earlier, you might think you don't but I bet you've got something.

If your script is about crime and you are a policeman or policewoman in real life, mention it. That adds credibility to the story.

If it's a courtroom drama and you are an attorney, that's good fodder for the credits paragraph, and so forth. We've all had life experiences that lend credence to our writing.

Which brings us back to the question, what does a query letter do? What's its real purpose?

Agents, producers, and managers really do not want to read scripts. Reading scripts all day can get old in a hurry. What they want is to read a *few good* scripts that will make them money! Your query letter must convince them, as realistically as possible, as close to the truth as possible, that this script will make them money.

That's what it's all about, and it can't be just your opinion either. You have to show these jaded film folk that you've written a winner.

As mentioned earlier, keeping your query (which probably will turn into several drafts and versions) in your Celtx container makes it a lot easier to find. It also lets you see and track your marketing efforts as a whole.

Here's my current query for Portals in the Celtx container. I've added a PRODUCTION BENEFITS line because this script really is a high concept (movie with some scope), but with low cost special effects. A doorway, a green screen, and some stock footage of places like Paris, Washington D.C., Asheville, and Seattle, and we've got movie magic! It does not hurt to point things like that out.

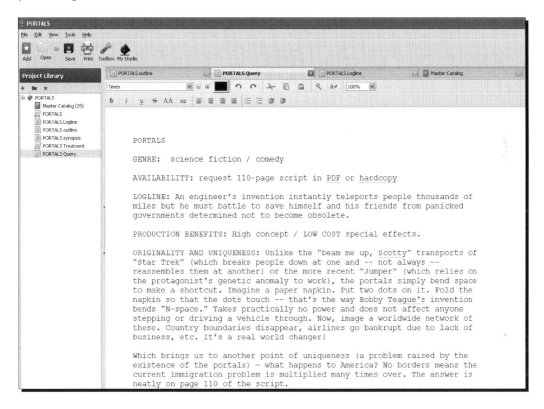

I'm sending the preceding query out with (in my opinion at least) the evocative e-mail title of PORTALS across oceans in a single step.

Your logline and the few other paragraphs in your queries are what will get attention and sell your script. Write, rewrite, and polish them until they sparkle. I keep honing mine.

Here are some articles I've found useful, where you can find out more about writing query letters on the Internet:

- "Query Letters" by Alex Epstein, author of *Crafty Screenwriting*: *Writing Movies That Get Made*—`http://www.craftyscreenwriting.com/query.html`

- "How To Submit Your Screenplay Query Letter To Agents" by Ashley Scott Meyers—`http://www.sellingyourscreenplay.com/screenwriting-faq/how-to-submit-your-screenplay-query-letter-to-agents/`

- "Writing Successful Query Letters" by Susan Kouguell—`http://www.writersstore.com/writing-successful-query-letters`

- "The Quest for a Winning Query Letter" also by Susan Kouguell, it's Chapter 5 of her book, *The Savvy Scriptwriter*—`http://bit.ly/a0wRkW` (takes you to Google's Inside the Book of Chapter 5. Buy the complete book on `Amazon.com`).

Some words about legalities. Agents, producers, and managers are much more worried about being sued than you should be about them stealing your idea.

The hundred thousand dollars or so a producer might pay you for a script is (to him or her) nothing compared to the millions they will spend on making the film. Besides, it is usually not their money anyway but rather that of investors or a studio. So they're not likely to stiff the writer.

What they do worry about (a lot) is being sued because they read a script similar to a movie they are currently making. When that movie comes out, someone screams "that was my idea, your read my script and stole it!"

So, most of the major studios and producers and agents have "no solicitation" policies, where they say they'll not even read queries. If you send a query to them, you'll get a nasty message back from their legal department confirming their policy.

Does that mean the majors do not look at queries? Nah, despite what they say, they're in the movie business. If it's really good, they request the script. Persistence pays—more about that later.

In general—in sending queries to agents, producers, and managers—you are thus giving them a legal opportunity to request and read your script in a manner that protects both sides.

Learn how to write good queries and send out bunches. In the *Places to get leads* section of this chapter that's coming up, I'll show you where to find regular mail addresses, e-mail addresses, and fax numbers.

First, there are ways of getting agents, et al, to notice you and request your script without you ever having sent them a query in the first place.

Ways to get noticed

If you want a jump start in marketing your script, that is, getting it out to as many qualified agents and producers as possible, preferably a thousand, a number of services on the Internet will do that for you, for pay.

There are basically two types of these (and the ones I mention here are ones I've used and had good results from).

First are the "mailers" who e-mail your query to hundreds or thousands of qualified markets and the read requests come directly to you, such as **Script Delivery** which is shown in the following screenshot:

I used this service last year for my script *The Farmer and the Alien* and got a pleasing number of read requests. If you do not want to accumulate your own lists, a service like this one is quite good because they have insider connections hard to find outside of Hollywood.

Then there are those like InkTip (the main webpage is shown in the following screenshot), which provide sites that have qualified members who are producers and agents. You (for a fee) can post your logline and other information about yourself and your script on the site and (in the case of InkTip) your entire script.

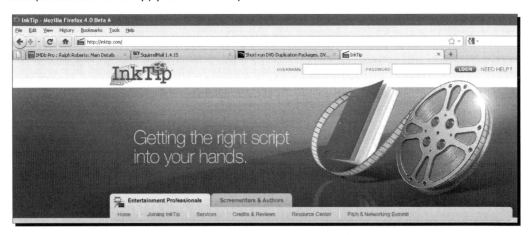

You can log in and see who looks at the logline and who actually reads the script. It's a good concept providing industry professionals a safe way to look at concepts, which have been vetted and are presented to them in a legally safe manner. I ran *The Berkeley Berserkers* on InkTip and it got a nice, long list of respectable professionals looking at it.

A third type of site, such as VirtualPitchFest.com shown in the following screenshot, allows you to pitch (present) your project in a more extensive and personal manner to major players in the entertainment industry. I have not used such a site yet, but I will probably give these guys a try soon. Read these sites for more details on how they work, costs, and so on:

Such sites as those just discussed, stress that they can get your query, script, or pitch before people you cannot on your own.

Other types of screenplay marketing websites offer *script doctoring* (suggestions on how to rewrite your script into a more marketable form), coverage (a qualified script reader who grades your script based on structure, characterization, grammar, theme, and so forth and gives a *Recommend* or *Pass*, which can then be touted to agents and producers), and other services for money, including even ghostwriting (someone writes a script based on your idea for you).

Google *screenplay marketing* to open up the world of these sites.

The drawback, of course, is that all these sites cost money. So, do your research and decide, based on your own marketing strategy and available budget.

Film festivals

Films festivals are good ways to promote your script. Disclosure: I am the Director of SkyFest. Read more about our film festival at `http://SkyFest.net` (see the following screenshot):

For a wide range of film festivals to enter, see `http://withoutaBox.com`

Film festivals usually cost from $20 to $50 to enter. Many take both films and scripts, and there are various screenplay-only contests. At SkyFest, we get more script entries than anything.

The benefits of competing in film festivals include awards, trophies, laurels (award graphics you can include in promoting your work, see the following screenshot), contacts with people in the industry, and a sense of accomplishment to keep you going. The latter can be really important—breaking into Hollywood is a long, hard, lonely road.

Places to get leads

Leads are simply names, addresses, phone numbers, fax numbers, and/or e-mails of agents, managers, producers, or anyone else who can help you sell your script. Thanks to that wonderful 24/7 research library in a case on our desktop or even our Smartphone— our Internet connection—we can Google or Bing or Yahoo or whatever and find literally thousands of addresses.

The best starting place (and fascinating entertainment about entertainment) is the Internet Movie Database (now in its 20th year) or IMDb.com. The following screenshot shows an example page, that of Charlie Chaplin:

IMDb has literally millions of pieces of information about practically every movie ever made and all the people who are in those movies, wrote them, directed, produced, designed sets, did stunts, composed the soundtracks, and so forth. More importantly to those of us trying to sell screenplays, you can also find current production companies, agents, managers—the leads we need to see out scripts!

While you can find all these companies and people in the free IMDb, to get their addresses and other information about them, such as the movies they've made, the budgets of those films, and much more, you must subscribe to IMDbPro, a for pay service. It is both reasonably cheap (I pay $15 per month and use it almost every day) and pretty much indispensible.

The following screenshot shows the top of my own IMDbPro page:

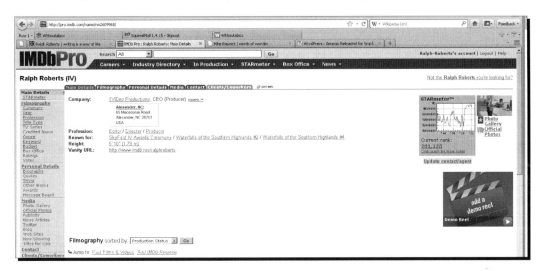

I like to think of IMDbPro as being the base of my lead-finding efforts.

Here's an example of how it works for me in finding leads. Find a good message board devoted to screenwriters. Let me give another shout out to http://donedealpro.com (their forums are free).

The following screenshot shows the subforum relating to the business of selling your work:

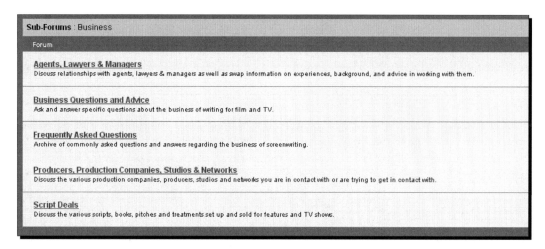

Reading the messages posted in these forums will give you all sorts of leads as people mention this agent or that production company. You'll find out who's looking at queries, which production companies are approachable—all sorts of valuable information.

What you won't get through casual reading are the addresses (e-mail or otherwise) to contact these agents, producers, and managers. That's where your IMDbPro subscription pays off. Search IMDb and find out more information about the agent or production company, including what they've done, what type of stuff they do, names of contacts, addresses, and e-mails (not always but some).

Getting leads to people who can do you good requires constant searching and detective work. However, it's rewarding (really big time if your script sells) and it costs you little but your time.

Places to get leads for money

There are also subscription databases on the Internet, where you can search and find the Big Three Categories—agents, managers, and producers. These databases provide some contact information (and you can get more through IMDbPro) and are usually inexpensive.

I belong to several and recommend two. The first is `DoneDealPro.com` (home of my favorite free forums as well).

The other is Writers Little Black Book, `http://writerslittleblackbook.com`

However, the preceding is only a start. Use the Internet to its full potential and you'll have no lack of places to send your queries.

Getting support from your fellow writers

You also do not need to be alone in the process of selling your scripts. Thousands of us out here are trying to do the exact same thing. So back once more to `DoneDealPro.com`. The free forums there and the others devoted to screenwriters on the web give you great scope for interaction with those of us who, just like you, scrabble around attempting to find that big sale!

To get, you must give. Where you can provide information or answer a question, post a message. By being helpful, you'll soon find yourself exchanging marketing tips and addresses with other board members. The following screenshot shows the one that I posted as an example:

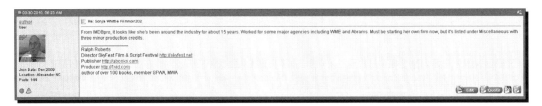

Time for action – marketing using Celtx files

Okay, back to Celtx. Marketing is where **Text** (called Novel from Celtx 2.9 on) really helps us out. As we've seen earlier, **Text** is an unformatted script—in essence, a standard word processor built into Celtx.

We add a **Text** object to the **Project Library** by clicking on the big blue **Add** button to the top left of the Celtx screen, selecting **Text** in the **Add Item...** dialog box, typing in the title we want, and clicking on **OK**, as shown in the following screenshot:

In my case here, I've made a Text document for the first version of my query letter for Portals (you'll go through numerous versions, I do), as you hone and polish the query.

Once the **Text** document is available, use it as you would Word or any other word processor.

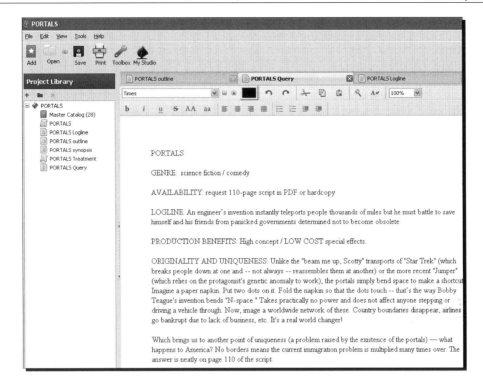

Whenever you find an e-mail address of an agent, producer, or manager to send the query to, just:

1. Left click on any in your query letter in Celtx.

2. Use the key combination *Ctrl+C* to copy.

3. Open your e-mail program.

4. Press *Ctrl+V* to paste into the e-mail body.

5. Add e-mail address, the subject line, and send.

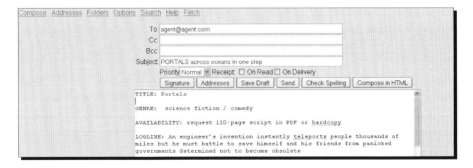

Remember also that you can have as many files as you like in a Celtx script container. So, use **Text** to create files to track the results of your queries, accumulate addresses, make notes about comments on your script, and so forth.

Be persistently persistent

Now we come to the final component of marketing your scripts and I can give you no greater gift than revealing this, the real secret of marketing.

Be persistent!

The word persistent means never give up, always keep trying. It is the only way you'll ever succeed and it is why so many people try and fail—they give up way too soon.

Immerse yourself in the business. Learn how it works. Use Celtx to your full advantage to both look professional and be professional.

However, above all, as the great British leader in World War II, Winston Churchill said, "Never give in. Never give in. Never, never, never, never—in nothing, great or small, large or petty—never give in, except to convictions of honor and good sense. ..."

As screenwriters, I believe we can ignore the "good sense" part, eh?

However, *never give up*. Keep writing! And I'll be watching your movie along with all those who kept telling you it would never happen. They were wrong! Make them buy their own darned popcorn.

Summary

In this chapter, we learned that appearances are everything! How your script looks is critical in all meanings of that work. Celtx helps by properly formatting scripts to industry standards.

We also saw that getting attention is important, and proper loglines and queries e-mails or letters do that.

I gave you a good start in finding places to get leads for producers, agents, and managers to pitch your great scripts to and showed you how persistence pays off.

Also, we delved into marketing using Celtx and how to get support from your fellow writers.

This chapter gets you started with selling scripts, and if it doesn't make you more than the price of this book, you really shouldn't have accepted that first offer, eh?

Conclusion

So, that's it. Thanks for reading my book.

All the best of luck in writing, producing, and selling scripts the Celtx way!

—Ralph Roberts

A

List of Recommended Books on Screenwriting and Productions and Online Resources

Here are some recommended books, which will help you continue to learn and grow as a screenwriter and/or movie professional. For more details about each book or to purchase, check them out on Amazon.com.

Screenwriting

*"Must have" books

Cinematic Storytelling: *The 100 Most Powerful Film Conventions Every Filmmaker Must Know* by Jennifer Van Sijll

Crafty Screenwriting: Writing Movies That Get Made by Alex Epstein

Horror Screenwriting: The Nature of Fear by Devin Watson

How Not to Write a Screenplay: 101 Common Mistakes Most Screenwriters Make by Denny Martin Flinn

*How to Write a Movie in 21 Days by Viki King

Mind Your Business: A Hollywood Literary Agent's Guide To Your Writing Career by Michele Wallerstein

Save the Cat! Goes to the Movies: The Screenwriter's Guide to Every Story Ever Told by Blake Snyder

*Save the Cat! Strikes Back: More Trouble for Screenwriters to Get into ... and Out of by Blake Snyder

*Save The Cat! The Last Book on Screenwriting You'll Ever Need by Blake Snyder

Screenplay: The Foundations of Screenwriting by Syd Field

Screenwriting for Teens: The 100 Principles of Screenwriting Every Budding Writer Must Know by Christina Hamlett

Story: Substance, Structure, Style and The Principles of Screenwriting by Robert McKee

The 101 Habits Of Highly Successful Screenwriters: Insider's Secrets from Hollywood's Top Writers by Karl Iglesias

The Coffee Break Screenwriter: Writing Your Script Ten Minutes at a Time by Pilar Alessandra

*The Screenwriter's Bible: A Complete Guide to Writing, Formatting, and Selling Your Script by David Trottier

The Screenwriter's Workbook (Revised Edition) by Syd Field

The Writer's Guide to Writing Your Screenplay: How to Write Great Screenplays for Movies and Television by Cynthia Whitcomb

*Your Screenplay Sucks!: 100 Ways to Make It Great by William M. Akers

Production

* = must have

Designing Movie Creatures and Characters: Behind the Scenes with the Movie Masters by Richard Rickitt

*Direct Your Own Damn Movie! (Your Own Damn Film School {Series}) by Lloyd Kaufman, Sara Antill, and Kurly Tlapoyawa

Film Editing: Great Cuts Every Filmmaker and Movie Lover Must Know by Gael Chandler

*How to Make a Movie With a Very, Very, Low Budget by Michael P. Connelly

*Make Your Own Damn Movie!: Secrets of a Renegade Director by Lloyd Kaufman

Master Shots: 100 Advanced Camera Techniques to Get an Expensive Look on Your Low-Budget Movie by Christopher Kenworthy

The Complete Film Production Handbook, Third Edition by Eve Light Honthaner

The DV Rebel's Guide: An All-Digital Approach to Making Killer Action Movies on the Cheap by Stu Maschwitz

The Independent Film Producer's Survival Guide: A Business and Legal Sourcebook (Omnibus Press) by J. Gunnar Erickson, Mark Halloran, and Harris Tulchin

The Pocket Lawyer for Filmmakers: A Legal Toolkit for Independent Producers by Thomas A. Crowell

The Production Assistant's Pocket Handbook by Caleb Clark

What They Don't Teach You at Film School: 161 Strategies For Making Your Own Movies No Matter What by Camille Landau and Tiare White

Who Needs Hollywood: The Amazing Story of a Small Time Filmmaker who Writes the Screenplay, Raises the Production Budget, Directs, and Distributes the #3 Movie of the Year by Joe Camp

Online resources

The following is a list of some useful online resources:

- `http://1vid.com/`: Ralph's video production company's website.
- `http://www.blakesnyder.com/`: Home of the Save the Cat books and software; lots of good information on writing screenplays that sell.
- `http://celtx.com`: Home of Celtx. Lots of information, good forums.
- `http://donedealpro.com`: Ralph's favorite screenwriters' forums and a great reference site for what's happening in the movie industry and to get leads on marketing scripts.
- `http://www.dvinfo.net/`: Information on video equipment and software (very active and informative forums).
- `http://hcdonline.com/`: Hollywood Creative Directory, extensive online subscription directory of the movie industry.
- `http://www.imdb.com/` and `IMDbPro.com`: The ultimate movie database, indispensible for anyone working in the entertainment industry.
- `IMDb.me/ralphroberts`: Ralph's IMDb page.

- `http://inktip.com/`: A subscription website where you can post your loglines and even entire scripts for qualified movie agents, managers, and producers to look at.

- `http://moviebytes.org/`: Scriptwriting contests and markets online.

- `http://www.packtpub.com/`: Packt's official website.

- `http://screenwritersutopia.com/`: Screenwriting news and tips.

- `http://www.screenwritingbasics.com/`: Hundreds of articles and other information about writing screenplays.

- `http://screenwritingu.com/`: Lots of information about how to write scripts.

- `http://scriptdelivery.net`: A website that, for a fee, e-mails your query to thousands of qualified agents, managers, and producers.

- `http://scriptshack.com/`: A website where you can buy scripts of movies already made to see how they were written.

- `http://skyfest.net/`: A home of the SkyFest Film and Script Festival.

- `http://sydfield.com/`: A homepage for one of the most famous screenwriting gurus.

- `http://www.theindiefilmblog.com/`: Interesting website with information about indie (independent) films and filmmaking.

- `http://virtualpitchfest.com/`: A website letting you (for a fee) present your ideas to professionals in the movie industry.

- `https://withoutabox.com/`: A website that lists and lets you enter thousands of film and script festivals!

- `http://writerslittleblackbook.com/`: A good subscription website providing leads to agents, managers, and producers.

- `http://www.zoetrope.com`: A website sponsored by the Coppola Companies (as in Francis Ford Coppola). Tons of stuff there for scriptwriters and indie producers!

B
Celtx's New Web Look and Smartphone Apps

Of course, I'm almost finished with this book and the website design of `Celtx.com` *gets changed. Luckily for me, only the look of the site changed and not the actual links given earlier.*

So, at least I don't have to go back through the book and change a bunch of illustrations.

Here are a few examples of the new appearance.

- ◆ **The new homepage**: The following screenshot shows the new look of the Celtx website's homepage:

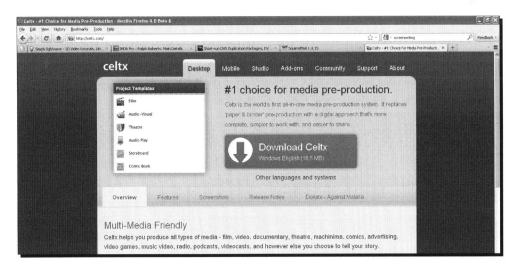

◆ **The download page**: The new look of the download page is shown in the following screenshot:

As shown in the preceding screenshot, the dialog box to download the latest version of Celtx pops up. By the way, the version is still 2.7, the one we've been using throughout this book.

◆ **The Support page**: The following screenshot shows the new appearance of the support page:

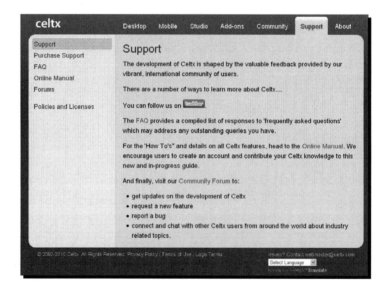

◆ **The Community page**: The new look of the community page is shown in the following screenshot:

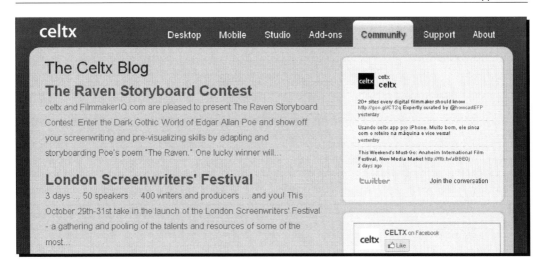

However, the online manual (the Celtx Wiki) still looks the same, as shown in the following screenshot:

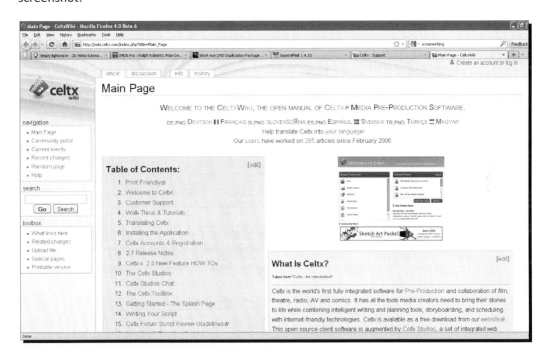

The forums are also unchanged.

Again, all links remain the same.

Celtx on Smartphones!

Celtx has also added a new add-on, not covered previously in this book. It's an **app (application)** that allows you to write scripts on your Smartphone and synchronize it with Celtx on your desktop or laptop computer.

So far, this app is only available for the Apple iPhone, but a number of us in the Celtx forums are asking for an Android app (I love my Droid 2).

The following screenshot shows the new `Celtx.com` page, which is about the iPhone app:

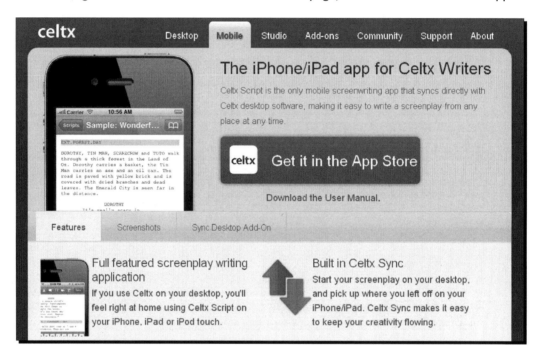

This application is aimed at the iPhone and iPad and is only $9.99. It can be purchased at the iTunes Apple apps store (link from the Celtx site), shown as follows:

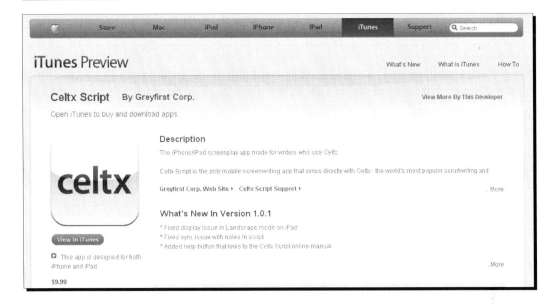

Finally, the following are a couple of screen captures of the app in action from the `Celtx.com` website:

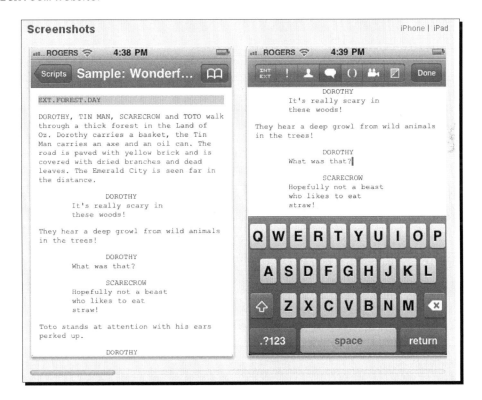

C
Future Development of Celtx

Celtx 3.0

This book is based on the current Celtx Version 2.7. However, sometime in 2011, Celtx 3.0 will be released with some additional features. To quote the only information given so far on the new release on the Celtx website (`http://celtx.com`):

> *"Work on the new version of the Celtx desktop software is going well. Among other things, we are adding support for* **Novels***, a new design for the* **Media** *and* **Breakdown** *sidebar, and tackling some of the remaining bugs."*
> *"New export options will enable you to more easily share data from a Celtx Project to your team."*

Check the Celtx website (`http://celtx.com`) periodically to see when the new version will be released. The update, like Celtx currently, is open source (free).

Thank you!

Thanks again for buying and reading *Celtx: Open Source Screenwriting*. If this book has been helpful, I would be pleased to hear from you. My e-mail address is `ralph@abooks.com`.

D
Pop Quiz Answers

Chapter 5: Tooling Up for Scriptwriting

1	Use the **File** menu or the Splash page that comes up when Celtx first starts.
2	Right click on the script's title in the **Project Library**, left click on **Adapt To..**, left click on the type of script you want.
3	d

Chapter 6: Advanced Celtx

1	Celtx projects are called "containers" because they can contain any mix of scripts of varying sorts, storyboards, sketches, documents, notes, media files, and so forth—literally thousands!
2	Celtx uses fewer resources (memory, disk space, computing power) because features, such as PDF formatting especially, are done out in the "cloud" (that is, on servers accessed through the Internet, a free service provided by the developers of Celtx)

Chapter 8: Documentaries and Other Audio-Visual Projects

1	d (is not an A/V production as it is audio only)
2	a

Chapter 9: Raising the Curtain on Plays

1	d (since plays can be one, three, or five acts)
2	b

Chapter 10: Audio Plays, Podcasts, and Other Great Sounds

1	c
2	b
3	d

Chapter 11: WAP! POW! BANG! Writing Comic Books with a Punch

1	b
2	c

Index

iPads 239
iPhone Apps 19
iPhones 239
items
  deleting 105

J

Just in Time scheduling 106-110

K

key shortcuts, assistant
  Ctrl+1 44
  Ctrl+2 44
  Ctrl+3 44
  Ctrl+4 44
  Ctrl+5 44
  Ctrl+6 44
  Ctrl+7 44
  Ctrl+8 44

L

layer tools 74
leads
  about 328
  categories, searching 330, 331
  IMDbPro page 329
  searching 328
line tool 71
Linux
  Celtx, installing on 18
  Celtx, system requisites for 13
local document
  printing 133
local print job
  previewing 132
  printing 132
log lines
  about 25, 315
  elements, requiring 317
  examples 318
  need for 317
  posting 319

M

Mac OS X
  Celtx, installing on 18
  Celtx, system requisites for 12
Master Catalog
  about 32
  manual catalogs, adding 38, 39
  project, saving 33-36
  updating 144
media files
  adding 68, 89-93
menus, Celtx
  about 117
  edit 117, 134
  file 117, 118
  help 117, 154, 156, 158
  script 117, 140, 141
  tools 117, 147-154
  view 117, 138, 139
movie making, Celtx used
  action 220
  character 222
  dialog 225
  hard copy, printing 231
  Parenthetical script 227
  scenes 214
  screenplay, writing 191
  shot 228
  text 230
  transition 229
multimedia show 236
multiple project containers
  working with 171, 172
multiple projects
  creating, in single project container 168-170
Music formats 286
My Way
  scripts, importing with 176, 178

N

Netbooks
  about 13
  Celtx, installing on 19
new project
  starting 119, 120

new project types
  creating 122

O

one-act play 259
online resources
  references 339, 340
Option tabs, tools menu
  General 152
  Privacy 154
  Production 153
  Script 153

P

page breaks 45
page element 303, 304
pages
  deleting 307
  navigating 307
  reordering 307
  setting up 128, 130
pagination
  about 45, 46
  scenes, numbering 46, 47
pagination option 146
Palettes window 76
panel element 304
Parenthetical element
  using 227
Parenthetical script element 252, 270, 285
paste tool 75
PC
  Celtx, installing on 16, 17
  Celtx, system requisites for 12
PDF
  creating 287
Pick a Colour dialog box 62
play, elements
  about 266, 267
  Act 268
  Character 270
  Dialog 270
  Parenthetical 270
  Scene Heading 268
  Stage Direction 269
  Transition 271

plays
  about 255, 256
  example 257
  outlining 263-265
  printing 271, 272
  writing 256-258
play's outline
  about 264
  catastrophe 265
  denouement 265
  exposition 264
  falling action 265
  resolution 265
  rising action 264
playwright 259
podcasts 275
portals7-14-10 122
Privacy tab 154
production
  book references 338, 339
production note 284, 285
Production Note script element 284, 285
Production tab 153
project
  closing 122
  opening from Celtx Studio 124
  project, opening from Celtx Studio 124
  saving, to Celtx Studio 125
  saving, under another name 121, 122
project file
  displaying 133
Project Library
  about 95-104, 117, 159
  folder, adding 104, 105
  items, deleting 105
  project templates 96
Project Library window 192, 203
project templates, Project Library
  about 96
  audio-play 96
  audio-visual 96
  comic book 96
  film 96
  storyboard 96
  text 96
  theatre 96

theatre project
  starting 259-261
  title page, creating 261-263
theatre projects, Celtx 27
Tiger 12
title page
  creating 261-263
  adding, to scripts 241-245
  creating 300-302
Toolbox feature, Celtx 95, 114, 115
tools menu
  about 117, 147
  Options selection 150-154
  Toolbox selection 147-150
top buttons 117, 158
transition 229, 230
Transition script element 271
TypeSet/PDF button 241

U

undo tool 75
ungroup tool 74

V

View menu
  about 117, 138, 139
  options 139
VirtualPitchFest.com 326
Voice script element 285, 286

W

War of the Worlds radio program script 278, 279
WDK 196
wildcards 185
workspace
  customizing 118
Writer's Development Kit. *See* WDK
writer support
  marketing, Celtx files used 331-334
  obtaining 331

Thank you for buying
Celtx: Open Source Screenwriting Beginner's Guide

About Packt Publishing

Packt, pronounced 'packed', published its first book "*Mastering phpMyAdmin for Effective MySQL Management*" in April 2004 and subsequently continued to specialize in publishing highly focused books on specific technologies and solutions.

Our books and publications share the experiences of your fellow IT professionals in adapting and customizing today's systems, applications, and frameworks. Our solution based books give you the knowledge and power to customize the software and technologies you're using to get the job done. Packt books are more specific and less general than the IT books you have seen in the past. Our unique business model allows us to bring you more focused information, giving you more of what you need to know, and less of what you don't.

Packt is a modern, yet unique publishing company, which focuses on producing quality, cutting-edge books for communities of developers, administrators, and newbies alike. For more information, please visit our website: www.packtpub.com.

About Packt Open Source

In 2010, Packt launched two new brands, Packt Open Source and Packt Enterprise, in order to continue its focus on specialization. This book is part of the Packt Open Source brand, home to books published on software built around Open Source licences, and offering information to anybody from advanced developers to budding web designers. The Open Source brand also runs Packt's Open Source Royalty Scheme, by which Packt gives a royalty to each Open Source project about whose software a book is sold.

Writing for Packt

We welcome all inquiries from people who are interested in authoring. Book proposals should be sent to author@packtpub.com. If your book idea is still at an early stage and you would like to discuss it first before writing a formal book proposal, contact us; one of our commissioning editors will get in touch with you.

We're not just looking for published authors; if you have strong technical skills but no writing experience, our experienced editors can help you develop a writing career, or simply get some additional reward for your expertise.

OpenSceneGraph 3.0: Beginner's Guide

ISBN: 978-1-849512-82-4   Paperback: 412 pages

Create high-performance virtual reality applications with OpenSceneGraph, one of the best 3D graphics engines.

1. Gain a comprehensive view of the structure and main functionalities of OpenSceneGraph

2. An ideal introduction for developing applications using OpenSceneGraph

3. Develop applications around the concepts of scene graphs and design patterns

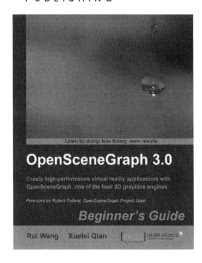

SketchUp 7.1 for Architectural Visualization: Beginner's Guide

ISBN: 978-1-847199-46-1   Paperback: 408 pages

Create stunning photo-realistic and artistic visuals for your SketchUp models

1. Create picture-perfect photo-realistic 3D architectural renders for your SketchUp models

2. Post-process SketchUp output to create digital watercolor and pencil art

3. Follow a professional visualization studio workflow

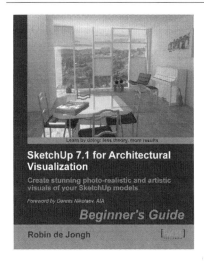

Please check **www.PacktPub.com** for information on our titles